W9-ASP-931
A 2180 245731 3

you can RENEW this item from home by visiting our Website at www.woodbridge.lioninc.org or by calling (203) 389-3433

The Brain Defense

The Brain Defense

MURDER IN MANHATTAN AND THE DAWN OF NEUROSCIENCE IN AMERICA'S COURTROOMS

Kevin Davis

PENGUIN PRESS | New York | 2017

PENGUIN PRESS
An imprint of Penguin Random House LLC
375 Hudson Street
New York, New York 10014
penguin.com

Copyright © 2017 by Kevin Davis
Penguin supports copyright. Copyright fuels creativity, encourages diverse voices, promotes free speech, and creates a vibrant culture. Thank you for buying an authorized edition of this book and for complying with copyright laws by not reproducing, scanning, or distributing any part of it in any form without permission. You are supporting writers and allowing Penguin to continue to publish books for every reader.

LIBRARY OF CONGRESS CATALOGING-IN-PUBLICATION DATA
Names: Davis, Kevin (Kevin A.), author.
Title: The brain defense : murder in Manhattan and the dawn of neuroscience in America's courtrooms / Kevin Davis.
Description: New York : Penguin Press, 2017.
Identifiers: LCCN 2016043485 (print) | LCCN 2016044316 (ebook) | ISBN 9781594206337 (hardback) | ISBN 9780698183353 (ebook)
Subjects: LCSH: Weinstein, Herbert—Trials, litigation, etc. | Trials (Murder)—New York (State)—New York. | Insanity (Law)—New York (State). | Forensic neurology—New York (State). | Brain—Diseases—Law and legislation—New York (State). | BISAC: LAW / Criminal Law / General. | PSYCHOLOGY / Cognitive Psychology. | POLITICAL SCIENCE / Public Policy / General.
Classification: LCC KF224.W395 D38 2017 (print) | LCC KF224.W395 (ebook) | DDC 345.747/02523—dc23
LC record available at https://lccn.loc.gov/2016043485

Printed in the United States of America
10 9 8 7 6 5 4 3 2 1

Designed by Gretchen Achilles

This one's for Sonny

Contents

Introduction

On December 17, 2014, Eric Williams, a former justice of the peace in the small town of Kaufman, Texas, was sentenced to death for assassinating a local district attorney, his wife, and a prosecutor. The killings, which had terrorized the town, were part of a complicated revenge plot for which Williams's wife, Kim, was also convicted. A month after a judge ordered Williams sent to death row, his defense lawyer declared that newly discovered evidence showed his client's brain was "broken" and demanded a new trial. Attorney John Wright filed a motion in court stating an MRI had revealed that part of Williams's brain had atrophied due to prior head trauma, thus impairing his ability to regulate his emotions, behavior, and judgment. The judge denied the motion for a new trial.

Williams's broken brain claim was another in a growing number of attempts to bring neuroscience into the nation's courtrooms to explain or diminish a defendant's criminal responsibility. Defense attorneys are looking to neuroscience, and hiring experts, to support claims of brain dysfunction—whether caused by traumatic brain injury (TBI), a tumor, cancer, drug or alcohol abuse, or a genetic anomaly—and argue that the effects should be considered in determining their clients' culpability and the severity of their sentences. The number of such cases has risen steadily in the past decade. Nearly 1,600 judicial opinions issued in U.S. courts between 2005 and 2012 mention neurobiological evidence, such as images of a person's brain structure, its level of functioning, or the presence of abnormalities, according to Nita Farahany, a professor of law and philosophy at Duke University. In more than 250 opinions issued in 2012, defendants argued that their "brains made them do it," more than double the number five years earlier. Defendants in about 5 percent of all murder trials and in 25 percent of death penalty cases made bids for lighter punishment using neurobiological data. The actual number of brain defense cases is likely much higher. Farahany had to rely on published judicial opinions, the only source from which she could comprehensively search. Not all brain defense cases are reported, and many trials in which neuroscience is used likely remain unnoticed unless picked up in the media. Farahany had just finished collecting new data on this phenomenon when I spoke with her in July 2016. Her preliminary figures indicate that use of the brain defense had doubled to four or five hundred per year since her last study. "It's a trend that's not going away," she told me.

The increasing use of neuroscience in the courtroom has far-reaching implications. It suggests that concussions play a role in violence perpetrated, for example, by football players off the field, and it shows that TBI and post-traumatic stress disorder (PTSD) among combat veterans may be a factor in why some become violent at home. Neuroscience also sheds light on adolescent brain development, suggesting that the unfinished brains of juvenile offenders render them unable to manage their impulses or make wise decisions in the face of peer pressure. As a result of these developments, judges and juries are being asked to consider complex science, evaluate conflicting opinions about human behavior, and ponder whether there is such thing as free will.

Having covered crime for many years as a journalist, I've seen all manner of violent and destructive behavior—often the result of poor choices made by people who claimed to have been damaged in some way, blaming their crimes on an abusive childhood, poverty, alcohol, drug abuse, or the bad company they kept. For some, their stories bring understanding and compassion, earning them treatment instead of incarceration. Others encounter only cynicism in an overburdened criminal justice system. Researchers and policy makers continue to struggle to understand the underlying causes of criminal behavior and the remedies to control it. And so we, as a society, are asked to decide to what extent we should hold people responsible for their deeds, and how we are to treat, punish, or seek to rehabilitate them. Neuroscience shows us that a person's decision to commit a crime, or to do anything in life for that matter, is triggered by a series of chemical and electrical interactions in the brain, but it cannot settle the ongoing debate over whether those decisions are made freely or independently of a person's will. Every thought, decision, and action springs from complex processes in our brains that are influenced by both nature and nurture.

I wanted to explore this idea further, so I set out to learn what neuroscience can really tell us, to better understand its value as well as its limitations, and to meet the people behind the kinds of cases that Farahany cites in her studies. I was curious to know whether the brain defense has merit: whether people who claim to have been driven by forces beyond their control should be considered less culpable than others in the eyes of the law, and why.

As I delved into the realm of neuroscience and law, I kept coming across the case of Herbert Weinstein, known in the legal and medical literature by his pseudonym, Spyder Cystkopf. His case appears in scores of textbooks, magazines, scientific journals, and law reviews. In 1991 Weinstein, a sixty-five-year-old retired advertising salesman from New York, killed his wife during an argument. He had a clean record and no history of violent behavior. His lawyer claimed that Weinstein had gone temporarily insane due to a cyst in his brain, then sought to prove it using brain scans and other scientific evidence. It was the first case in the United States in which a judge ruled that PET (positron-emission tomography) scan images could be shown to a jury determining a defendant's guilt or innocence. These images, Weinstein's lawyer argued, demonstrated that an anomaly in his brain accounted for the irrational, impulsive act of killing his wife.

The case evolved into a highly charged, contentious battle in which the lawyers debated the value and admissibility of such evidence. That debate continues over the use of neuroscience in court and whether it offers real insight into human behavior or is just a defense tactic to sway juries with colorful images. In 2007 Jeffrey Rosen observed in the *New York Times Magazine* that "when historians of the future try to identify the moment that neuroscience began to transform the American legal system, they may point to a little-noticed case from the early 1990s"—that is, the Weinstein case.

While Weinstein's is one of the most frequently cited case studies on the use of neuroscience in the courtroom, the story behind it was largely untold. Most accounts reveal little about who the man was, what brought him to that moment when he snapped, how his trial unfolded, and who the people were behind the legal battle. This book explores the human side of his case, as well as the science introduced in his defense, and addresses deeper issues about crime, personal responsibility, and the possibilities of law and neuroscience.

KEVIN DAVIS

July 2016

CHAPTER 1

We Found Something in Mr. Weinstein's Brain

Herbert Weinstein was the only person who could explain to police what had happened on that winter afternoon inside his Upper East Side apartment. The other person was dead.

She had fallen twelve stories through the cold January air and now lay sprawled on the sidewalk in front of their twenty-eight-story apartment building at 220 East 72nd Street near Second Avenue, a few doors west of the Catholic Church of St. John the Martyr. Barbara Weinstein—fifty-six years old, Mr. Weinstein's second wife, whom he married after his first wife died of cancer, the woman he told everyone he deeply loved—was gone. It looked as if Barbara had hurled herself out the window in a dramatic public suicide.

The case began, as many do, with a call to 911. It was January 7, 1991, about one-fifteen P.M., when people along East 72nd Street noticed the body on the sidewalk. A short time later New York City police officers Dominick Avallone and Warren Elliott, partners in the

Nineteenth Precinct, were called to respond to a "jumper," police shorthand for a suicide jumper. When they pulled up to the redbrick apartment building, a few officers already were milling around the body of a red-haired woman in a blue nightgown on the sidewalk. Avallone looked up and saw a window open on the twelfth floor. He went into the building and asked the doorman if he knew the woman on the sidewalk. He said he didn't.

As they headed to the elevators to go up to the twelfth floor, the officers saw a tall, older white-haired gentleman talking to two women in the lobby. The doorman dashed over to the officers and asked them to hold on a minute. In a nervous voice, he pointed to the white-haired man and said that he lived on the twelfth floor and was acting very suspiciously. Avallone walked over to the white-haired man and asked whether he lived on the twelfth floor. Yes, the man said, he did. His name was Herbert Weinstein. He lived up there with his wife, Barbara.

The officers noticed that Weinstein was holding a briefcase. Was he going somewhere? Weinstein explained that he had been on his way to work but had stopped in the lobby to look for his wife before leaving. She was not in the apartment upstairs, and he didn't know where she'd gone. The officers listened to his story, then told Weinstein they were going up to the twelfth floor to look around and ask building residents some questions. Would Mr. Weinstein mind coming along? Sure, he said, and they got into the elevator together.

As they stood in the car, Avallone noticed scratch marks on the right side of Weinstein's face. "What happened to your face?" the officer asked.

"I got it while playing football the other day," Weinstein said.

Avallone was surprised by this answer. But Weinstein was a big man and seemed to be in good shape, so maybe it was possible.

Weinstein seemed impatient and fidgeted as the three rode up to the twelfth floor. He kept saying that he was late for work and needed to find his wife. Though the woman on the sidewalk had not yet been positively identified, Avallone was pretty sure it was Mrs. Weinstein, but he didn't let on. The doors opened, and Weinstein escorted the officers into his apartment and down the hallway toward his study. Avallone felt a chilly breeze run through the apartment. As he passed the bedroom, he looked inside and saw that the window onto 72nd Street was open.

Avallone and Weinstein went into the study, which Weinstein used as an office. He was retired from the advertising business but kept a few clients to bring in extra income. Avallone asked Weinstein about his wife. How was she feeling lately? Just fine, Weinstein said. Did she suffer from any physical or mental ailments? None, Weinstein replied. The officer asked how long they'd been married and how they got along. Weinstein pointed to a photo of his wife in the study and said she was quite healthy. "We've been married for eight great fucking years," he blurted out, "and we get along fucking famously."

Weinstein began to breathe heavily, and the officer asked if he needed medical attention. Weinstein said no, he was fine. Weinstein asked what was going on. Why were there cops all over the place? The officer explained there was a dead woman on the sidewalk. Weinstein asked if it was his wife. Avallone said he didn't know. Did Weinstein want to call a family member to come over to be with him? Weinstein said yes and paged his thirty-two-year-old son, Nelson, who was at one of the Laundromats he operated in Brooklyn Heights.

When his son called back, Avallone overheard Weinstein say, "Please come over, a terrible accident has happened to Barbara."

The Weinstein apartment started to get crowded with cops. A sergeant asked Weinstein if his wife was depressed or was seeing a psychiatrist. Weinstein said no. What about marital problems? Weinstein said their marriage was the envy of many friends. In fact, they never fought. Had Weinstein got the scratches from shaving that morning? "Yes, among other things," he said.

The sergeant looked around the study. When had Weinstein last seen his wife? he asked. About one-fifteen, Weinstein said, but she had left without kissing him good-bye, which was unusual. Why was the bedroom window open on such a cold day? Weinstein explained that his wife often got warm in the apartment, and the air helped cool the place down.

As the sergeant questioned Weinstein, three more detectives pulled up to the building, took Polaroids of the body on the sidewalk, then went up to the twelfth floor. Detective Denise Jackson noticed some dark stains on the bedroom carpet, which looked to her like blood. She also noticed that the window curtain had been drawn back. Weinstein offhandedly mentioned that his wife might have been feeling a little down lately because they had spent New Year's Eve home alone after a party they had planned fell through.

Around that time Weinstein's son, Nelson, arrived. The detectives brought him into the kitchen. Nelson asked the detectives whether his father needed a lawyer.

"He appears to be in control of himself," one of the detectives said. "He's a smart man. If he wanted a lawyer, he'd ask for one."

A few minutes later Detective Frank Connelly arrived and went into the bedroom with the open window; it was getting colder now. He noticed the bloodstains on the carpet near the window and the bed and thought it looked as if someone had tried to clean it up.

Detective Connelly then went to the study to talk to Weinstein. He studied the scratch marks on the man's face carefully. There was one under each eye, and one over his right eye, as well as on his cheek and chin. Connelly thought they looked fresh, most likely defensive wounds or from a fight.

He asked Weinstein what had happened. Weinstein said he had been in his study working on some advertising contracts when he came out to look for his wife, who had a dental appointment that afternoon. He thought she might have gone to a neighbor's apartment, then went downstairs to talk to the doorman. That's when he'd seen the police.

Detective Connelly got a legal pad, wrote something down, and asked Weinstein to review and sign it. He explained that the note would grant permission for the police to conduct a crime scene search of the apartment. Weinstein signed it.

Connelly left the room, then returned with a card on which was printed the Miranda warnings. He read Weinstein his rights and asked if he understood. Weinstein seemed to get nervous and shaky, but he said he'd be willing to answer the detective's questions.

"So, Mr. Weinstein, how did you get those scratches on your face?" Connelly asked.

"Shaving," Weinstein said.

"That seems unlikely," the detective said.

Weinstein told the detective he had sensitive skin.

"C'mon," Connelly said, "that seems unlikely, too."

"Okay," Weinstein said. "I got the scratches while watching a football game and poked myself while cheering."

Connelly said those scratches didn't look like they came from either shaving or cheering. They looked like a person had scratched him.

Weinstein got up and looked at himself in a mirror.

"Where did the stains on the carpet come from?" Connelly asked.

"I don't know," Weinstein said.

Connelly said they were going to check Barbara Weinstein's blood type and check for skin under her fingernails to see if it matched Mr. Weinstein's. He then left the study. Another detective told Connelly that the crime scene detectives had found blood on a slipper. And there was something else. A witness across the street on East 72nd told police she had seen a man throw a woman out the window.

Connelly went back to the study. "Mr. Weinstein, do you know why there's blood on your slipper?"

"No, I don't."

"Mr. Weinstein, we have a witness across the street who said she saw a man throw a woman out the window. Do you know anything about this? Tell me the truth. What happened?"

"What did this witness see?" Mr. Weinstein demanded.

"Why don't you tell me?"

"I don't know what the witness saw."

Connelly again asked Weinstein about the scratches on his face.

Weinstein stood up and put his hands on a chair. Connelly noticed his hand was black and blue and had a spot of blood on it.

Weinstein sat back down and began to unburden himself. They had been arguing about his son, Nelson, he said, and Barbara had been criticizing his weight and his career choices. She was yelling. Weinstein didn't like it but remained calm. Her temper flared, and she scratched his face, and then he hit her, he said. He hadn't meant for it to go that far. She fell to the bed, then to the floor. He grabbed her by the throat. She was motionless, and he realized she was dead.

In a panic, he began to clean up the mess, using paper towels to wipe up the carpet. He put the bloodstained bedcovers into a bag and hid them in the front closet. He looked himself up and down and saw no blood on his clothes and so did not change. About fifteen minutes later, he said, he dragged his wife's body over to the window and threw her out to make it look like a suicide or an accident. It was, he said, a panic-driven, irrational act.

Connelly asked Weinstein to show him where the sheets were

stashed, and Weinstein led him to the closet. A few minutes later Weinstein signed his statement. Connelly left the study and told the others what had happened.

Detective Jackson came in and asked Weinstein why he had decided to throw his wife out the window. To cover up the crime, he said. How had he been able to do it? He said he picked her up underneath her arms, dragged her to the window, placed her on the sill, grabbed her legs, and flipped her out.

Satisfied they had their story, the detectives told Weinstein they were going to take him to the Nineteenth Precinct. Weinstein took off a ring and his watch, remarking that he wouldn't need them where he was going.

Diarmuid White had started his legal career a little later than most of his colleagues who worked criminal cases in the New York Supreme Court building on Centre Street. For seventeen years he had worked in advertising, selling network television airtime. It was a good job, but he thought advertising was pointless and grew bored. With a wife and four children, he had to boost his income. He had a gnawing desire to move into a career with a social conscience that also could be lucrative. Criminal law seemed a good fit. He liked to challenge authority, and he liked the idea of being a watchdog of overzealous cops and prosecutors. When he saw lawyers at work, he thought to himself, "Hey I could do that, and do it even better."

So at age forty he went to Brooklyn Law School at night while working at his advertising job during the day. In his third year of law school, he landed a job at Lipsitz, Green, Fahringer, Roll, Salisbury & Cambria, a high-priced firm known for handling well-to-do clients. The firm was headquartered in Buffalo, and White was one of two lawyers based in Manhattan. The other was Herald Fahringer, who had built a reputation as a First Amendment lawyer defending purveyors of X-rated entertainment, including magazine publishers Larry Flynt and Al Goldstein. Fahringer had represented Claus von Bülow, who was acquitted of trying to kill his socialite wife, known as Sunny, and Jean Harris, convicted in the 1980 shooting of Dr. Herman Tarnower, author of *The Complete Scarsdale Medical Diet.*

With Fahringer as a mentor, White took on criminal cases right away, representing clients accused of everything from murder to stock fraud. On January 7, 1991, he had been at the job for about six years when one of the lawyers in his firm called him to take the case of a Mr. Herbert Weinstein, who had been arrested on suspicion of murdering his wife and was to be arraigned the next morning.

White met his new client in a holding cell a few minutes before the arraignment. He was struck by how unusually calm and unconcerned Weinstein seemed, despite having been charged with murder. The man was emotionless, expressionless, and apparently oblivious to what was happening to him.

White went over the charges against Weinstein and asked him to repeat what he had told police. Weinstein explained that he had confessed. White said that it didn't matter and instructed Weinstein to plead not guilty. They could discuss it later in more detail and work on building some kind of defense.

Inside the courtroom, Weinstein's son, Nelson, and daughter, Joni, from his first marriage, were sitting on benches waiting for the proceedings to begin. Weinstein stepped up before the judge to hear the charges. The district attorney charged him with two counts of second-degree murder: one count for intentional murder, the other for depraved indifference to human life. If he was convicted, Weinstein faced the possibility of life in prison. Because he had no criminal past and was not considered a flight risk, the judge set bail at $100,000.

Weinstein posted a portion of his bail and was released from Rikers Island. The judge permitted him to live with close friends who pledged to watch over him.

A few days later Weinstein met with White at his Madison Avenue office to discuss his legal options. When he arrived, he was amiable, even cheery. White thought again that Weinstein's demeanor seemed incongruous with what had just happened—he acted as if this were a business meeting. Weinstein appeared to be a decent man, not a tightly wound person prone to explosive or violent behavior, certainly not a murderer. Yet he seemed oddly disengaged, White thought. It occurred to him that Weinstein might be mentally unstable, perhaps even suffering from a mental disorder. White suggested that he get a psychiatric evaluation.

A week after being released on bail, Weinstein went to see Dr. Daniel Schwartz, director of forensic psychiatry at Kings County Hospital in New York. Schwartz was well known in New York City's courts and one of the go-to psychiatrists for criminal defendants in insanity cases. He didn't favor sides. He testified for anyone. Defense lawyers, prosecutors, and judges often called on him to offer his professional opinion on whether defendants were mentally competent to stand trial or met the legal standard of insanity. Schwartz had testified in many high-profile cases, including the murder trials of David Berkowitz, the "Son of Sam" killer; and of Mark David Chapman, who assassinated John Lennon.

Schwartz began by asking Weinstein about his medical history. Weinstein told him he'd been hospitalized in 1948 after experiencing severe headaches caused by some unusual neurological disorder. Besides the headaches, his symptoms included a bit of amnesia and aphasia, or a loss of ability to speak or understand speech. But the symptoms had passed and never returned.

Weinstein described to Schwartz what had happened in the apartment that day with Barbara, explaining that he had remained calm as they argued but lost control when she scratched him in the face. "I couldn't stop myself," he told the doctor. Weinstein said he was aghast that he had gone so out of control for the first time in his life.

Schwartz found nothing wrong with Weinstein. In his opinion, the man was articulate, smart, and seemingly in control. He could find no evidence of mental illness, psychopathy, organic mental disorder, or psychosis. He reported to White that Weinstein was fully alert and quite cooperative, though his mood was "neutral." He noted, however, that Weinstein didn't show any feelings about his wife's death, "no manifestation of guilt, depression or anxiety," as he wrote in his report. Still, Weinstein exhibited no serious type of disordered thinking or delusions, and his judgment seemed to be perfectly intact. Schwartz suggested that Weinstein be further evaluated by a neuropsychologist, who could test him for cognitive, behavioral, and brain dysfunction. It was still possible that Weinstein had some kind of brain disorder.

The neuropsychologist's exam yielded nothing unusual, though Weinstein's visual memory was better than his verbal memory, and he had a small left-hand advantage even though he was right-handed. She referred Weinstein for more tests, including a brain scan.

At New York Hospital–Cornell Medical Center he underwent more psychiatric exams, as well as tests of his memory and motor skills. The doctors found no indication of brain dysfunction or mental disturbances, other than his uncharacteristically violent reaction during the fight with his wife. Weinstein's psych exams revealed nothing unusual, either. When he took the Purdue Pegboard Test, which measures gross motor skills by having patients place a series of pegs into holes during a specified time, he again showed better skills with his left hand than his right, even though he was right-handed.

Finally, Weinstein underwent magnetic resonance imaging (MRI) to see whether an image of his brain would reveal any anomalies. A technician slid him into a tunnel where a powerful magnet and radio waves scanned his brain. The image that appeared on a screen in the next room was stunning. There was a growth the size of an orange over Weinstein's left temporal lobe.

"HIGH-RISE HORROR" blared the front page of the *New York Daily News* the day after Barbara's death. The headline took up the top half of the page; the other half featured a picture of Herbert Weinstein attempting to bury his face inside his overcoat, while a beefy cop in suit and tie led him from the courthouse after his arraignment.

It was completely out of character—he had to have been out of his mind. That's how Weinstein's friends and neighbors reacted to news of his arrest. His closest friends, Morton and Cecile Wagner, who had known him for more than thirty years, were convinced that he had blacked out or something when he strangled his wife. Rather than distance themselves from him, the Wagners embraced him like family. They were so sure that dear Herbie was blameless that they told the judge at his arraignment that he could live at their home in Queens while awaiting trial.

Weinstein remained upbeat after his arrest, retaining his wry sense of humor with his friends. A week after he was released on bail, he stopped at his Upper East Side apartment to get some things before going to the Wagners' house. He showed up at their home with a tin of caviar. "This is what Barbara and I were going to have on New Year's Eve," he said to Cecile. "Why let it go to waste? You guys ought to have it."

Cecile joked that if she weren't such an upstanding, law-abiding citizen, she'd gladly take Herbie to a country that had no extradition agreement with the United States.

A few weeks after his neurological tests, Weinstein got some good news. The large growth on the left side of his brain was not a cancerous tumor, his doctors said. It was a benign growth called an arachnoid cyst, a puffy sac of tissue filled with fluid. The cyst got its name because it rests in the arachnoid mater, a spiderweb-like protective lining that covers the brain. Arachnoid cysts usually develop at birth and are found in 0.5 to 1 percent of the population. For the most part, they are harmless. Their effects and symptoms vary, based on their size and location; they have been associated with everything from headaches and seizures to ADHD (attention deficit hyperactivity disorder) in children and dementia in seniors.

Weinstein decided not to have the cyst drained or removed because those procedures carried risk, especially for a man his age. Draining the cyst, doctors explained, would leave a large space inside his skull and might cause his brain to shift to fill the void, possibly causing serious damage that could lead to catastrophic neurological complications or death.

In defending Weinstein, Diarmuid White didn't have many legal options because Weinstein had already confessed to police. White could try to get the confession thrown out, but that didn't seem promising because Weinstein had understood his rights and spoken freely to the police. But when he learned about Weinstein's cyst and saw the striking MRI image of the orange-size growth on the left frontal lobe, he knew he had something powerful. How could a person's behavior *not* be affected by that?

White realized that he could use this brain anomaly either to play down Weinstein's responsibility or to absolve him altogether. Much like Weinstein's friends and neighbors, White took the position that his client was out of his mind at the time he killed his wife. A decent, law-abiding citizen until that fatal January day, he had been driven to kill her because the cyst pressing on his brain had caused him to act out of character, irrationally, without control during their argument. White thought he could call the murder an instance of insanity. Weinstein wasn't insane in the classical sense—his mental health evaluations confirmed that. But Weinstein, he could argue, had been temporarily insane—at the time of the crime, Weinstein had not been Weinstein.

The theory wasn't far-fetched. Aberrant and antisocial behavior had been linked to brain injuries, particularly in the left frontal lobe, in many research studies. But using a brain injury to explain temporary insanity, and ultimately, to excuse a crime, was novel and risky. Tying the injury to a specific act at a precise moment was untested in the courts. To support it, White would need some hard science and willing experts.

The roots of the neurological theory that Weinstein might not have been Weinstein can be traced back more than 160 years to a fellow named Phineas Gage, whose case became one of the most famous and studied in the annals of neuroscience. On September 13, 1848, Gage, a twenty-five-year-old worker for the Rutland & Burlington Railroad of Vermont, was serving as the crew foreman for a gang whose job was to blast away rock. Gage and his crew were clearing a path to lay down tracks near the village of Cavendish. Gage was using the blunt end of a tapered iron rod to tamp down an explosive charge. His tamping iron scraped a rock, causing a spark, which set off an explosion of packed combustible power. The tamping rod was three feet, seven inches long, 1¾ inch in diameter, and was sharpened to ¼ inch at the end. It shot through Gage's face like a rocket, entering beneath his left cheek. It continued behind his left eye, traveled through the front of his brain, and burst through the top of his skull, coming to rest about a hundred feet away, covered, as one eyewitness said, with blood and brains.

His coworkers were stunned to see that Gage remained conscious. He had been thrown back and convulsed for a few moments but was alert and able to speak. The men loaded him onto an oxcart, in which he rode sitting up to a tavern in Cavendish. He was able to get off the cart with little assistance and sat down to wait for a doctor. As he waited, he told incredulous bystanders what had happened and assured them he would be fine. When a doctor approached, Gage was reported to have said, "Doctor, here is business enough for you." He seemed hardly affected, except for having a gaping bloody hole in his head, through which the doctor could see his pulsating brain. Gage recounted the accident as the doctor cleaned and dressed the wound.

In the coming days, Dr. John Martyn Harlow, Gage's treating physician, worked to remove as many bone fragments as possible from his brain to reduce the risk of infection. Harlow kept the wound clean and disinfected, changed the dressings often, and kept Gage in a semirecumbent position so that the wound could drain properly. He also employed the ancient technique of bloodletting, which was presumed to prevent or rid the body of disease. During the first few weeks after the accident, Gage suffered from high fevers and an abscess inside the wound, which Harlow drained and disinfected.

According to Harlow's account, about nine weeks after the accident, Gage became restless and left his lodgings to get out and about, despite Harlow's warnings that he avoid "excitement and exposure." One cold and wet day he walked half a mile without an overcoat to buy some things at a store and came back with a chill. Still, he seemed all right overall, and his memory was intact. A few months later he pronounced himself ready to go back to work.

Harlow would later write extensively about this most unusual case.

He attributed Gage's amazing survival and recovery not to his own treatment methods but to *vis conservatrix,* or the inherent power of the body to resist the effects of injury and heal with its own natural abilities. He said he did little to interfere with Gage's recuperative powers. Gage's strong physique and willpower certainly helped, the doctor said. The absence of whatever portion of brain matter was lost or irrevocably damaged by the rocket-propelled tamping iron seemed not to have affected Gage in any significant way.

But then Gage began to have personal troubles. He tried to go back to work, but contractors were put off by disturbing changes in his personality. Before the accident, he had been a highly regarded, capable railroad foreman with a well-balanced mind. But afterward he became "fitful, irreverent and grossly profane," according to Harlow. The once-amiable Gage now showed little deference to his coworkers and was antisocial. Unable to find work, he traveled around New England, and Harlow believed he had exhibited himself at Barnum's American Museum in New York City. Other accounts had him working in circus freak shows on the East Coast, though no one knows for sure. The details of Gage's subsequent life are even sketchier. In early 1851 he reportedly found work as a stagecoach driver, first on the East Coast and later in Chile. He then came back to the States and settled in San Francisco, where he died in 1861. Harlow learned of his death five years later. He asked Gage's family to have the body exhumed so that he could use the skull for medical research, and they agreed. They also handed over the tamping iron, which Gage had saved.

Harlow did not publicly reveal the case details until after Gage's death, and his account has influenced the study and understanding of localized brain function to this day. In an oft-quoted paper from 1868, Harlow wrote that Gage's friends declared that Gage "was no longer Gage," a line that has been continually cited as evidence linking Gage's brain injury to changes in his personality. It has been widely accepted in medical and neuroscientific communities that the change in Gage's behavior was tied to the damage in his prefrontal cortex. Because no autopsy was performed, the damage to Gage's brain was never measured with precision, leaving much to speculation. Still, the case was the first to suggest that an injury to the frontal lobe could compromise reasoning and regard for other human beings. Neuroscientists have latched on to the Gage case ever since, and contemporary researchers have conducted empirical studies that support the theory that the prefrontal cortex is the area of the brain responsible for rationality, morality, and intellect. Many have used Gage's preserved skull, along with Dr. Harlow's papers, to further study the implications of his case.

The extent of Gage's personality changes may have been exaggerated over the years. Second- and third-hand accounts have portrayed Gage as irrational and unsocial, impulsive and uninhibited, thus giving rise to the idea of frontal lobe syndrome, or Gage syndrome. Some have taken Harlow's accounts of Gage's personality change to make him into a sinister person. Malcolm Macmillan, an Australian psychologist who may be the most knowledgeable Gage scholar on the planet, sorted through the scientific and popular accounts of his story and found them to be inconsistent and often poorly supported by firsthand evidence. Most of the accounts of Gage's life after the accident, he wrote, were strange mixtures of "slight fact, considerable fancy, and downright fabrication." Of the greatest concern, he said, was the fact that Harlow had waited twenty years to report anything about Gage's supposed aberrant behavior. There should have been more information about his behavior at the time, McMillan argues. Why didn't others report it?

Fact, fiction, or something in between, the Gage case helped push brain research into a new era, prompting scientists to probe the links between personality and behavior and the front parts of the brain. If

Gage was no longer Gage due to a brain injury, then why couldn't Weinstein no longer have been Weinstein when he killed his wife?

While the case of Phineas Gage was groundbreaking, connecting specific parts of the brain with specific cognitive functions was not an entirely new idea. The field of phrenology, developed more than fifty years earlier, linked certain functions with configurations of the skull. Its chief advocate, the Austrian physician Franz-Joseph Gall, believed that the brain contained many different organs, each of which was connected to a specific human characteristic. He and his colleagues identified thirty-seven mental and moral faculties that they thought were represented in the exterior surface of the skull. These faculties were divided into several spheres: intellect, perceptiveness, mental energy, moral faculties, and love. They were further divided into more abstract personality traits such as cautiousness, spirituality, destructiveness, and something he called marvelousness—belief in the doctrines of religion. Gall also named parts of the brain for combativeness, covetousness, and secretiveness.

During his early studies, Gall visited jails and lunatic asylums to examine inmates. He claimed to have identified the part of the brain responsible for criminal behavior, including what he called an organ of murder, later called the "organ of destructiveness." In 1834 a criminal defense attorney in Maine claimed that the organ of destructiveness contributed to the violent disposition of a nine-year-old boy who was on trial for savagely attacking a classmate. The boy, his lawyer explained, had suffered a head injury when he was younger, which caused permanent swelling over the organ of destructiveness and triggered violent behavior. The judge, however, dismissed the so-called phrenological evidence, and the boy was found guilty.

While phrenology has long since been discredited, neuroscientists have been connecting specific regions of the brain with specific functions, including emotions, behavior, and decision making. At the time when Herbert Weinstein was arrested for murder, Antonio Damasio, a researcher and head of the neurology department at the University of Iowa, was studying the behavior of patients who suffered from various brain lesions, including tumors. Damasio was interested in whether the injuries and behaviors could be connected and how they might affect the way people make decisions.

In the summer of 1991 Damasio got a phone call from a lawyer in New York asking whether he could see a patient who had been arrested for murder and had a tumor pressing into his frontal lobe. By all means, Damasio said—bring him to Iowa.

CHAPTER 2

Lawyers, Brains, and Colorful Pictures

Geoff Aguirre, a cognitive neuroscientist at the University of Pennsylvania, is standing before lawyers, judges, and other criminal justice professionals packed into a conference room at a Chicago hotel. He's giving them a crash course on brain-imaging techniques and basic brain anatomy, tossing out terms like *gyrus* and *sulcus, axons* and *dendrites, white matter* and *gray matter,* and introducing them to the electrochemical activities of neurons. It's a complex and challenging subject for those in the room, but Aguirre, a professor of neurology—a medical doctor *and* a PhD in neuroscience—is keeping them engaged.

Aguirre is explaining fMRI (functional magnetic resonance imaging) and how the data from such scans are transformed into colorful pictures that reveal activity—or the lack of it—in specific areas of the brain. He calls fMRI "the grand pooh-bah" of brain-imaging techniques because of its ability to provide sharp structural images of brain anatomy and illuminate its functioning. These giant electromagnetic machines allow scientists, researchers, and now lawyers and juries to view brain activity, detected through blood flow, as people react to various circumstances and stimuli while being scanned. The images offer a window into which areas become active when we're thinking or feeling something in particular.

"Changes in brain activity cause changes in blood flow," Aguirre explains, while pointing to a color-enhanced image of a human brain—the brain of a psychopath—on a screen behind him. The fMRI scanner, he continues, detects the iron content in the blood through the scanner's magnetic coils. Blood flow can indicate what regions of the brain are most active at a given point in time. "Where the flowers in the brain are thirstier, the garden hose is made wider to provide more water," he says.

With his talk, "Brain Basics: Neuroscience and Neuroimaging for Lawyers," Aguirre is leading the first session of a sold-out conference in April 2013 called "The Future of Law and Neuroscience." The demand for such events has steadily increased because the use of brain scans in the courtroom is one of the most contentious issues in both the legal and scientific communities. Aguirre has been on a cross-country speaking circuit to educate the legal community and other interested people. He's attempting to bring insight, excitement, and a dose of caution to this shifting legal landscape. Melding law and neuroscience has meant reassessing how the legal system views human responsibility, the concept of free will, and the role of the brain in our being.

What excites scientists like Aguirre, not to mention the many lawyers in this room, is the possibility that new technology can help answer some of the lingering questions that humans have posed for as long as they have tried to understand one another's behavior. Is it possible, they wonder, to somehow collect hard evidence that shows whether people are really responsible for their actions? Can we know what was going on inside a person's head at the time he committed a crime, for instance, and whether it was conscious or involuntary?

The psychopath whose brain scan Aguirre is showing to his audience is a convicted killer named Brian Dugan. At trial Dugan's lawyer wanted jurors to view scans of his brain so that they might see him as a sick man whose condition was not his fault and who thus should be spared the death penalty. The scan was taken by Kent Kiehl, a researcher at the University of New Mexico who had been scanning the brains of psychopaths for years and had found evidence that their brains were structurally and functionally different from those of the general population.

For the fMRI test, Dugan was placed inside a machine and shown a series of pictures of people with facial expressions ranging from extremely fearful to neutral. The theory is that psychopaths, when looking at someone who's fearful, won't register an emotional response, thus demonstrating their characteristic lack of empathy. The amygdala, an area of brain associated with emotional responses, will therefore show less activity, and less blood flow, than that of those who are emotionally healthy. The amygdala of a psychopath won't be very thirsty for blood, to borrow Aguirre's metaphor.

After a brain scan like Dugan's is completed, Aguirre explains, the raw data are run through a computer to assemble an image, which gets color-coded and then fashioned, or smoothed, to show clean images on a model. Most images in brain scans are simplified, Aguirre says. They do not, as many believe, actually show the brain "lighting up" in response to various stimuli. They have been crafted so that they're clear and easy to follow, according to what he calls "neuroaesthetics."

In Dugan's case, the judge did not allow the actual brain scans to be presented but did allow Kiehl to describe what he saw in them and to interpret their meaning. During the sentencing hearing, Dugan's lawyer argued that criminal psychopaths like Dugan show less activity than noncriminal control subjects in specific emotion-processing areas of the brain. Dugan's abnormally functioning brain, therefore, was good reason not to sentence him to death. Even though he might have committed a horrible crime, it was not entirely his fault. The jury was not persuaded and sentenced Dugan to death.

Aguirre says Dugan's brain scans proved nothing. "This is taking group-based research and applying it to individuals," he says. "I would use caution. There are very few examples of this imaging that are so well articulated that they can say something about an individual."

Caution is a term often used at the conference, and if lawyers have come here expecting to gain some dazzling new defense techniques, they're bound to be disappointed. The conference is meant to be both illuminating and sobering. It's being sponsored by the MacArthur Foundation Research Network on Law and Neuroscience, a cooperative of scientists, lawyers, and researchers operating on a multimillion-dollar grant to better understand this intersection of modern neuroscience and criminal law.

Among those attending is James Castle, a criminal defense attorney from Denver who specializes in capital murder cases. "Lawyers, we love toys, bells and whistles, something new to show the jury," he tells me after the conference. "And when something first comes on board, we tend to rush to it like moths to a flame. Our goal is to win our case and to get our client off death row, and so we don't necessarily wait until the science is perfected. . . . It's probably no more complicated than what we try to do to figure out what's going on in people's minds without it."

Antoinette R. McGarrahan, a mitigation specialist, traveled to the conference from Dallas. Mitigation specialists work mostly on death penalty cases: they are hired by defense attorneys to help persuade juries and judges to spare the lives of their clients. McGarrahan tells me she will soon be working on a case in which brain science may be crucial in helping save her client. Before he was charged with shooting two people to death in Waco, Texas, her client twice had brain surgery to remove an abscess. His defense team argues that as a result, he was brain damaged and demonstrated impaired judgment.

Because neuroscience has been steadily finding its way into criminal courtrooms, the MacArthur Foundation in 2007 decided to fund the Law and Neuroscience Project with a three-year $10 million grant. The project represents the first systematic effort to bridge the fields of criminal law and science in considering how courts should deal with new brain-scanning techniques. "Neuroscience could have an impact on the legal system that is as dramatic as DNA testing," MacArthur president Jonathan Fanton said in announcing the project. "Neuroscientists need to understand law, and lawyers need to understand neuroscience."

The project originated at the University of California, Santa Barbara, and drew scientists and legal scholars from more than two dozen universities. Michael S. Gazzaniga, director of the SAGE Center for the Study of the Mind, served as the first director and principal investigator. Walter Sinnott-Armstrong, a professor of philosophy and legal studies at Dartmouth College, codirected the project. "Neuroscientific evidence has already been used to persuade jurors in sentencing decisions, and courts have admitted brain-imaging evidence during criminal trials to support pleas of insanity," Gazzaniga said at the time. "Without a solid, mutual understanding of each other's fields, lawyers and judges cannot respond in an informed way to developments in neuroscience, and scientists cannot properly advise lawyers or recognize the legal relevance of their current and future research."

Sinnott-Armstrong pointed out that the criminal justice system incorporates assumptions about behavior that are often centuries old.

"The legal system assumes that people make deliberate choices and what we choose determines what we do," he said. "However, neuroscience indicates that our choices sometimes are based upon electrical impulses and neuron activity that are not a part of conscious behavior. This includes not only criminal activity, but also decisions made by police, prosecutors, and jurors to arrest, prosecute, or convict."

Provocative statements like these—that behavior may not always be conscious or deliberate—are at the root of the conflict over the value of neuroscience in the legal world. Such issues were far from being resolved by the time the initial MacArthur grant ran out after three years. The foundation didn't want to lose any momentum and awarded Vanderbilt University a $4.85 million grant to continue the work by managing the newly established MacArthur Foundation Research Network on Law and Neuroscience. The network is led by Owen Jones of Vanderbilt University, who is one of the nation's few professors of both law and biology. Jones has been the public face of the network since designing and launching it in 2011 and has helped organize conferences like the one in Chicago.

"Why law and neuroscience? Well, you may have noticed that suddenly, brains are everywhere," Jones says during his remarks to the group. "Even the president has jumped on board with a major brain initiative." He's referring to President Barack Obama's $100 million BRAIN Initiative, launched just three weeks before the conference, to fund brain research to better understand the mind and treat brain disorders. "The criminal justice system in many ways is obsessed with brains," he says. "A lot of the questions we care about really devolve to questions about what's happening in someone else's head."

Jones describes the increasing interest in neurolaw as "this Technicolor blossoming of hope" that neuroscience can answer some of the perennial questions of law. "How do we navigate between the promise of the technology and the peril in either misunderstanding it or misapplying it to the legal issues before us?"

Jones later tells me that the research network is not an advocacy group designed to support the use of neuroscience in the courtroom but rather a collection of scholars entrusted to monitor and evaluate its use or misuse. In fact, one of the network's most vocal members has been largely dismissive of the use of neuroscience in determining cause and culpability in criminal acts. Stephen J. Morse, a professor of law and psychiatry at the University of Pennsylvania, is one of the field's most renowned skeptics. He has long argued that brains don't commit crimes—people do. Even the latest neuroscientific research and imaging techniques, he says, cannot answer questions about responsibility or legal competence.

The problem is that some defense lawyers are making giant leaps from the science. "Lots of people are making extravagant claims about what it can do for us. They're based on insufficient or irrelevant science or people are making moral inferences that the science does not entail," he tells me in an interview after the conference. Certainly brain damage can cause people to lose their judgment and inhibitions—that it can has been well documented. Morse's point is that we don't know whether or how those people try to control their impulses or whether they have lost their sense of right and wrong. "Causes are not excuses," he says.

Bringing brain images before judges and juries may unduly influence their decisions. Those images may be powerful and convincing, but they don't show us what's really going on inside a person's head at the time he commits a crime, Morse argues. Nor are they compared to images from other people's brains who might suffer from similar damage or anomalies but do not commit criminal acts.

Back at the conference, Jones clicks to the next image in his presentation. A picture of a white-haired man in a suit and tie appears on the screen. "This fellow is Herbert Weinstein," Jones says to the audience. "An otherwise unremarkable, calm, cool, collected individual who came home one day, strangled his wife, and threw her out the twelfth-story window of their apartment."

He clicks again, and a color image of Weinstein's brain appears on the screen, clearly showing a big black space occupied by his cyst. "A lot of people to whom I show this image vote with their hands to say they would at least be willing to give this guy some kind of inferential break . . . on the theory that he is not rowing with all of his oars in the water. He is just not the same as the rest of us."

CHAPTER 3

A Charming Man

Joni Weinstein's phone rang at her apartment around nine-thirty P.M. It was her brother, Nelson. His voice sounded odd—not the voice she knew but a scared voice, a shaky voice suggesting that he was about to deliver some bad news. Nelson told her to sit down.

"What's the matter?" she asked.

"Barbara's dead."

It took a minute to register. *Okay,* Joni said to herself, taking a deep breath, *Barbara's dead.* Then her body felt cold, a mild shock. Maybe it was a car accident. She couldn't quite envision it. What about Dad—where was he?

Just as she was going to ask Nelson what had happened, he broke in.

"Dad's in jail for killing her."

"What? What happened?"

"Barbara either jumped, fell, or was pushed out of their bedroom window."

Nelson told his sister to walk over to their aunt Esther's apartment, which was in the complex where Joni lived in Hackensack, New Jersey. Esther was their birth mother's sister and had always been close to the family.

"There's been a terrible tragedy," Joni said when she arrived at Esther's. "Barbara's dead, and my dad is in jail."

They turned on the television and watched the ten o'clock news. There, near the top of the broadcast, was the story about Barbara's death. It was being reported as a murder, not an accident or suicide, as Nelson had suggested it might be. The camera panned a shot from the street level up to the twelfth-story window.

Joni hadn't seen her father for months. She'd been busy with her career as vice president of corporate communications for a marketing company. She had her own circle of friends, and her father had an active social life with Barbara, who had come into Joni's life long after she had reached adulthood. Joni was not close to her stepmom—she felt she had an Upper East Side sort of arrogance. She accepted Barbara as part of their family and was polite and kind to her because her father loved her. That her father was happy was more important. Joni had never thought Barbara could provoke her father into killing her—that was crazy. Not only that, her father was unflappable. He hardly ever got angry. As long as Joni could remember, he had prided himself on his self-control and his ability to extricate himself from brewing conflicts and encounters, large and small. If her father and Barbara argued, Joni thought he'd either walk away or give in to keep the peace. That was his style. And he never spoke ill about Barbara.

Joni felt badly for Barbara's family. To lose a loved one to murder seemed unthinkable. Barbara had her own children who loved and cared for her. As Joni thought about it, anger at her father began to build. What the hell had happened? What had he done? she wondered. How could he have lost it like that? Could he really kill someone?

Other family members and friends confirmed that Herb and Barbara had exhibited a loving marriage during their eight years together, and that neither had physically or verbally attacked the other. Weinstein used to say that his marriage to Barbara worked well because it was a second marriage for both of them. They were free from the kinds of conflicts that first married couples had over money and children. Their kids were grown, and they were financially independent. Their romance appeared genuine. Rita Levy, Barbara's cousin, told the *New York Daily News* that, just a few weeks earlier, during the holidays, Herbie and Barbara had been holding hands while on a double date with Levy and her husband. They all attended a screening of *Bonfire of the Vanities,* and things seemed normal that night. A neighbor in their high-rise told the *Daily News* that about ten days before her death, Barbara had accompanied Herb to an audition for the television show *Jeopardy!,* though he was not accepted as a contestant. Levy also said that Barbara and Herb were planning a trip to Puerto Rico and told friends they intended to visit Atlantic City in the coming weeks.

To hear his friends and family tell it, Weinstein was a gentleman: charming, smart, a lover of books, and a lifelong student of self-improvement. Among his favorite books was Dale Carnegie's *How to Win Friends and Influence People.* Another was *Language in Thought and Action* by professor and former U.S. senator S. I. Hayakawa—it examines how language affects thought and influences behavior and can be used for cooperation and understanding rather than confrontation and conflict.

Weinstein dedicated much effort to speaking precisely and eloquently, and Hayakawa's book helped him improve those skills. Joni noticed that he often seemed attentive about the words he chose and the way he said things. While his language could be elegant, his demeanor often seemed detached, disaffected, and even flatly emotionless. Professionally, his attention to the economy of language served him well in the advertising business, where the right words were necessary for him to negotiate deals and land good clients.

He was the youngest of three brothers, born in New York City to Lithuanian immigrants. His father worked as a heating and plumbing contractor, and his mother worked as a seamstress. Weinstein attended public school in Manhattan and later in the Bronx. He liked school and had a near perfect attendance record.

His quest for self-improvement likely sprang from the fact that his physical imperfections and shyness made him feel like an outcast. As a youngster, he was a tall, overweight nerd, as he told the doctors who examined him after his arrest. By the time he was twelve, he weighed more than two hundred pounds. He characterized himself as a "fat and extremely sensitive" child, easily brought to tears by the verbal abuse of others. He never cared much for sports, preferring to busy himself with reading and schoolwork.

Nothing in Weinstein's past, from childhood through adulthood, suggested a predilection toward violent behavior. He admitted to being involved in two violent incidents in his life besides the killing of his wife. The first occurred when he was about eight. When another boy punched him, Weinstein said, "my middle brother Lou told me to hit him back. I bloodied his nose." The other incident occurred when he was ten and had just moved to the Bronx. Because he was the new kid on the block, he said, he often got teased. One boy bullied him and swung a jai alai cesta at him, which broke over Weinstein's arm. The other boy started to cry—presumably because he was upset at breaking the cesta. Weinstein later told a psychologist that "those two incidents are the totality of violent incidents in my life."

Weinstein called himself a perfectionist. It was an attitude he developed as a young man in response to his early years of low self-esteem and weight problems. He developed an emotional shield, purposely numbing his feelings so that he would not be provoked to anger. He decided he would not raise his voice, and he very rarely cried, except at age eighteen, when his father died. He told a psychiatrist that he was "very disciplined, very organized, very reliable."

He went to radio school to become a Merchant Marine officer and served overseas during World War II. In 1949 he earned a bachelor's degree in economics and English from New York University and went into the advertising business, specializing in creating outdoor signs and billboards, as well as ads for buses and bus shelters. In 1955, when he was thirty, he married his first wife, Belle, and they had two children, Nelson and Joni. They eventually settled in Englewood Cliffs, New Jersey, where they lived a comfortable suburban existence.

While growing up, Joni remembers her father being unusually upbeat. If someone asked him how he was doing, he never offered a simple "fine." His usual response was an enthusiastic "Fantastically well." Sometimes he would say, "Fantastically well and hoping to improve as the day goes on." Joni thought he was the most positive person she had ever met.

On the other hand, he could be strangely detached, even stoic in the face of crisis. During a violent thunderstorm, a willow tree in their yard toppled onto the roof of their home. While his wife was in hysterics, Weinstein barely registered a reaction. "That's interesting," he said. He called the insurance company and the appropriate people to repair the deck and got things back the way they were. He attached no emotional response to the problem.

Weinstein liked to gamble—craps was his favored game—and the family came along during some of his gambling trips. He took them to Las Vegas twice each year. The lights and the bells and buzzers of the casinos were fun for the children, who often accompanied their parents to the casino floors. Weinstein always started his bets at two dollars. If he won a few rounds, he would increase them. But if he and

Belle lost their daily self-assigned gambling allowance, they stopped playing craps and spent time with the children at the pool, went to restaurants, and visited other hotels. Weinstein was never happy about losing money but would justify the losses by pointing out that he was treated as a casino regular. The family always traveled on junkets with free airfare. They stayed in suites with two bedrooms, a large living room, and three bathrooms. They ate in fine restaurants around Las Vegas and got to see headline entertainment. And on some occasions the family left Las Vegas as winners. That's when Joni remembers her mother and father at their happiest.

Weinstein's weight increased as he got older. This was the one part of his life over which he had no self-control. He loved to eat so much, Joni recalls, that he once went to an Italian restaurant with a friend who was also overweight. Weinstein instructed the waiter to bring them every entrée on the menu. The ones listed above the halfway point of the menu would be served to his friend and those below the line to him. They told the waiter to bring the entrees to each of them one plate at a time.

At his heaviest, Weinstein weighed about 260 pounds. When he turned forty, his doctor insisted he go on a diet. He prescribed a plan that Weinstein referred to as "the Prudent Diet," involving balanced and reasonable portions. Following that diet, he shed fifty or sixty pounds. The weight loss left him looking very trim on his six-foot-two-inch frame. He was adamant about sticking to his diet. Losing the weight and keeping it off was a source of pride, prompting him to visit Brooks Brothers for a suit. After trying on several, he discovered he didn't like their style, so he hired a tailor who styled and custom-made suits for him. They accentuated Weinstein's lean figure and gave him a look and feeling of class.

After Weinstein lost the weight, he was stuck with piles of clothing that no longer fit him. He knew a police officer in the neighborhood who was as large as Weinstein used to be and gave him thousands of dollars' worth of his best clothing. Weinstein liked to give things away and make people feel good. Because of his job in the advertising industry, his clients often gave him tickets to events at Madison Square Garden, such as the Ice Capades and the circus; he donated them to the police and fire departments.

This was the father Joni knew: gentle and kind. He held doors for ladies and stood until all the women at a table were seated. Throughout her childhood and even as a young adult, she would hear her father tell her not to sweat the small stuff. When conflicts arose, he often would say, "It doesn't matter, it doesn't matter." Not even traffic disputes riled him. Joni never remembered hearing him raising his voice, ever. The children called him Mr. Zen because he was so even-keeled.

Life in suburban New Jersey was pretty good. His children attended private school. He sent them on vacations with their classmates to Italy, England, and Greece and had memberships at two country clubs. He bought Joni thousands of dollars in camera equipment to encourage her interest in photography and took her to New York City to visit galleries and museums.

But in 1987, Belle, the love of Weinstein's life, was diagnosed with an aggressive cancer that spread from her lungs to her liver and then her brain. Weinstein accompanied her to every doctor's appointment and chemotherapy session. Her decline was rapid. He hated to see her suffer. He stayed by her side, administering morphine to ease the pain, until she died at home. Though Weinstein often tried to suppress or hide his emotions, it was too much for him at Belle's funeral. He sat next to Joni in the front row holding hands. Joni felt her father's body quickly rising and falling. She looked at him and saw he had tears in his eyes. She was happy for him that he was able to cry.

After her mother died, Joni encouraged her father to go on dates.

He met Barbara through a mutual friend, and they seemed like a good match. Barbara was divorced and, like Weinstein, had two grown children, a son and a daughter. Barbara had always been considered an attractive woman, standing about five foot six, svelte, with luxuriant strawberry blond hair and blue eyes. She came from a moneyed past, having grown up on the Upper West Side, where her father owned a successful clothing business.

Before she met Weinstein, she had been married to Jerome Glazer, a New Orleans businessman who was chairman and chief executive of Glazer Steel and Aluminum. He was also a successful real estate developer and was active in political and civic affairs, counting district attorney Harry Connick, Sr., among his friends. Barbara had reluctantly moved to New Orleans after they married, and there they raised two children, Kim and Bradford. Barbara always yearned to return to New York, while Jerome felt deeply connected to New Orleans and his business. They divorced after twenty years, and Barbara moved back to New York with Kim, while Bradford went off to college.

Barbara and Kim got an apartment on the Upper East Side on East 72nd Street, the one where Barbara and Weinstein would eventually live together. Weinstein got along well with Kim, and she liked his sense of humor. Kim never saw Weinstein raise his voice, argue with her mom, or exhibit any kind of behavior that would be cause for concern. About the only thing she heard her mother complain about was that Weinstein's son was working as a croupier, assisting with bets and payouts at gaming tables, in Atlantic City. She thought Nelson could do better for himself.

Weinstein eventually sold his house in New Jersey, moved into Barbara's apartment, and took over the lease. He told his children that he loved her, and a year after Belle died, he announced that he was going to marry Barbara. Joni didn't like Barbara, whom she perceived as snobbish, and she didn't want her father to marry her. But she kept her opinions to herself, and the couple got married in the Crystal Room at Tavern on the Green on a blustery, snowy day in February. Afterward Joni didn't visit her father as much as she used to.

After her father was arrested for murder, Joni struggled with her feelings about him. As much as she loved him, she was repulsed when she read in the police account that he had confessed to choking Barbara and heaving her out the window. She thought he should go to prison. She even thought he might deserve the death penalty.

A few days after her father's arrest, Joni went with him and Nelson to attorney Diarmuid White's office to discuss the case. During a break, she privately asked her father what had happened.

He told her that Barbara had scratched his face and he had reacted without thinking. "I knew it was wrong, and I couldn't stop," he said.

"Was it an out-of-body experience?" Joni asked.

"I guess so," he said flatly. He told her that Barbara had initiated the argument and had been trying to get a rise out of him.

Joni knew there had to be some other explanation. *It's just not him,* she thought. He didn't get angry like that. But he really did kill Barbara—that was a fact.

When Joni learned that White was going to use the brain cyst to explain her father's actions, she thought it preposterous, a high-priced lawyer's desperate attempt at a defense that was going to cost a lot of money. She knew nothing about neuroscience. Nor had she given much thought to the possibility that her father's brain might yield clues to his homicidal behavior.

The case would take months to proceed, and Joni decided not to stick around for it. At the time of Barbara's death, she had been thinking about moving to San Francisco. She had already been preparing herself for being away from her father. Now she hastened the move. She was still angry when she left, asking herself what could have compelled her father to commit the most hideous of acts against another human being. Could he really have done it because that cyst in his brain caused him to become temporarily insane? She didn't give the theory much credence.

In fact, the basis for the defense that Weinstein's lawyer intended to use was centuries old, nearly as old as the legal system itself.

CHAPTER 4

The Brain Blame Evolution

The idea that the law might excuse a person for committing a crime because something was wrong with his brain has its roots in ancient Greece. In creating their public court system, the Greeks sought to turn the people's thirst for vengeance and retaliation into a more reasoned system of justice—a system that held offenders accountable for their actions but also tried to understand their minds. The Greeks thought the reasons people committed crimes were worthy of consideration. They recognized that those suffering from diseases of the mind should not necessarily be held responsible for their actions to the same degree as their mentally healthy counterparts, that these unfortunate lawbreakers deserved some measure of mercy because they lacked the ability to make rational or voluntary choices. Madness or insanity didn't exempt criminals from facing all consequences for their deeds, but it was considered a mitigating circumstance that could raise the possibility of alternatives to the harshest punishments.

Responsibility was not just a legal question but also a moral one. Aristotle wrote in 350 B.C. that moral responsibility depended on both intention and knowledge; these concepts became the foundation of most contemporary laws addressing criminal culpability and insanity. That is, holding an accused criminally responsible required proof that he committed the act (*actus reus*), and proof that he committed the act of his own free will, that it was intentional (*mens rea*). *Mens rea* translates, literally, to "guilty mind." In Aristotle's view, "pardon and sometimes pity" should be bestowed on those who commit involuntary deeds. Around the same time, Plato pondered the possibility that sickness might lead to bad behavior. "For no man is voluntarily bad," he wrote, "but the bad becomes bad by reason of an ill disposition of the body."

The Romans also supported leniency for those who suffered from madness. To be mad was considered by some as a punishment in itself. Accused criminals could be judged *non compos mentis* ("without mastery of mind") and thus not guilty for their criminal actions. Those who committed nonviolent crimes would often be sent home to their families. Criminals who were considered dangerous faced imprisonment. The Romans had no particular test or set of guidelines for determining madness. It was an affliction that they simply observed, long before anyone was administering diagnostic tests or peering into brains with scanners.

It wasn't until the eighteenth century that Britain began to establish legal guidelines for insanity. Under British law, a person's madness had to be obvious and overwhelming to serve as an excuse for a criminal act. The accused, through the questioning of the court, had to be judged incapable of distinguishing between good and evil or of grasping the consequences of his actions. In 1724 the English courts developed a standard that became known as the "wild beast test." It came out of a murder case, *Rex v. Arnold,* in which a man was tried on charges of shooting an English lord. Under the wild beast test, a person could be found insane if judged to be "totally deprived of his understanding and memory and not to know what he is doing any more than an infant, a brute, or a wild beast."

From the wild beast test came the "irresistible impulse" standard, which was first used successfully in 1840 during the trial of Edward Oxford, an Englishman who attempted to assassinate Queen Victoria. The court found that "if some controlling disease was . . . the acting power within him which he could not resist, then he will not be responsible."

For a time, lawyers who put on insanity defenses proved successful in a majority of cases. In the latter half of the eighteenth century, for example, one hundred recorded pleas of insanity were entered at the Old Bailey, London's Central Criminal Court. Of them, sixty resulted in acquittals, a success rate more than double that of today, in which 15 to 25 percent of such cases lead to a verdict of not guilty by reason of insanity. An acquittal at the Old Bailey meant the defendant could go free without any confinement to a mental institution or asylum, a policy that created public resentment and fear. However, if the person was considered too dangerous, the court could convene a separate civil hearing to determine whether he or she should be held at a lunatic asylum. There was no consistency in how these cases were handled. In most instances, the insane were sent home. Others were placed under the care and protection of friends or relatives. A handful were confined to asylums or chained to the walls of churches or public places.

The insanity defense became even more contentious when lawyers not only presented them but began to explore the *causes* of their client's irrational behavior in an effort to excuse their actions. One of the earliest legal attempts to explain that a brain injury led to crime-inducing insanity occurred in England in 1800. On May 5 of that year, James Hadfield, a veteran of the king's army, shot at King George III as he entered the royal box at the Drury Lane Theatre in London. The king was bowing to the audience at the time Hadfield fired a shot and was not hit. Hadfield was captured and charged with a capital crime, even though he had missed his intended target. He was also charged with high treason, a political crime that afforded him a key benefit under English law: he was allowed to put on a defense with an outside counsel. (Had he shot at an ordinary citizen, he would have been tried at the Old Bailey, where he would have been required to put on his own defense.) Hadfield also had the right to require the court to pay attorney fees to the counsel of his choice.

He picked the renowned lawyer Thomas Erskine. Erskine learned that Hadfield had suffered serious head wounds during a military campaign against the French. His head injuries had such a profound effect on his mental state that the army had discharged him; his face was permanently disfigured, and those in his community were quite sympathetic toward the veteran after he returned to civilian life. Erskine urged Hadfield to plead insanity, concluding that he had been delusional at the time he shot at the king: Hadfield had said he believed that if he killed the king, the world would come to an end and would result in the second advent of Christ.

The prosecutor, John Mitford, argued that while Hadfield may have been delusional or even insane, in order to be found not guilty he must also suffer from "an absolute privation of reason," an inability to distinguish between good and evil. But Lord Erskine countered that all mad people retain some ability to understand and reason, that they need not always be in a state of frenzied madness; delusions were characteristic of insanity, not total incapacitation. He went on to explain to the jury that Hadfield's insanity was not his fault; he had valiantly served king and country and was honorably wounded at the battle of Lisle against the French.

Erskine may have been among the first to call medical experts to testify about brain damage in a criminal case. The distinguished surgeon Henry Cline testified that several of the head wounds that Hadfield suffered during battle were bad enough to cause brain damage. Cline suggested that he was permanently damaged. Another physician testified that he had not the "smallest doubt" that Hadfield was insane and that his condition was most likely caused by his war wounds.

The evidence supporting Hadfield's insanity was strong. The chief judge, anticipating an acquittal, was concerned about his being released if found not guilty. An assistant prosecutor suggested to the judge that if the jury explained its reasoning for the verdict, then the court would have reason to detain Hadfield because he was insane and might pose a danger. The conversation between the judge and prosecutor was within earshot of jurors, likely by design, so they might consider an option that would serve everyone's interests. The jury returned a verdict of not guilty, explaining that it reached the verdict because Hadfield "was under the influence of insanity at the time the act was committed." This may have been the first time such a verdict was read with an explanation, and it set the foundation for the modern not-guilty-by-reason-of-insanity verdict, which carries with it a justification to detain the defendant in a mental health institution to protect himself and society from future harm if deemed necessary by the court.

Hadfield's acquittal caused concern among the government and its prosecutors, who did not want him freed. Attorney General Mitford introduced a bill in the House of Commons that changed the crime of murder or attempted murder against the king from an act of treason to a regular felony, which meant defendants would not be afforded the privilege of legal counsel that Hadfield had been given.

The measure also required that those found not guilty by reason of insanity be held in confinement, and it gave the government power to preventively detain mentally ill persons charged or even those just suspected of crimes. The bill created a special verdict of insanity that empowered the king to confine someone acquitted by reason of insanity and made it retroactive so that it applied to Hadfield. That person could be confined until "His Majesty's pleasure be known." From then on, people found not guilty by reason of insanity could be held indefinitely and sent to prison or an asylum. The belief was that even a mentally ill person could be deterred from committing a crime by the threat of punishment.

Five months after firing a shot at the king, Hadfield, considered insane, was sent to Bethlem Hospital, the asylum known locally as Bedlam. He spent forty-one years in confinement before dying of tuberculosis in 1841. The fallout from his case was inconsistent, and the courts did not follow a discernible pattern in dealing with insanity cases, which varied often according to the whims of judges.

Across the Atlantic in New York, another case would soon unfold that would bring to light the growing conflict between the medical community's interpretation of insanity and the legal community's definition of criminal responsibility. Pleas of insanity were commonly met with skepticism, anger, and even ridicule among a public hungry for justice and seeking retribution. In one instance, such a plea almost sparked racially charged mob justice.

On the evening of March 12, 1846, William Freeman, an ex-convict of African and Indian descent, arrived at a farmhouse in Fleming, New York. A fresh layer of snow blanketed the ground. Freeman crept toward the house carrying two knives. Sarah Van Nest stepped out her back door, where Freeman had been standing. Without word or warning, he plunged a knife deep into her abdomen. The woman screamed, stumbled to the front of the house, and collapsed.

She bled to death in a few minutes. Freeman walked into the house through the back door. Sarah's husband, John G. Van Nest, confronted Freeman, who stabbed him in the chest, piercing his heart. Freeman continued through the house. He found the couple's sleeping two-year-old son, George Washington Van Nest, and put a knife through him, killing him. A hired hand named Cornelius Van Ardsdale heard the commotion and came inside the house to investigate. Freeman stabbed him in the chest, though not fatally. The wounded Ardsdale chased Freeman from the house.

Outside, Sarah's mother, Mrs. Phoebe Wyckoff, who had heard the screams, was waiting, armed with a butcher knife. Freeman attempted to slash her, but she was able to slice his wrist during their struggle. The wounded woman ran a quarter mile to the next house for help. Freeman stole her horse and rode off the property to escape. When the first horse gave out, he stole another and continued riding into the night.

Lawmen tracked Freeman down and arrested him the next day, about forty miles from the Van Nest home. They took him back to the scene of the crime, where a mob had assembled, thirsty for vengeance. Members of the crowd proposed lynching Freeman, burning him, or putting him on the rack to suffer a painful death. The lawmen who captured him feared they might lose him to the impatient mob. As some men in the crowd readied a lasso to try to snatch Freeman, the authorities moved in quickly and carted him off in a wagon. The mob chased them all the way to the nearby town of Auburn, where Freeman was jailed and charged with multiple murders.

Freeman needed a lawyer, but the case was so hideous, the crime so awful, that no one stepped forward to offer legal representation. One man eventually volunteered: William Seward, the former governor of New York who would later become Abraham Lincoln's secretary of state. Seward was sympathetic to Freeman, who exhibited symptoms of mental impairment and seemed shamed and unusually shy. Seward learned something else that disturbed him. As a youth, Freeman had been sent to prison for horse thievery, but his conviction had been questionable. Moreover, during his five-year confinement, he had suffered beatings that might have led to or exacerbated his mental condition. In one altercation, a guard had beaten him on the head with a board. Freeman became partially deaf and, according to townspeople, slow-witted and detached. The facts of the Van Nest murders were such that seemingly only a sick mind could have committed them. Freeman never denied his actions.

As governor, Seward had devoted a good deal of energy to improving life for the mentally ill, inspired in part by the mental health crusader Dorothea Lynde Dix. Seward took on Freeman's case with a special understanding of mental illness and compassion for those who suffered from it. But elsewhere compassion for Freeman was all but nonexistent. He was a black man charged with killing a white family in a peaceful rural community, and the pressure to convict him was immense.

During the arraignment, Freeman entered a plea of insanity—his condition, his lawyer argued, was caused by the harsh and abusive beatings he had suffered in prison. Seward contended that Freeman's murder spree was the result of an impulse to avenge both his unjust imprisonment for horse thievery and the beatings he suffered there. The well-connected Seward arranged for the best expert witnesses he could find.

Freeman's murder trial opened on June 25, 1846, with a preliminary trial to determine first whether he was sane. The prosecutor was state attorney John Van Buren, son of former president Martin Van Buren. Both sides called witnesses to discuss Freeman's life and mental condition before, during, and after the murders. The witnesses included friends, family members, fellow prisoners, police officers, local townspeople, and prison employees. The judge learned that Freeman had had a seemingly normal and happy boyhood, though he was intellectually simple. He often had a vacant stare and what people described as an idiotic smile. He had an aunt and uncle who were considered insane, and it was possible, his lawyer said, that his mental state was a family trait. Others who knew Freeman said in court that his behavior changed markedly after he was beaten on the head in prison.

An official at the prison where Freeman served his five-year sentence, Capt. James E. Tyler, testified that during the prisoner's first year, he had decided that Freeman should be flogged for not doing all his assigned work in the shop. Tyler said that he ordered Freeman to take off his clothes, and when he turned to get his whip, he felt a blow to the back of his head. As Tyler turned around, Freeman hit him on the back. Tyler kicked at Freeman and knocked him over. Freeman got up and dashed for a knife inside the shop, grabbed it, and lunged toward Tyler. "I took up a piece of wood lying on the desk, went down, and met him. It was a basswood board, two feet long, fourteen inches wide, and half an inch thick," Tyler said.

Tyler got closer to Freeman. "I struck him on the head flatwise, split the board, and left a piece in my hand four inches wide," he told the jury. "I hit him eight or ten more times with the remaining board." He then flogged Freeman about a dozen times: "A black man's hide is thicker than a white man's, and I meant to make him feel the punishment." Following the fight and the flogging, Freeman behaved as if all his interest in other human beings had been beaten out of him. From then on he walked with his head down, his demeanor flat.

The preliminary trial continued as attorneys from both sides brought medical experts to the witness stand to present contradicting evidence about Freeman's mental state. Seven of them declared that Freeman was insane, while six testified that he was not. After jurors announced that they were unable to reach a decision, Judge Bowen Whiting tried to simplify their task. He instructed them that the main question was whether Freeman knew right from wrong. If he did, then he was sane. About an hour later, the jury came back and said he did know the difference between right and wrong. Seward objected but to no avail. Freeman would have to go to trial.

If Freeman's sanity had been a contentious issue on its own, the underlying racism made the case against him even more difficult. On the day of the trial, a local mob burned him in effigy. The prosecution prepared to stoke the fires of racism, lining up experts prepared to testify that Freeman's speech impediment and lack of emotions were linked to his descent from African slaves and "savage" Native Americans.

The jury faced a daunting and laborious task. Most of the witnesses from the preliminary trial returned to testify. In all, there were 108 witnesses. The basic facts of the crime were not in dispute, as Freeman had admitted his role in the killings. The trial was largely a debate among physicians over his state of mind. Seventeen physicians testified, though many of them had limited experience in observing or treating insane or mentally ill people.

Prosecution witness Leander B. Bigelow, whose background included experience as a prison surgeon, was blunt and hardly scientific. Among his self-proclaimed skills was detecting fakers of insanity. He visited Freeman on several occasions and, after examining him, concluded that he "is an ignorant, dull stupid, morose and degraded negro, but not insane." Dr. Samuel Gilmore also examined Freeman in prison and found that, while his crime may have been depraved, his apparent planning for the murders and the skill with which he carried them out suggested he was sane. Dr. Thomas Spencer, who "bestowed much mental labor on this case," showed the jury a chart to help them sort out the brain's functions. The diagram identified what he called the thirty-six faculties of the mind, divided into three classes: involuntary, voluntary, and intermediate. He gave the jury a lesson in how they worked and applied it to Freeman, who, he concluded, was sane.

Seward, who challenged Spencer on cross-examination, put up his own experts. Dr. Blanchard Fosgate, who had treated Freeman's wounded hand in the jail and visited him several times, described him as out of touch. "I think he does not comprehend the idea of right and wrong," Fosgate testified. "He has no moral sense of accountability." Seward had persuaded Dr. Amariah Brigham to come in from Utica, thirteen hours away by train, to testify. Brigham clearly was the most accomplished expert in this area: he had published writings on insanity, edited *the Journal of Insanity,* and worked as superintendent of an insane asylum. During his physical examination of Freeman, he had noted that his skin had a peculiar pallor, which suggested insanity, possibly an inherited condition. But most obvious was the character transformation in Freeman from "a lively active, sociable lad," before his wrongful conviction and time in prison, to the man who became "taciturn, dull and stupid."

Seward then called to the stand Dr. John McCall, president of the Medical Society of New York. This esteemed physician declared that Freeman's brain was diseased and that the beatings he had suffered in prison might have injured it further. Freeman had been under an insane delusion—possibly an irresistible impulse—when he murdered Van Nest and the others, he said, and should not be held responsible. But perhaps most significantly, McCall pointed out that knowing the difference between right and wrong, as Freeman apparently did, did not preclude him from being insane. "I do not consider a verdict of sanity. It falls far short of it."

The trial went on for thirteen days before the lawyers made their closing arguments. Seward told jurors that Freeman was not faking insanity and reminded them about the medical testimony they heard suggesting otherwise. Van Buren said "criminal responsibility is a question of law, not medicine." He concluded, "If the punishment of crime is to be determined by medical rules, the professors should sit upon the bench and fill the jury box."

Judge Whiting was careful to instruct the jury on the question of insanity, expanding his instruction from the preliminary trial. Sanity started with whether a person knew right from wrong, he said, but it also consisted of possessing memory, intelligence, reason, and will. "If sane, he is guilty. If insane, he is not guilty. There is no middle ground."

On July 23, 1846, the jury came back with a guilty verdict. The next day the judge sentenced Freeman to hang by the neck until dead. But Freeman did not go to the gallows right away. Seward appealed the case to the New York Supreme Court on a writ of error. On February 11, 1847, the court reversed the judgment and ordered a new trial. Seward, intent on not letting Freeman suffer the fate of being hanged, once again called his friend Dr. Brigham. He asked Brigham to get him the names of one hundred of the most intelligent physicians in New York and abroad who might provide evidence on Freeman's behalf. It turned out to be unnecessary. Freeman's health went into rapid decline. He died in his cell, in chains, on August 21, 1847.

But the questions of Freeman's sanity and the state of his brain remained. On the morning of his death, a group of physicians assembled for a postmortem. They removed his brain and put it on ice to prevent any deterioration before Dr. Brigham and a colleague arrived that evening. A crowd of lawyers and doctors gathered to watch the autopsy and observe Brigham dissect the brain. Afterward Brigham prepared a statement, signed by himself and the other physicians, that said Freeman's brain appeared to show chronic disease, including a thickened arachnoid membrane and a medullary portion of "unnaturally dusky color, harder in places, as if parboiled." There was no question that this brain was diseased. Brigham, in a later statement, said that based on all the evidence and on Freeman's history, "this was a case of insanity—that Freeman had disease of the brain, and was deranged in mind, from a period some time previous to his leaving prison, until the time of his death."

Seward might have been vindicated, but he felt the wrath of much of his community. His attempt to understand why his client had committed murder and to seek a measure of mercy for him brought down anger, hostility, and verbal abuse on himself and his family. He wrote afterward, "I rise from these fruitless labors exhausted in mind and body, covered with public reproach, stunned with duns and protests."

Yet Seward's willingness to defend Freeman created a larger public discussion about the insanity defense that would intensify in the years to come. His work on the case also drew widespread admiration and helped propel his legal and, eventually, political career. Twelve years later President Abraham Lincoln appointed him secretary of state.

Though insanity defenses had become part of the legal landscape in the United States and Britain by the time of the Freeman trial, lawmakers in both countries had not created definitive rules to regulate its use or definition. Britain was the first to codify the legal insanity defense, prompted by the case of a man charged with attempting to assassinate the prime minister. In 1843 a Scottish laborer named Daniel M'Naghten went to 10 Downing Street and fired a pistol at the back of a man he believed to be British prime minister Robert Peel. It wasn't the prime minister—M'Naghten killed Peel's secretary, Edward Drummond. Before he could fire another shot, M'Naghten was captured and charged with first-degree murder.

M'Naghten had the means to assemble a first-rate team of barristers and medical experts to claim he had been insane at the time of the shooting. At his murder trial, his legal team argued that M'Naghten was in the midst of a paranoid delusion and believed the prime minister wanted to kill him. His medical experts testified that he was psychotic. The evidence was overwhelming that M'Naghten was mentally unstable, and he was found not guilty by reason of insanity. The public was outraged. Even Queen Victoria expressed her displeasure, and members of Parliament were indignant at what they perceived as a gross miscarriage of justice.

M'Naghten was not released, however. The judge sent him to the lunatic asylum at Bethlem Hospital, where James Hadfield had been sent following his acquittal forty-three years earlier.

Immediately after M'Naghten's acquittal, the House of Lords established specific guidelines for dealing with criminal defendants who might use the same defense. Under the new rules, insanity claims would be judged on whether defendants knew what they were doing when they committed the crime and whether they knew it was wrong. If one or both of those questions was answered no, a defendant would have the basis for an insanity defense.

The M'Naghten rule hinges on cognitive factors, meaning it can absolve people from legal responsibility if they lack the capacity to understand the meaning of a crime. For more than one hundred years, courts in Britain, as well as the United States, used M'Naghten as a guideline for the insanity defense. In 1962 the American Law Institute broadened the insanity defense to include cases in which a person could not control his or her impulse to act because of a psychiatric disorder. It made room for those who might have an understanding of a criminal act and its consequences but were unable to inhibit impulsive, destructive behavior. The thinking was that people who cannot control their actions should be treated rather than punished.

Determining whether a person was sane has been, and continues to be, based mostly on observed behavior and diagnosis by trained mental health professionals. In the late eighteenth and early nineteenth centuries, however, doctors and scientists delving into the causes of psychiatric disorders discovered that biological, psychological, environmental, and genetic factors play a role. When imaging technology allowed researchers to see inside the brain, new theories sprang forth about physiological characteristics that might explain why some people were insane.

The public got its first glimpse of the courtroom battles to come during the trial of John Hinckley, Jr., who was tried for attempting to assassinate President Ronald Reagan in 1981. Hinckley's defense lawyers, using the insanity defense, brought in medical doctors to support a diagnosis that he had had schizophrenia and been delusional when he shot the president and wounded three others. Dr. William Carpenter, a University of Maryland psychiatrist who specialized in schizophrenia and the lead expert for the defense, diagnosed Hinckley with major depressive disorder and "process schizophrenia," which he described as beginning in adolescence or early adulthood and progressing to a severe disorder typically characterized by breaks from reality, magical thinking, and delusions.

Hinckley's lawyers then sought to introduce into evidence CAT (computerized axial tomography) scans, which provided structural images of Hinckley's brain. Federal district judge Barrington D. Parker initially refused to allow the scans but later changed his mind, saying they might help give jurors a complete picture. They could reach their own conclusions about the scans' value. Legal scholars believe this was the first time such evidence was used in a criminal trial,

The CAT scans, Hinckley's lawyers claimed, showed evidence of a shrunken brain, which some researchers believed occurred more frequently in schizophrenics than in normal men Hinckley's age. Dr.

Marjorie LeMay of Harvard Medical School testified that Hinckley's brain was "'shrunken' to an unusual degree," though she stopped short of saying that it could be associated with schizophrenia.

In the end, the brain scans were not critical to Hinckley's defense. His lawyers had built a substantial case that he suffered from a diminished mental state. Psychiatrists and mental health experts who testified portrayed him as a man battling an intense internal struggle and full of despair. Prosecutors argued, however, that Hinckley's assassination attempt had been a deliberate, well-planned bid for fame, motivated by his desire to impress the actress Jodie Foster. Most crucially, they said, Hinckley knew right from wrong.

The jury deliberated for four days and came back with a verdict of not guilty by reason of insanity. Judge Parker ordered that Hinckley be committed to a hospital for the mentally ill until he was no longer considered a threat to himself or to others.

The use of brain scans during Hinckley's trial proved less controversial than the verdict itself. News that the man who had tried to kill the president would not go to prison unleashed a storm of protests, letters, phone calls, and demands for reform of the insanity defense, much as the M'Naghten verdict had 140 years earlier. People around the country, outraged by the apparent coddling of a dangerous criminal, bombarded their local legislatures with requests to eliminate the insanity defense altogether.

Government responded. At the federal level, the Reagan administration proposed redefining the rules so that juries had less discretion to acquit those deemed insane. Congress passed restrictions on the insanity standard, shifting the burden of proof. Prior to Hinckley, prosecutors had the burden not only to prove a defendant was guilty but also to *disprove* an insanity claim. Now it would be up to defense lawyers to put on an *affirmative defense,* meaning they carry the burden to prove that a defendant was insane. The majority of states followed Congress's lead requiring an affirmative defense.

In the first three years after the Hinckley verdict, about half the states enacted further limitations on the insanity defense. Some abolished its use altogether. Others passed legislation giving juries the option of rendering a verdict of guilty but mentally ill, which acknowledged that defendants could have mental health problems but were not absolved of responsibility. Those found guilty were required to receive psychiatric treatment in prison or in a secure mental health facility until they were well enough to serve the remainder of their sentence in prison.

Despite its controversial nature, the insanity defense is rarely used. Fewer than 1 percent of criminal cases involve an insanity plea, and the majority of these cases end up with a verdict of guilty. In the rare instances in which a defendant is found not guilty by reason of insanity, the law allows judges to commit those persons to treatment centers or mental health institutions until officials pronounce they no longer pose a danger to themselves or others, as was the case with Hinckley. In 2015 his family began efforts to seek his release. On July 26, 2016, a federal judge determined that Hinckley, at sixty-one, no longer posed a danger to himself or others and ordered him released from a government psychiatric hospital to live full time with his mother.

Though Hinckley's lawyers had mounted a successful insanity defense, insanity, as it is now defined, is tough to prove. Herbert Weinstein was taking a huge gamble with his defense. Not only was he claiming insanity, he was claiming that he had been temporarily insane, and that his condition had been triggered by a cyst in his brain. As far-fetched as his strategy sounded, Weinstein's attorney was going to seek experts who could support that theory or were willing to try.

CHAPTER 5

Inside Weinstein's Brain

For the most part, defense attorney Diarmuid White was less concerned with what went on inside his clients' prefrontal cortexes than with keeping them out of prison. He spent his days laboring in New York's criminal justice system and navigating the crowded courtrooms of Lower Manhattan, where his clients were a revolving lineup of rough characters accused of murder, rape, fraud, and various felonies involving dangerous weapons. Neuroscience meant about as much to him as rocket science.

That all changed with Herbert Weinstein, the strangely emotionless white-haired gentleman from the Upper East Side who was willing to pay for a complicated and expensive murder defense. So by necessity, White found himself immersed in brain science. He wanted to understand how the giant cyst inside Weinstein's skull might be used to absolve him. He checked out medical books from the library, read specialized medical journals, and studied neuroscience textbooks at night and on weekends. He pored over their dense pages looking for ideas. He kept a medical dictionary at his side, consulting it frequently, whenever he got stuck in jargon.

During his crash course, White learned that the area of the brain that was being squeezed by Weinstein's arachnoid cyst was associated with judgment and decision making, functions that could be compromised or altered by injury. Case studies showed that damage to this area not only could cause a person to lose powers of forethought but might also prompt them to become violent. White decided to build his case on the theory that the pressure from the cyst had so damaged Weinstein's prefrontal cortex that it affected his powers of reason and impaired his ability to control his impulses during the argument with his wife; Weinstein's brain was so disorganized and his thoughts so disinhibited that he had gone temporarily insane and killed her. White would have to prove that at the time of the murder Weinstein lacked the mental capacity to realize that he had committed a crime and that what he did was wrong. For that to work, White would need support from experts and, ideally, some kind of diagnostic proof that such growth in the brain could prompt a person to commit murder.

White knew he was taking a big chance. Most defendants found not guilty by reason of insanity were seriously mentally ill, having been diagnosed with a chronic, long-term mental illness such as schizophrenia before they committed crimes. Weinstein certainly wasn't schizophrenic; nor did he have any other diagnosed mental illness. He showed no evidence of delusions or other mental impairments. He was very much aware of what he'd done to his wife, though he acted quite undisturbed when speaking about it and appeared to be lacking in emotion and spirit. But he understood what was going on around him. By any standards he was competent to stand trial and capable of assisting in his legal defense.

But White wanted to dig deeper into his mind, insistent that while Weinstein's brain functioned and allowed him to live normally to all appearances, it became compromised, agitated, and illogical amid the stress of fighting with his wife. He would have to prove that Weinstein was temporarily insane at the moment he killed his wife. Little did he realize that the scientific evidence he needed had already been accumulating.

While Weinstein was out on bail, his personal physician referred him to a neurologist to evaluate the cyst and its possible long-term effects. Dr. Norman Relkin was an associate professor of neurology at New York Hospital–Cornell Medical Center and coordinator for the Neurobehavior Evaluation Program at Cornell University. He was one of an esteemed group of neurologists, psychologists, and neuropsychologists who treated patients with brain disorders.

Upon examining Weinstein's MRI image, Relkin was struck by the size and placement of his cyst. He'd never seen one this large, and he could see that it was pushing on Weinstein's frontal lobe, parietal lobe, and temporal lobe. He estimated that the temporal lobe was displaced backward, and to some extent upward, by about three centimeters. The part of the left frontal lobe known as the orbitofrontal cortex (called orbital because it's close to the eye, or orbit) was also pushed up about a centimeter. The cyst was like a hard rubber ball putting pressure downward on a softer but larger ball.

After meeting Weinstein, Relkin described him in his notes with dry, clinical language as "a well-dressed elderly male with a normal head circumference without significant skeletal or muscular asymmetry." During their conversation, he noticed that Weinstein repeatedly made facial tics, as if he were grimacing, and sniffed loudly and regularly. The doctor asked him about it. Weinstein explained that the sniffing was a long-standing habit that got worse in stressful situations. Relkin wondered whether Weinstein had Tourette's syndrome but decided it was unlikely, as there was no family history of the disorder, which is believed to be inherited. Relkin went through a series of general neurological tests to gauge Weinstein's sensory and motor skills and nerve function. Based on these tests, he concluded that Weinstein was pretty much normal—nothing seemed wrong with him.

Relkin asked Weinstein to review his medical history. Weinstein told the neurologist about being hospitalized in 1948 when he was in his twenties. He'd been in excellent health as a young man but began developing headaches, strangely and suddenly, mostly on the left side of his head. The headaches increased in severity and intensity. Then, some months after the initial onset of these headaches, he had what appeared to be a seizure, as well as other neurological problems that lasted for a few weeks. His left eyelid drooped. He had some difficulty naming things. He experienced memory problems. The symptoms had come without warning, occurring spontaneously and unpredictably over the course of several weeks. The records showed that Weinstein's doctors had ordered an EEG (electroencephalograph) to record electrical activity in his brain, along with a spinal tap and cerebral angiogram. The spinal tap showed some bleeding in Weinstein's central nervous system, though the exact site was unclear. The angiogram on the left side of his brain showed that the shape of his cerebral vasculature was normal. Relkin surmised that the cyst had developed and expanded later in Weinstein's life.

He asked Weinstein whether he had any current or past homicidal or suicidal thoughts. Weinstein said no. The doctor noted that Weinstein's mood seemed neutral, devoid of much emotion. He didn't seem nervous, sad, or remorseful about the recent tragedy in his life. Relkin would later say that Weinstein's affect seemed inappropriate when he was discussing his wife's death. He spoke of her strangulation and the disposal of her body in a deadpan, dispassionate tone. After the murder, he said, he recalled an outward sense of dismay at losing control of himself, but he did not elaborate and stopped himself from sharing any further self-reflection. Relkin concluded that Weinstein seemed to appreciate the moral implications of what he had done but could not explain or fully understand what had driven him to it.

After the exam, Relkin thought about how the cyst might have affected Weinstein's brain, and possibly his behavior. He knew that arachnoid cysts like Weinstein's had been associated with brain dysfunction. Some scientific papers had examined the possible link. One of them documented the experiences of eight patients with intracranial cysts who had suffered from psychiatric disturbances. A more recent report presented the case of a seventeen-year-old boy whose behavior had become unusual and difficult to explain. His doctors were puzzled, unable to connect his behavioral problems with any psychiatric diagnosis, which prompted them to order a CAT scan. There they discovered an arachnoid cyst, similar to Weinstein's, on the right side of his temporal lobe. After surgeons removed the cyst, the boy's symptoms showed a gradual improvement. Based on such reports, Relkin had reason to believe that arachnoid cysts could indeed compromise brain function and their removal could restore patients to some normalcy.

Relkin and his colleagues at Cornell met to discuss the Weinstein case in detail. They invited Weinstein to sit in for part of the meeting. He mostly listened and didn't say much. One doctor asked whether he had any regrets with regard to the death of his wife. Weinstein replied matter-of-factly that he regretted he had lost control of himself that day. A few beats later, as an afterthought, he said he regretted that he killed someone he loved. As before, he offered no indication of remorse and showed no emotion.

The doctors thought his responses were unusual, perhaps an indication of brain dysfunction. Lack of remorse and lack of empathy were among the known effects of frontal lobe syndrome, which could explain Weinstein's flat demeanor. A psychiatrist in the group suggested that Weinstein, in an effort to avoid painful feelings about killing his wife, was using a psychological defense mechanism known as "isolation of affect." While he was able to clearly and clinically recite details of the murder, he blocked, or steered himself away from, the emotional charge connected with it.

The doctors also talked about Weinstein's medical history and recent psychological testing. They were particularly interested in the results of the Wechsler Adult Intelligence Scale, which measures verbal skills, memory, vocabulary, and reasoning through a series of exercises involving reading, writing, solving math problems, and completing visual puzzles. Weinstein scored twenty-one points higher on the verbal portion than on the performance portion, a gap the doctors considered significant. Perhaps the cyst had altered his brain function early in life. Perhaps it shifted his left brain function, including linguistic skills, to the right side, due to the phenomenon of brain plasticity. When the right side is crowded with more functions than it normally handles, right-sided functions can be compromised. Therefore, the theory went, Weinstein was less capable of carrying out nonlinguistic functions than linguistic ones because the damage on his left side overtaxed his right side. But this was just a theory, and nothing at this point could support it with anything close to definitiveness.

Relkin wanted to probe deeper into the effects of the cyst on Weinstein's brain to see if there was evidence of dysfunction, so he recommended that Weinstein get a PET scan. Until the advent of X-rays and other noninvasive imaging techniques, the only way to observe brain damage had been to see its physical results. The Phineas Gage case, as we have seen, opened the doors for a sort of brain mapping that helped scientists and physicians tie specific parts of the brain to specific behaviors. By observing changes in a person due to a lesion or trauma, they could link an area of the brain to its function. But at the time of Weinstein's case, peering inside the head of a live person to detect brain activity as it was occurring was relatively new and its implications were still unclear.

Standard MRI and CAT scans provide static, structural images of the brain. PET scans, by contrast, are capable of measuring activity inside the brain such as blood flow, oxygen use, and glucose metabolism, all of which could help identify any abnormalities in brain function. PET images, obtained through radiation, had the potential to reveal metabolic changes occurring at the cellular level, allowing Relkin to determine how well Weinstein's brain was working, especially around the area of the cyst. A lack of metabolic activity could confirm dysfunction.

Relkin scheduled a PET scan for Weinstein at New York Hospital-Cornell Medical Center on the Upper East Side. Dr. David Eidelberg, the director of neurological PET scanning, would oversee the procedure. Dr. Eidelberg injected Weinstein with a small dose of flourine-18 deoxyglucose, a radiotracer that would travel through his body to his brain, where it would be visible through the radiation-based scanning process. He lay on his back on a movable bed that would be wheeled so that his head was surrounded by a large doughnut-shaped halo. When the radiotracer reached Weinstein's brain, it would be metabolized in the same way that glucose is metabolized, thus showing where there was brain activity. The scanner picked up the radioactivity emitted from Weinstein's brain where it was metabolizing glucose. Using a computer, a technician converted the radioactive energy into 3-D images for the doctors to evaluate.

When Relkin and his colleagues looked at the images of Weinstein's brain, they found areas of significantly reduced glucose metabolism. The reduced activity, as Relkin suspected, occurred around the cyst and, to a lesser extent, in regions on the other side of Weinstein's brain. Eidelberg found that as a result of the cyst, glucose metabolism in some regions was below normal by greater than two standard deviations. Such weak activity confirmed the neurological diagnosis of frontal lobe impairment.

This was good news for Weinstein and Diarmuid White. But using the PET scan images in court to prove that a defendant was temporarily insane and not criminally responsible would be uncharted territory.

White was planning to argue that his client had simply lost it on the day he killed his wife. Herbert Weinstein was otherwise a kind, law-abiding, peaceful, intelligent man. Could White prove that his damaged brain had caused him to commit an uncharacteristic act? Could an otherwise balanced, gentle person commit an act of savage violence triggered by a growth in his brain?

CHAPTER 6

"That's Not My Dad"

Late one night in June 2012, David Alonso was watching TV in his small Cape Cod–style home in Bloomsbury, New Jersey, when he dozed off on the living room couch. He woke up early the next morning and trudged upstairs toward the bedroom. Groggy and unsteady, he tripped and tumbled backward, striking the base of his skull on the wooden floor at the bottom of the stairs. His wife, Debra, heard the noise, rushed down, and found him unconscious. She tried to revive him and saw that his eyes were flickering. She called 911, and paramedics took him by ambulance to a local hospital.

In the ER, a doctor told Debra that her husband, age forty-eight, had fallen into a coma and could wake up in minutes, hours, days, or months. David spent about six more hours at the hospital before regaining consciousness. He was disoriented when he awoke, according to his wife, but doctors could find no reason to keep him at the hospital any longer, and a neurologist authorized his release. Because he had mentioned feeling a lot of anxiety lately, a psychiatrist prescribed antidepressants and suggested he go home to rest.

But something wasn't right. Once he was home, David acted oddly, curling up on the sofa and saying he was afraid to go outside. His balance wasn't good, and he stumbled into doorways as if he were drunk. He was tired and withdrawn and felt an inexplicable paranoia. He told Debra that he suspected someone was coming to kill the family. He wanted her and his twenty-four-year-old daughter, Malori, to leave the house and hide.

Five days later, just after sunrise on June 13, Malori was stirred awake by the sound of painful moans coming from her parents' bedroom. She sat up in her bed and heard footsteps coming down the hall toward her room. A large figure stood in her doorway holding something above his head. He walked over and swung the object toward the back of her head. She felt a sharp blow—a force so hard that it knocked teeth from her mouth. Then it registered: the man striking her was her father. He was in his pajamas and holding something that looked like a pepper mill. When she saw the dark, dilated pupils of his blue eyes, she thought, "That's not my dad."

Malori felt more blows to her body and head. David never said a word. Neither did she. She felt confused. This all seemed incongruous. She tried to shield herself with her hand as her father kept hitting her. She counted twenty blows before he turned around and left the room, clutching what was in fact a five-pound metal dumbbell.

Despite the many hits to her head, Malori remained conscious. She stumbled down the stairs and saw the family dogs, along with a digital clock that read 6:50. Her leg was numb. She went back upstairs to look for her mother. David was in the bedroom in a strange, disengaged, catatonic-like state.

Debra walked out of the bedroom in a daze. David had smashed her head with the dumbbell, too.

Malori turned to see her father hitting himself in the head with the weight, never flinching. She and Debra retreated downstairs and managed to dial 911 before going out onto the front lawn. A neighbor who was walking her dog saw the two and later described it as like a scene from the movie *Carrie*.

When police arrived, David Alonso was at the top of the stairs repeatedly pounding his head with the weight, smashing his skull and further damaging his brain. He chanted "OCC," for Ocean County College, a construction project he was working on.

He didn't put up a fight. He dropped the weight and just stood there. His injuries were so severe that he had to be taken twenty-five miles by helicopter to St. Luke's Hospital in Bethlehem, Pennsylvania, where he underwent emergency brain surgery. Malori was also taken by helicopter to the hospital. Debra was transported by ambulance and underwent head surgery. All three family members were listed in critical condition that night.

To the police, neighbors, and outsiders, what happened inside the Alonso home that morning appeared to be a case of domestic violence by a deranged and dangerous man. The Hunterdon County prosecutor's office charged Alonso with attempted murder.

The state police asked Malori a lot of questions as she recovered from her injuries. (Debra was still in no condition to talk.) Were there problems at home in her parents' marriage? Did her father have any motives to harm her or his wife? No, Malori insisted, he did not: "My dad is strong guy, and if he wanted to kill me, he would have killed me."

It was, Malori—and later Debra, too—told authorities, as if David had turned into a different person. The only explanation anyone could think of was the fall down the stairs that he had experienced three days earlier. He must have hurt his head more than the doctors at the hospital had thought. He must have sustained a traumatic brain injury. David had had a CAT scan after that fall, but the image had revealed no structural damage to his brain. Still, the fall could have caused a traumatic brain injury, which is often hard to detect because it involves the shearing of tiny connections in the network of neurons. David's self-inflicted damage to his brain after he attacked his wife and daughter was so severe that further diagnostic tests, such as PET scans or fMRI, would not reflect the state of his brain before he attacked himself.

The attack in the Alonso home that morning raised many puzzling questions for his family, friends, and authorities. None of it made sense, they said. Alonso wouldn't hurt anyone. He was a sensitive man. He cried at movies. He had a steady job as a construction project manager and was drummer in a rock-and-roll band with middle-aged pals who played at local clubs from time to time. He'd never been arrested and had no record of violent behavior or mental illness. He liked to eat cupcakes and ice cream like a kid. His daughter called him her teddy bear.

How could an otherwise normal person, a nonviolent person, commit such a horrific act? Could a knock on the head, a brain injury, or some other neurological anomaly cause such uncharacteristic and violent behavior? But even scarier for the family was the fact that David was facing attempted murder charges. If his brain was damaged, to what extent should he be held responsible? He had committed a serious felony that, in the eyes of the law, demanded prosecution.

The Hunterdon County prosecutor's office faced a dilemma when both Malori and Debra Alonso declined to pursue criminal charges against David. But regardless of their wishes, it was the prosecutor's responsibility to thoroughly investigate what had happened.

David Alonso's initial head injury was not uncommon. Every year in the United States, more than 1.7 million people suffer brain injuries, from mild concussions to more serious traumas that require hospitalization. Many of these injuries can trigger physical and cognitive problems ranging from minor to severe. The top cause of brain injury is falls, followed by motor vehicle accidents, collisions with or blows struck by objects, and assaults. Other causes include stroke and surgical complications. The Centers for Disease Control reports that more than 5.3 million Americans are currently living with a disability related to traumatic brain injury (TBI). In mild cases, TBI can cause brief mental health changes. In severe cases, people with TBI can suffer from bouts of unconsciousness or amnesia and seriously impaired cognitive and motor skills. TBI often triggers behavioral changes that cause struggles in a person's relationships with family and friends or diminish a person's ability to work, socialize, and perform household tasks and daily activities. Some TBI sufferers cannot control their thoughts or conduct. One study found that TBI is frequently accompanied by psychiatric disturbances, which can range from relatively minor to radical, including otherwise unexplained hostility and aggression.

Most people who sustain brain injuries do not become violent or commit crimes, so assuming cause and effect is not so simple. Each person brings his or her own mental, environmental, and physiological baggage to the table. In the early 1980s, David Alonso served time in Beirut as a U.S. Marine, though he never had a documented head injury or showed signs of PTSD, mental illness, or psychiatric distress. About the most serious mental affliction he faced was professional stress at his construction job and accompanying insomnia.

Researchers have investigated a possible link between TBI and criminal behavior. Since the 1980s, dozens of studies have found that people in prison have higher incidences of TBI than the general population, but the numerical results vary widely: anywhere from 25 percent to 87 percent of inmates report having experienced a head injury, compared to about 8.5 percent in the general population. In 2011 a meta-analysis (a study of studies) of twenty-six research papers found "a significantly higher prevalence of traumatic brain injury in the incarcerated groups compared to the general population." But most of the twenty-six studies relied on prisoners' self-reporting their injuries, and their claims could not be independently confirmed with medical records. Moreover, the researchers did not know whether the prisoners had shown a propensity to violence before or after their self-described injuries. The studies also failed to answer whether the kind of behavior that leads people to prison could also lead to head injury. The meta-analysis pointed out that people at risk for TBI are similar to those people at risk for behavior leading to prison: low socioeconomic status, low education, male, and a propensity to engage in risky behavior.

Given that those who suffer from TBI can undergo behavioral changes and act out in ways they may not have before, their cases pose unusual challenges in a criminal justice system that is rooted in the idea that people have the free will to choose their behavior. In the David Alonso case, prosecutors would have to grapple with whether he had attacked his wife and daughter willingly or had been driven, perhaps because of a TBI, by some force he could not control.

Alonso spent five months in a rehabilitation hospital recovering from his head injuries before he was able to come to court to face charges. He told doctors, as well as visiting friends and family members, that he had no memory of what happened the night he was taken to the hospital. No one had talked to him about it yet. But he would soon be released from the hospital, and the police would have to arrest him. When Malori learned her father was to be released in late November 2012, she arranged to visit before the police arrived so that she could tell him what happened first.

She sat down across from him in his room. He was wearing a protective helmet, still healing from his head injuries. "Dad, I have to tell you something," she began. "You didn't mean to, but you hurt me and Mom." She did not offer details.

David wanted to know more. She just said it was bad.

"I would never hurt you," he said.

"I know. It's okay," she said. "It's not your fault. You didn't do it."

David cried. The police came for him a short time later. Detectives cuffed him, covered his shackled hands with a blanket, and rolled him in a wheelchair out to a waiting SUV with pillows where he could rest his head. Malori noticed that the officers were treating him kindly and respectfully. Perhaps they saw him as a victim the same way his family did.

David's first court appearance was at the Hunterdon County Courthouse in Flemington, New Jersey. Eighty years earlier, in the old courthouse down the street (now a historic landmark), Bruno Richard Hauptmann had been tried for the kidnapping and murder of Charles Lindbergh's son, in "the trial of the century." In 2012 in the modernized court building, a judge told David Alonso that he was being charged with attempted murder and set bail at $250,000. He ordered David to undergo a mental competency evaluation at a state hospital. But David had to wait nearly two months until a bed was available at a secure mental health facility, and because he could not afford to post bond, he was held at the county jail in a medical unit. The Alonsos hired an attorney from Newark, Joseph Ferrante, who discussed the case with prosecutors and raised the possibility that he would pursue an insanity defense.

I first visited Debra and Malori Alonso in the spring of 2013. At that time David was being held at New Jersey's Ann Klein Forensic Center, a secure state mental health facility that houses convicted sex offenders and mentally ill detainees with violent histories. The Alonsos were clearly a close family, and both women believed that David would never harm them intentionally. They felt different effects from their head injuries. Malori told me she had trouble sleeping and wasn't sure how she would feel when she woke up each day. She startled easily and suffered from loss of taste and appetite. Debra had memory problems and was sometimes a bit slow in reacting to conversation. Her left eardrum had been ruptured, and she had to relearn how to talk and eat.

David and Debra had been married for twenty-five years. They met in their early twenties in Raritan, New Jersey, at a nightclub where Dave was a bouncer and she was a cocktail waitress. He had joined the marines after graduating from high school, served in Beirut, and came home to work as a carpenter. She liked his energy and humor and that he was game to do the things she enjoyed, like bike riding. After they married, Debra worked as a health and fitness trainer. Malori was their only child, and the three of them, Debra says, had always been very close. They took vacations together on Cape Cod and frequently went to New York City to see plays and enjoy walking around Manhattan. They had lived in the house in Bloomsbury, a town of about 850 people, for the last twenty-two years. David kept a drum set in the garage where he could practice and hit the skins as loud as he wanted.

During my visit, they told me that Dave was doing well at the Ann Klein Center, going to church services there, mentoring a young man to help him learn to read construction documents, and making friends. Debra had refused to allow the center to give David antidepressants, which she didn't think he needed. She and Malori tried to visit him a few times a week, and it was always heartbreaking to see him, especially when he wanted to talk about what he had done on the night he attacked them. He told them he was ashamed and often cried.

"I knew right then and there, he was not in the right state of mind, his eyes had changed," Malori told me while recalling the morning of the attack. "It was not him."

Malori assured her father that they knew he had not been himself, but it offered little consolation.

Hunterdon County assistant prosecutor Deborah Factor had never seen a case like this before. Before moving forward with a criminal prosecution, she consulted with medical experts and Alonso's attorney. She found no independent evidence of domestic abuse or anything else to suggest that David would intentionally attack his wife and daughter. She was convinced he had suffered some type of psychiatric episode, triggered by something unknown. She agreed to make a deal with David's lawyer. She would not seek an attempted murder conviction and instead would agree that David was not guilty by reason of insanity. Through his attorney, David waived his right to a jury trial and agreed to proceed with a bench trial. The judge accepted the plea deal and found David not guilty by reason of insanity. Factor's boss, prosecutor Anthony Kearns III, released a statement to the media a short time later. "The investigation and medical evidence revealed that Mr. Alonso did not know what he was doing at the time of the incident. Hopefully he can get the treatment he needs and his family can continue on the road to recovery."

The ruling brought great relief to David's family and friends. But the question remained of whether his brain injury and his mental state might render him once again a danger to himself or others. Was he capable of snapping? Should he even be released? The judge said David would continue to be held at the secure Ann Klein Center until a hearing determined that he was mentally fit to be released. He would have to undergo months of psychiatric care and therapy before a judge could consider releasing him to his family.

Four months after he was officially found not guilty by reason of insanity, David Alonso returned to the Hunterdon County Courthouse with his lawyer, asking to be released. Dozens of friends and family members packed the courtroom. Alonso arrived dressed in a charcoal jacket, jeans, and a white shirt, his hair cut short on the sides and a scar visible across his head. Malori, Debra, and Alonso's family sat in the gallery, nervous on the day they had been anticipating for nearly a year.

Dr. Elaine Martin, a clinical psychiatrist who had been observing David at the Ann Klein Center, testified that the most pronounced, lingering effect of his brain injury was some impairment to his ability to put words and sentences together. David could communicate, but he sometimes struggled to articulate the things he wanted to say.

New Jersey Superior Court judge Stephen Rubin asked Martin whether David's cognitive abilities were impaired. Martin said they were not, adding that he understood the nature of the court proceedings. "His behavior has been appropriate. He's pleasant, cooperative. He's not violent," she told Rubin. "I have seen no aggressive behavior."

"Is he a danger to anyone?" Rubin asked.

"He's not psychotic. He's in touch with reality." Martin explained that David had no history of mental illness, but since the incident, he had suffered from depression, which was now in remission. She recommended outpatient treatment.

"Would you have any hesitation if he were released today?" the judge asked.

"No."

Prosecutor Deborah Factor asked Martin the same question, pointing out that Alonso would go home with his wife and daughter. "Do you feel any hesitation that he is a danger to them?"

"No."

"To others?"

"No."

"To himself?"

"No."

The prosecutor called Malori to the stand. "You were the victim of an assault," the judge said. "How have you been doing since then?"

Malori pointed to her father. "My only inclination is to support him." She said her relationship with her father had not changed. "We were very close. He's my best friend."

"You have no hesitation of him coming home?"

"It's all I want."

"Does your mother have any hesitation of your father coming home?"

"Absolutely not."

"Fear?"

"No."

The prosecutor asked Malori to describe what happened to her father that night.

"It was out of character. Unfortunately, I'm the only one who remembers what happened," she said. "I knew right then and there that it wasn't him. I just knew it." She finished by making a plea to the judge. "Me and my mother will do whatever it takes to make sure he gets the treatment he needs. All I ever wanted was for him to come home."

The judge needed no more convincing and released Alonso with the requirement that he begin psychiatric treatment within twenty days. "The testimony is clear that Mr. Alonso is not a danger to himself and others," he said. "My hope is that you can find the road to recovery. That's what everyone wants for you. I'm satisfied that it's in everybody's interest at this time."

Those in the courtroom broke into applause, and many began weeping. Then one by one they stood up, continuing to clap in a tear-filled standing ovation. David Alonso cried with them. When he walked out into the hallway, he was enveloped by family and friends, and he cried some more. That night he went home with his wife and daughter.

David Alonso's unusual case is a dramatic illustration that an injured brain can drive a person to do something out of character, and can trigger a person to lose all rational control without understanding the nature or consequences of his actions. It was also a rare instance in which an insanity defense worked, and the defendant got what he needed: psychiatric care and compassion.

Alonso's case resembles another rare phenomenon, parasomnia, in which sleepwalkers demonstrate involuntary behavior, sometimes seriously harming themselves or others. In one renowned incident in 1987, a Canadian man afflicted with parasomnia, Kenneth Parks, woke up, got in his car, and drove fourteen miles to the home of his in-laws. He went inside, strangled his father-in-law, and bludgeoned his mother-in-law with a tire iron. He then stabbed them with a kitchen knife. The father-in-law survived, but the mother-in-law died of her injuries. Parks, covered in blood, drove to a police station and appeared thoroughly confused. Officers noticed he had severed tendons in his hands but seemed unaware of and unbothered by his wounds. Police found that Parks had no motive to kill his in-laws, whom he had always liked. At trial, experts testified that he had been sleepwalking during the attack and was not conscious of what had happened. He was found not guilty because he had no intent and had not acted willfully.

David Alonso and Kenneth Parks clearly lacked the ability to freely make decisions and control their actions. The ability (or inability) to freely make choices is where the brain defense becomes contentious. Judges and juries are being asked to ponder whether defendants on trial had any independence in making their choices and committing their criminal actions. Could their actions have been determined or influenced by a biological or physical force beyond their control—an arachnoid cyst, a TBI, or a frontal lobe dysfunction caused by any other factor?

This question alludes to the concept of free will—whether we act, or choose to act, freely or are driven by something outside our power. Philosophers, scientists, and other thinkers have grappled for centuries with this question. They have argued over whether the brain and mind are intertwined or are separate entities. Many scientists cannot reconcile the idea that electrical and chemical reactions in the brain allow us to freely determine our actions, suggesting that a physical explanation for behavior exists outside our recognition of it.

One neuroscientist in particular has suggested that our brains make choices for us before we know it. Benjamin Libet, a researcher at the University of California at San Francisco, pioneered testing this theory in the 1980s. He had volunteers wear EEG leads on their scalps to pick up brain activity while asking them to perform movements with their hands and fingers. As they sat in front of a timer, Libet and his associates asked them to press a button, flex a finger, or flick a wrist whenever they wished. As soon as the subjects made a move, Libet instructed them to note the exact time they had formed the intention to act. He found that the subjects formed the intention to act after the EEG detected brain activity known to precede these kinds of movements. In Libet's view, the brain "decided" to initiate—or at least, to prepare to initiate—the act about a half second before the person was aware of making the decision.

Libet's findings were seen as evidence that decisions and intentions become conscious *after* actions are under way. While the subjects believed that they reported the moment they intended to act, they were, according to Libet, reporting the moment they became aware of a sequence of brain activity that was already in motion. While Libet's methods and conclusions have been frequently replicated by himself and others, some scientists challenged them, arguing, for example, that the electrical signals in a person's brain may have nothing to do with voluntariness but could reflect anxiety, tension, or anticipation that precedes a conscious choice to act. But in the experiments, the volunteers already knew what they were supposed to do, so it was a just matter of when.

Libet clarified his views, explaining that even though the volitional process was initiated unconsciously, people still had the conscious ability to stop the action or control it. They had a veto option. His subjects had reported that sometimes when they felt a conscious urge to act, they suppressed that urge and did nothing. Unconscious signals preceded actions, Libet explained, but "the role of the conscious free will would be, then, not to initiate a voluntary act, but rather to *control* whether the act takes place. We may view the unconscious initiatives for voluntary actions as 'bubbling up' in the brain. The conscious will then selects which of these initiatives may go forward to an action and which ones to veto and abort, with no act appearing." He was saying, in effect, that we have "free won't," which "is actually in accord with religious and ethical strictures. These commonly advocate that you 'control yourself.' Most of the Ten Commandments are 'do not' orders."

By contrast, other scientists argue that people have no free will—they never really act voluntarily, because physiological and biological causes underlie all action and behavior. Networks of firing neurons make us do things before we know it. In such theory, however, no one is responsible for deciding to do anything, good or bad. But discarding the idea of free will would undermine the entire criminal justice system and the notion of criminal responsibility. Finding a person guilty of a crime requires proving not only that she committed the action but that she did so intentionally—the idea of volition. If criminals can't help themselves, then one could argue that they must be locked up indefinitely: due to their inability to control their actions they would continually pose a threat. In our legal system, a person's guilt depends on his intentions, not just on the actions he took. Even though neuroscience suggests that our actions emanate from physical activity occurring within our brains, we still have the power to make choices.

Some people cannot voluntarily control certain actions, such as those with Tourette's syndrome, cerebral palsy, Parkinson's disease, or Huntington's disease—neurological conditions that cause involuntary movements of limbs and hands. If someone with one of these afflictions accidentally struck or hurt another person, we would not hold them criminally responsible, because they had no intent to harm and the muscle movement was involuntary. The legal system determined that David Alonso and Kenneth Parks could not voluntarily control their actions because they had observable mental impairments. Not only did they lack free will, they lacked the "free won't" to stop themselves.

Many believe that while debates over the existence of free will make for interesting conversation, they are irrelevant to the context of the criminal justice system. According to Michael Gazzaniga, neuroscience reveals that free will has no meaning, and its findings have no relevance to personal responsibility. Even though scientists can point to physical mechanisms in the brain that enable the mind, he writes in *Who's In Charge?,* "there is no one thing in us pulling the levers." Responsibility is not located in some specific region of the brain but is a social construct, an agreement among people who develop rules for society. Moreover, having "an abnormal brain does not mean that a person cannot follow rules," he insists. "Human nature remains constant, but out in the social world, behavior can change. Brakes can be put on unconscious intentions." No matter what their condition, most humans can follow rules or choose to break them.

No one knows what drove David Alonso to hurt the people he loves most, and it has hurt David even more. "I have felt so guilty," he told me as we sat at his dining room table a few months after his release. "I had no idea what happened. When I woke up in the hospital, I thought it was a dream and I was going to get up and go to work."

He wept when talking about it and spoke almost in a whisper. He's a big man with a friendly face who hardly seems a threat. "Not understanding is worse," he said.

He remembered the hospital staff asking him what happened, what he had done. "I was always crying," he said. "One day at a time. That's what got me through."

The Ann Klein Center was scary, he told me. He lived among sexual predators and patients with severe mental illness who were sometimes violent. "I kept my back to the wall," he said. "I wasn't sure I was coming home." Many of the patients detained there never received visitors. He shared food and books with other patients and always stopped himself from getting into fights, even if provoked, for fear that if the staff witnessed any violence, it would confirm that he was a violent person who had to be locked up. "Because they'd say 'aha!' "

As he sat at the table, David wondered aloud what had gone on inside his brain that night that made him into someone else. "I never thought about my brain until I came home," he said. "Is your brain who you are?"

CHAPTER 7

A Trip to Iowa

In the mid-1980s a forty-four-year-old man came to see Antonio Damasio in the neurology department at the University of Iowa. The man was struggling to understand whether something in his brain had caused him to become someone he was not. He explained to Damasio that he had experienced a change in personality so profound that it had destroyed his career, led him to lose his life savings, and prompted his wife and children to leave him. His problems, he told Damasio, began to develop after surgeons removed a tumor that had grown over his frontal lobes. Desperate and broke, he came to Damasio because he needed proof from a doctor that something was wrong with his brain so that he could receive disability payments.

Damasio realized that he had found a modern-day Phineas Gage. He had a long-standing interest in studying the connections between frontal lobe damage and behavioral problems. A handful of his patients had trouble making sound decisions, holding on to jobs, managing money, and keeping friends. They were smart, often accomplished people who later in life developed behavioral problems that Damasio believed were linked to frontal lobe damage. He described them as having "acquired" sociopathic characteristics, meaning they had exhibited normal personalities before experiencing some type of damage to their frontal lobes in the ventromedial cortex.

The man who came to see Damasio that day had led a so-called normal life. Elliot, the name Damasio used to protect his patient's identity, had grown up on a farm, had been happily married to his high school sweetheart, had two children and a good job as an accountant, and was active in his church. His siblings considered him a role model. But nine years before, he had begun to get hints that something peculiar was going on inside his head. It began with headaches, and he gradually lost his ability to concentrate as well as, strangely, his sense of responsibility. As the headaches persisted, Elliot fell behind at work and failed to complete tasks. His doctor suspected a brain tumor and sent him for a scan. Images of his brain revealed a growth about the size of an orange, much like Weinstein's arachnoid cyst, in membranes around the front of his brain. It was diagnosed as orbitofrontal meningioma, a benign tumor. It had compressed both frontal lobes, which likely caused the headaches and personality changes. Surgeons had removed the damaged frontal lobe tissue, along with the tumor, without complications. About three months after the surgery, Elliot seemed fine and went back to work, doing accounting and bookkeeping for a small construction company. Soon he uncharacteristically talked about investing in a business partnership with a former co-worker. His family thought the business partner was a man of questionable repute and recommended against the investment. Elliot went ahead anyway, investing everything he had. The business failed, and Elliot went into bankruptcy.

To survive, he took on a series of jobs—as a warehouse laborer, a building manager, and an accountant for an auto parts store. But he was often tardy and disorganized. He routinely spent hours getting ready for work in the morning, obsessed with shaving and hair washing. With his poor work habits and poor decision making, he got fired from most of his jobs. His marriage deteriorated, and his wife of seventeen years divorced him and took custody of the children. Two years after the surgery, doctors reexamined Elliot to see if the tumor had returned, but they found nothing. His neurological exam was normal, and there was no evidence of psychiatric illness. He still couldn't hold down a job. He remarried, only to divorce two years later. He also began hoarding junk—keeping dead houseplants, broken television sets, old phone books, cigarette lighters, and stacks of newspapers.

Elliot's free fall continued. Six years after his brain surgery, he went for another psych evaluation. Once again, doctors found no evidence of organic brain syndrome, or mental disorders caused by disease or injury to the brain. One report concluded that his problems "reflect emotional and psychological adjustment problems and therefore are amenable to psychotherapy." He was labeled as having a compulsive personality style. He tried therapy a few times, but the sessions proved ineffective. That was when one of his physicians referred him to Damasio.

Elliot was hoping that Damasio, one of the foremost experts in frontal lobe damage, could help him prove that he had a neurological condition that accounted for his unusual and self-destructive behavior. When Damasio interviewed him, he was struck by how pleasant and charming Elliot was, but that he was also emotionally contained, cool, and detached. He was respectful and diplomatic but had "an ironic smile implying superior wisdom and a faint condescension with the follies of the world." He was also intellectually engaging and enjoyed discussing current affairs.

Damasio knew that people like Elliot often performed well on psychological and intelligence tests even if they demonstrated severe abnormalities in their behavior and personality. What made Elliot's case so challenging was that the damage from the tumor and subsequent surgery had severely impaired his ability to make good decisions in social and personal matters. CAT scans and MRIs showed that the right and left frontal lobes were damaged, mostly in the prefrontal cortices, with the right side showing more injury. Damasio ventured to say that Elliot's injuries had compromised his free will, as Gage's had. The structures destroyed in both Gage and Elliot happened to be those necessary for reasoning and decision making. But how could the connection be proved?

It dawned on Damasio that he hadn't paid much attention to Elliot's emotions—or rather his seeming lack of them. Elliot spoke of the many tragedies of his life with utter detachment. When recounting the difficulties of his life, he was calm rather than disturbed. Why? Damasio had an idea. His colleague, Daniel Tranel, had been working on an experiment in which he showed people emotionally charged images of tragic events—such as injuries, burning houses, impending floods—and analyzed their reactions. How might Elliot react to such provocative pictures? Tranel tested him—and he barely reacted at all. Even Elliot realized that his own emotional reactions were flat. Damasio was astounded. Could this lack of emotion have played a part in Elliot's poor decision making? Damasio, along with his wife, Hanna, and Tranel, decided to include Elliot in a research study of four other brain-damaged patients who experienced behavioral problems. It would be a test of Damasio's somatic marker hypothesis.

The somatic marker hypothesis sought to explain the physiological processes behind reasoning and deciding. When people have to decide how to respond to a given situation, they assume they are consciously aware of their various options and the short-term and long-term consequences of each, then decide accordingly, using logic and reason. But Damasio thought emotions affect decision making in a powerful way, because people's bodies react to their various options.

When considering negative consequences to a course of action, such as stealing, people often experience a physical, bodily reaction. The reaction "marks," or is connected to, a specific mental image in the brain related to the course of action. In other words, people's past experiences are encoded in their bodily responses, which Damasio called somatic markers.

Damasio theorized that somatic markers work at the unconscious level by functioning as an automated alarm system that warns a person of danger if they choose a negative path. This automated signal, sorted out in the brain in milliseconds, leads people to immediately reject a negative course of action and move on.

A negative somatic marker may sound an alarm when a person is considering the outcome of one choice, but a positive marker can become an incentive to make another choice. Someone who is thinking of stealing may consider the costs of getting caught and the benefits of avoiding punishment and shame. Somatic markers do not deliberate for people, Damasio argued, but rather they assist the deliberation by highlighting options that are dangerous and quickly eliminating them from consideration. Thus, according to Damasio's somatic marker hypothesis, emotions and decision making are connected. A defect in emotion, or damage to an area in which somatic markers operate, can impair decision making, which may have been the case with Elliot. Damasio believes that somatic markers are processed in the ventromedial prefrontal cortex, one of the areas in which Elliot's brain was damaged by his tumor and subsequent surgery. That damage, Damasio theorized, could be related to the bad decisions he had made about his life and career.

To test this theory, Damasio and his team showed a series of images to their test subjects and measured somatic activation through skin conductance response (SCR), also known as galvanic skin response. A change in the skin's ability to conduct electricity, SCR is triggered by emotional stimuli. Scientists often use SCR testing for research in psychology and cognitive neuroscience. It is best known for its use in lie detection, which measures autonomic responses. Damasio and his colleagues considered SCR a biologically and psychologically relevant index for autonomic neural activity, the foundation for somatic states.

The five patients, including Elliot, had had normal personalities until undergoing some type of damage to the ventromedial cortex. Following the damage to their brains, the patients all had developed defects in decision making and abnormal social conduct, or what the researchers called acquired sociopathy. They also recruited a control group that included six people with damage to other areas of the brain who did not have social conduct problems, and five non-brain-damaged people as well.

The researchers attached electrodes to the subjects' hands, then showed them a series of slides—some neutral, some pleasant, and some disturbing—all intended to create a signal that activated SCR. The reactions were recorded on a polygraph-style machine. The doctors found that the SCR readings of the eleven subjects in the control group rose and fell normally, depending on the images. But the brain-damaged subjects showed little response, which Damasio and his colleagues reported as "defective somatic activation."

Months after the team published their paper, Damasio got a phone call from a neurologist in New York who asked whether he was interested in seeing a new patient with frontal lobe damage caused by an arachnoid cyst—a patient who happened to be a murder suspect.

On July 11, 1991, Weinstein, accompanied by his son, Nelson, traveled to the University of Iowa, where Damasio was the head of the department of neurology and directed the Division of Behavioral

Neurology and Cognitive Neuroscience. Weinstein's neurologist in New York, Dr. Norman Relkin, had arranged for the visit so that Weinstein could undergo the SCR experiment to test the possible connection of somatic markers to frontal lobe damage. The outcome might prove valuable to Weinstein's criminal defense.

When Weinstein arrived at the lab on the second floor of the hospital building, the research team saw a tall man who was polite but whose conversation seemed controlled and stilted. Weinstein was cooperative but not very friendly. After he washed his hands with a nonabrasive soap, the researchers attached an electrode, about a centimeter in diameter, to each of his hands and a ground to his arm. They connected the electrodes to a series of amplifiers, then to a polygraph recording device.

As Weinstein settled into a comfortable chair in a darkened room, the researchers calibrated the equipment, measuring spontaneous fluctuations in Weinstein's SCR to make sure they were normal under these neutral circumstances. They then darkened the room further and projected two kinds of slides. The target slides had high emotional value, meant to activate an SCR response: they contained images of social disaster, mutilation, and nudity. The nontarget, or neutral, slides featured placid images of farmland, nature, and animals. In between the target and the neutral slides, the researchers projected a cyan blue slide as a transition, so Weinstein could relax. The doctors asked Weinstein simply to view the slides and gave no other instructions. They repeated the same experiment over several days.

When Damasio and his colleagues reviewed the data, they found that Weinstein's responses to the target slides and the nontarget, neutral slides were the same. Normal test subjects, at least those without frontal lobe damage, registered sharp reactions to the socially charged scenes. Weinstein registered virtually no reaction at all. The researchers concluded that his autonomic response was impaired when it came to viewing socially charged scenes. His responses were identical to those of sociopathic patients whose personality changes were caused by specific brain damage, as documented in Damasio's research paper on acquired sociopathy. In fact, Weinstein's responses were the most dramatic example of the pattern they had seen in all cases of frontal lobe dysfunction.

Weinstein underwent other neuropsychological tests in Iowa. The researchers found evidence that his memory was slightly impaired, as were his executive functioning, prospective memory, sequential learning, and flexible responding to changing environmental contingencies. He was normal in social fluency tests, which measured his ability to generate possible responses to social dilemmas.

A psychologist administered more tests, including the Minnesota Multiphasic Personality Inventory, the California Psychological Inventory, the Eysenck Personality Questionnaire, the Tridimensional Personality Questionnaire, and the Schalling Multidimensional Inventory. These tests, standard in psychology and neuropsychology, ask hundreds of true-or-false questions to assess personality traits. Weinstein would read statements such as "I find it hard to keep my mind on a task or job," "I am liked by most people who know me," or "No one seems to understand me," and then check true or false.

Collectively, the test results showed that Weinstein's personality was excessively rigid. He seemed to be in denial of his emotions and psychological conflicts. The psychologist who tested him noted that he approached the questionnaires very carefully, and appeared circumspect before answering questions. That behavior was consistent with his highly controlled, dispassionate responses during interviews and other personal interactions with the staff. "Mr. Weinstein relies on rationalization and verbal agility to deal with psychological dissonance and emotional stress," Damasio noted in his report. "The results suggest an individual with a very low level of experienced anxiety or tension. Mr. Weinstein has very poor empathy."

In many ways, these were characteristics of a sociopath—though the tests were not designed to make that determination. The psychologist noted that "the results indicate a person who experiences little anxiety or fear and who has cultivated an overcontrolled rational approach to the world. His history, with the single exception of the murder of his wife, is remarkable for cool tempered and socially adequate behavior consistent with the results of our evaluation."

Damasio came to a similar conclusion. Weinstein was not a psychopath, either acquired or developmental, but "he does have a highly over controlled personality" and "his emotional range is minimal." Though he had mild defects in executive function and memory, his intellectual level was superior. And while he was socially fluent, he lacked the emotional markers to guide his behavior. Damasio's conclusion was consistent with how Weinstein's friends and family saw him: erudite, even-keeled, and emotionally flat.

Damasio thought it was reasonable to assume that Weinstein's inability to respond correctly during the conflict with his wife was part of the same defect that limited his emotional and psycho-physiological responses. He believed Weinstein's defect was caused by the cyst, which may have been worsening over time. "Confronted with an unusual provocation, he was unable to select the most appropriate response option," Damasio wrote. "The assault and killing of Mr. Weinstein's second wife constitutes a radical departure from his usual comportment."

Two months later in New York, Weinstein visited neurologist Dr. Daniel Schwartz for the third time. In preparation for the trial, Diarmuid White had asked him for a full psychiatric report. This time Schwartz had much more information to wade through than he had

had during his first exam, including the indictment against Weinstein, police records, medical records, mental health evaluations, brain scans, and a copy of Damasio's report.

Like the others who examined Weinstein, Schwartz found him to be quite cooperative, well groomed, and well spoken. "There is no manifestation of guilt, depression or anxiety over the present offense, and his present legal status," Schwartz wrote. He was not delusional and appeared to be otherwise normal in his thinking and judgment. Schwartz diagnosed Weinstein with an "organic mental disorder otherwise not specified" and "obsessive compulsive personality." For much of his life, Weinstein had shown a pervasive pattern of perfectionism and inflexibility. He called him a "Mr. Spock or a Mr. Data, if you will, which makes the present offense so markedly unique."

Weinstein had been a tough case to figure out because he showed no obvious or outward signs of mental incapacitation. However, Schwartz cited the cyst and Weinstein's low rate of glucose metabolism, as revealed from the PET scan, as capable of causing profound cognitive changes related to social behavior. Weinstein, the doctor said, had "dysfunctional frontal lobe pathways." That dysfunctional brain, along with Barbara Weinstein's "unusual and provocative behavior," the doctor concluded, "made it impossible for Mr. Weinstein to appreciate the nature and consequences of his conduct, or that it was wrong."

Schwartz's conclusion added to the growing body of evidence that Weinstein's frontal lobe damage deprived him of the ability to control his impulses or make the right decisions in a heated moment. In some ways, it was as if Weinstein had acted like a reckless, impulsive child.

CHAPTER 8

The Young Brain Defense

From the time he was a toddler, Ronnie Cordell lived in fear of those who were supposed to love him. He was the sixth of seven children in a working-class family in Wilmington, Delaware. His early years are a blur of memories. To this day, he doesn't know whether his parents were married or the name of the hospital where he was born. He was about three when he and his siblings were removed from their home by state child welfare workers. His father left Ronnie's mother and married another woman. Ronnie and his siblings wound up living with their father and new stepmother, along with her children.

It was an uneasy arrangement for everyone. Ronnie's mother didn't seem interested in seeing her children once they moved in with the other family. Life got darker for Ronnie and his brothers and sisters in their new home. He remembers that his father unleashed a rage the kids hadn't seen before. He punched them in the face and kicked them in the ribs for minor offenses. Ronnie's stepmother used switches and books to hit the children. Often the beatings were so severe that blood ran from their mouths, noses, and ears. When the kids looked as if they might require medical attention, their parents locked them in the house so that no else could see how injured they were.

As he approached his teen years, Ronnie started committing petty crimes like burglary and theft and was eventually sentenced to live in a reform school. By the time he was sixteen, he had made a series of bad decisions that would prove fatal. Early on the morning of June 4, 1982, he slipped out of his room at reform school and met up with a friend and their girlfriends. The group wandered around downtown Wilmington looking for something to do. As it started to rain, they dashed for shelter beneath an overpass of Interstate 95, just east of downtown, in an area known as Browntown.

As they sat under the highway, Ronnie saw a homeless man, apparently drunk, staggering around. Ronnie decided to impress his girlfriend by taunting the man. He crept up behind fifty-five-year-old Howard Marshall as he wobbled along, intending to scare him. Ronnie startled Marshall, who swung around to see who was behind him. Ronnie punched the man twice in the face and knocked him down.

Ronnie's friend, Charles "Rusty" Blizzard, seventeen, joined in. They beat Marshall as he lay on the ground, kicking and punching him in the ribs and throat. The boys wrestled ten dollars in change from his pockets and then dragged his body to a nearby lot, covered him with a blanket, and left him lying on the ground between several trash cans. A yard worker found the body later that day. Marshall had multiple broken bones in addition to fractures of the thyroid cartilage, which had caused his death.

The boys' girlfriends reported what happened to detectives. When the boys were arrested, they claimed they didn't know they had killed Marshall. The boys were charged with crimes that, under Delaware law, called for adult consequences. Both were indicted by a grand jury on charges of first-degree murder and faced the possibility of being put to death for their crimes.

Children and teenagers often make poor decisions, whether they commit felony murder or engage in reckless behavior on the playground. They're more susceptible to peer pressure and often act more impulsively than adults because they are, simply, immature. Adults have recognized the hallmarks of immaturity for centuries, and so has the legal system. That's why most countries around the world have separate juvenile justice systems that hold children accountable for their actions but also allow them a chance to grow up, learn their lessons, and have a shot at life as adults. Things get complicated, however, when young people commit violent crimes that are so serious that courts treat them as adults by holding them to adult legal standards and imposing adult punishments—from life in prison to the death penalty.

But advances in neuroscience have helped shift that thinking. Researchers now have a better understanding of adolescent brain development and its role in decision making and impulsive behavior. These new insights have led the courts to reconsider how to handle young offenders like Ronnie Cordell, how to determine the extent of their culpability, and whether they have the capacity to become better people as their brains become fully mature.

During the past two decades, a growing body of research has shown that the adolescent brain is not fully developed until a person is about twenty-five, and that as it's developing, many things can go wrong that can lead to psychiatric and behavioral disorders. Stress can inhibit proper brain development. Abuse, neglect, and mistreatment, like that suffered by Ronnie Cordell, can alter brain function and affect mental, emotional, and behavioral development. Even psychological abuse has been shown to have enduring negative effects on brain development, and scientists have found specific kinds of brain abnormalities in psychiatric patients who were abused as children. Feeling threatened or being hurt by people entrusted to care for them can leave long-term damage. Young brains develop based on experiences with caregivers, family, and community, and Ronnie had no positive experiences in this realm. He remembers that his parents had nothing but contempt for him and his siblings. They rarely spent time with the boy, engaged with him in any loving or meaningful way, or showed they cared about him.

Child psychiatrist and author Bruce D. Perry, who has worked with traumatized children for decades, has documented how early-life stress and violence affect the developing brain. In a 1997 examination of the cycle of violence carried out by children, he coined the chilling phrase "incubated in terror." A lack of nurturing combined with excessive exposure to traumatic violence, he concluded, will alter a child's developing brain and central nervous system, "predisposing to a more impulsive, reactive and violent individual." Dr. Martin H. Teicher, a psychiatry professor at Harvard, concluded from his research that the trauma of abuse "induces a cascade of effects," including changes in hormones and neurotransmitters that can derail normal brain development. That very well may have been what happened to the young Ronnie Cordell.

"Society reaps what it sows in nurturing its children," Teicher wrote. "Early abuse molds the brain to be more irritable, impulsive, suspicious, and prone to be swamped by fight-or-flight reactions that the rational mind may be unable to control." While abused children may know right from wrong, their brains are so irritable and the connections between hemispheres so tangled that they lack the ability to use logic and reason to control their aggressive impulses. Is it fair, he asks, to hold such children criminally responsible for actions that they lack the capacity to control?

Before he was arrested for murder, Ronnie Cordell faltered in school, was placed in special education classes, and eventually was kicked out. Sometimes he ran away from home, stealing food during the day and sleeping in parks, under hospital steps, or in hospital waiting rooms. Anything was better than living at home with his abusive parents. His brothers and sisters had trouble, too, and they all spent time in juvenile homes for truancy. For them, it was hardly punishment. They liked the juvenile facilities better than home because they felt safer there.

When Ronnie was fifteen, the state ordered him to undergo psychological tests. The results showed he was not developmentally on par with others his age and possessed below-average intelligence. Shortly thereafter he dropped out of high school and ran away from home. His siblings all had developed drug and alcohol problems and were building up arrest records. One of his brothers committed an armed robbery and was sent to prison for fifteen years.

Ronnie's delinquency, too, got more serious. He was arrested for burglary, receiving stolen property, resisting arrest, criminal trespassing, theft, criminal mischief, hindering, and escape. And then murder in the first degree. Being a teenager could not save him from the possibility of receiving the death penalty. Back then the United States still executed people who committed crimes as juveniles. In fact, the country had allowed the execution of children for hundreds of years.

English common law heavily influenced the laws that developed in the United States, including those for juveniles. Many American legal concepts and standards were gleaned from *Blackstone's Commentaries* in the 1760s, a primer on English common law. The author, William

Blackstone, declared that children under seven were incapable of "vicious will"—one of the requirements for being responsible for a crime. If children between seven and fourteen understood right from wrong, they could be held accountable to the same extent as adults, including being subject to the death penalty. According to Blackstone, the capacity for committing a crime was related less to age than to the strength of the person's understanding and judgment. "For one lad of eleven years old may have as much cunning as another of fourteen; and in these cases our maxim is, that *malitia supplet aetatem*"—malice supplies the age.

Children in England who committed capital crimes were frequently executed. Blackstone wrote of a thirteen-year-old girl being "burned" for killing her mistress, and of two boys, aged nine and ten, who were sentenced to death for killing their friends. They received the ultimate punishment, Blackstone reasoned, because their attempts to conceal the crime showed consciousness of guilt and an understanding of the difference between good and evil. In the case of a ten-year-old boy convicted of murder, Blackstone wrote, the judges felt that "sparing the boy merely on account of his tender years might be of dangerous consequence to the public, by propagating a notion that children might commit such atrocious crimes with impunity."

In colonial America, during the nascent years of its justice system and before Blackwell published his book, Americans were already following the lead of England and executing the young if their crimes were deemed worthy of capital punishment. The first documented execution of a juvenile offender in what would become the United States took place in 1642. He was Thomas Graunger, believed to be sixteen or seventeen years old, from Plymouth Colony, Massachusetts. Graunger was executed not for murder but for "buggery," or having sex with farm animals, including a mare, a cow, two goats, a sheep, calves, and a turkey. He confessed and was condemned by a jury and sentenced to death by hanging. William Bradford described the case in *Plymouth Plantation,* referring to the punishment as "according to the law" of God, citing Leviticus 20:15 of the King James Bible, which reads, "and if a man lie with a beast, he shall surely be put to death: and ye shall slay the beast." The animals were slaughtered in front of the boy before he was hanged. There was no mention of any protest against the boy's death sentence.

For more than one hundred years after the Constitution was ratified, the United States had no separate juvenile justice system. In the summer of 1899 a group of civic leaders helped found the nation's first juvenile court system in Chicago with the noble intent to both help children and families and to protect the public from young criminals. The idea was to give abandoned and orphaned kids a chance, to keep them out of the squalid and deplorable adult prisons where they were subject to abuse, and to offer them some hope for the future. The juvenile court system was rooted in the belief that children should be treated differently than adults. Children were still forming as human beings and thus had greater potential for rehabilitation. Chicago became a model for the nation and the world in adopting a philosophy of compassion for children rather than harsh punishment. Jane Addams, one of the court's founders, suggested that the court would serve as a "kind and just parent."

While the juvenile justice system brought reforms and protected the young, however, states still had the option of trying children in court as adults. A thirst for retribution and punishment often outweighed any reflection or consideration that young criminals might be helped or shown some measure of mercy. The Death Penalty Information Center, a Washington, D.C., nonprofit, reports that since the execution of Thomas Graunger in 1642, 364 persons have been executed in the United States for crimes they committed as juveniles. Twenty-two of those executions were imposed after the reinstatement of the death penalty in 1976. The youngest person ever executed in the United States was George Junius Stinney, Jr., an African-American boy who was fourteen when he was strapped into an electric chair in South Carolina in 1944. He had confessed to killing two white girls, seven and eleven years old. In the Jim Crow South, the hunger for lynch-style mob justice was insatiable.

At his murder trial, Ronnie Cordell admitted to beating up Howard Marshall, though he said he never intended to kill him or rob him. He had had no idea that the beating had left Marshall dead. He said he just wanted to get a laugh and watch the man stumble. When it came time to sentence Cordell, the judge had no choice: Delaware law mandated life without parole.

During his first year in adult prison, Cordell fought with other inmates—demonstrating a necessary survival skill—and showed little interest in doing much else. But a year after being sentenced, he started to shift his thinking and took steps to better himself. He enrolled in classes to earn a high school equivalency diploma. He eagerly participated in prison work programs. He worked in the auto body shop, learned welding, woodshop, and kitchen repairs, and worked in the laundry room. In subsequent years he learned auto mechanics and worked as a prison mechanic. Cordell went on to earn certificates in nonviolence and anger management workshops and other programs that promoted positive thinking and sensitivity. He didn't do these things because he was trying to impress a parole board. There would be no parole. He was a lifer.

As Cordell marked his time in prison, a movement took shape, supported by neuroscience, that would give hope to prisoners like him who were doing time for crimes they had committed as teens. It started in 2005 when the U.S. Supreme Court eliminated the death penalty for juveniles in *Roper v. Simmons,* concluding that executing youthful offenders was cruel and unusual punishment. The case stemmed from a murder in Missouri in 1993. Christopher Simmons, a seventeen-year-old high school junior, and two other teenagers broke into a house. Simmons had told his friends that even if they got caught, they would get off easy because they were minors. The burglary went awry when a woman inside the house recognized Simmons, and he decided he had to kill her. That the murder was callous and cruel was never in question, but condemning a teenager to die, the court found, was not in line with evolving standards of decency and did not acknowledge that juveniles are immature, vulnerable, and still developing a sense of responsibility.

The American Medical Association and the American Psychological Association (among others) filed briefs in that case, summarizing the most recent research on adolescent brain development, including neuroimaging studies showing significant differences between adolescent and adult brains. The role of the research in the justices' decision was not paramount, but it supported the logic behind the ruling. The decision was rooted in an earlier ruling that banned executions of the mentally ill, who were considered less culpable because of their limited mental and cognitive capacities. In that 2002 case, *Atkins v. Virginia,* the court ruled that executing the mentally ill violated the Eighth and Fourteenth Amendment prohibitions on cruel and unusual punishment because a majority of Americans found such executions unseemly.

When the Supreme Court ended the juvenile death penalty in *Roper v. Simmons,* Justice Anthony Kennedy, writing for the 5–4 majority, wrote that most states already rejected this particular form of punishment, and the trend was continuing toward abolition: "Today society views juveniles, in the words Atkins used respecting the mentally retarded, as 'categorically less culpable than the average criminal.' " Juveniles' susceptibility to immature and irresponsible behavior meant that "their irresponsible conduct is not as morally reprehensible as that of an adult." Therefore juveniles have a greater claim than adults to be forgiven for failing to escape negative influences in their environment.

With the death penalty eliminated, juvenile justice advocates moved to erase another punishment from the books: life without parole. Neuroscience once again appeared in the legal arguments. In 2010, in the case of *Graham v. Florida,* the Supreme Court was first asked to consider whether sentencing juveniles to life without parole was unconstitutional in instances that did *not* involve murder. Terrance Jamar Graham, like Ronnie Cordell, seemed destined for a life of crime through no fault of his own. His parents were addicted to crack cocaine, using it during his early childhood. In elementary school, Terrance was diagnosed with attention deficit hyperactivity disorder. He began smoking cigarettes and drinking alcohol at nine and was smoking marijuana at thirteen. In 2003, when he was sixteen, he and three other teens tried to rob a barbecue restaurant in Jacksonville. Terrance and one of the other boys went in wearing masks while the rest waited in a car. The other boy beat the manager with a steel bar, causing him severe head injuries.

Terrance took a plea agreement. He wrote a letter to the court saying, "This is my first and last time getting in trouble. . . . I've decided to turn my life around." He promised God and himself that if he got a second chance, he'd do whatever it took to become an NFL player. The judge sentenced him to a year in jail and three years' probation, giving him a chance to mend his ways and grow up.

Terrance's freedom was short-lived. Less than six months after his release, at seventeen, he committed a home invasion robbery with two twenty-year-old men. They held two men hostage at gunpoint while searching the home for money, then locked them in a closet and fled. Their crime spree continued. Terrance and his friends attempted another robbery, and one of them was shot in the melee. Terrance dropped off his wounded accomplice at a hospital and left. A police officer tried to stop him, sparking a high-speed chase then ended with Terrance crashing his car and getting caught while trying to escape on foot.

He faced a minimum of five years in prison and a maximum of life. At his sentencing, the judge said, "Mr. Graham, as I look back on your case, yours is really candidly a sad situation. I don't see where I can do anything to help you any further. You've evidently decided this is the direction you're going to take in life, and it's unfortunate that you made that choice. . . . The only thing I can do now is to try and protect the community from your actions."

This time the judge sentenced Terrance to life in prison. Florida had no parole system, so that was it—life without the possibility of parole.

Was that robbery an impulsive act by a youngster who deserved a chance at life as an adult? Or did Terrance merit this punishment because he had had his chance and didn't learn a thing? The case went on appeal. His lawyers argued that sentencing a juvenile to life without parole for a crime in which no one was killed constituted cruel and unusual punishment. They cited neuroscientific studies to support their arguments that the adolescent brain is not fully developed and that juveniles are immature, vulnerable, poor decision makers, and capable of change as they continue to mature. The American Medical Association and the American Academy of Child and Adolescent Psychiatry submitted an amicus brief similar to the one in the Simmons case. The organizations were not taking sides, nor did they have a formal position on sentencing juveniles, but they pointed out that "scientific evidence now sheds light on how and why adolescent behavior differs from adult behavior."

Among the neuroscientists whose work the organizations cited—and whose counsel the lawyers sought before submitting the brief—was Beatriz Luna, the director of the Laboratory of Neurocognitive Development, Western Psychiatric Institute and Clinic, at the University of Pittsburgh Medical Center. Cautiously, she helped write a letter to accompany the amicus brief, signed by a number of prominent researchers in adolescent brain development. It spelled out what they knew, what they didn't know, and what they felt comfortable stating conclusively for the purposes of the court case.

At the time, Luna was studying how teens act impulsively under pressure. She and her colleagues used eye movements, or saccades, to examine brain development during the transition between childhood and adulthood. Their test subjects were told to try to resist the impulse to look at randomly appearing spots of light. Adults succeeded about 90 percent of the time, while teens just 70 percent. The researchers used fMRI to scan their brains to determine what areas were active during the test. The scans revealed that while the architecture of the brain is mostly complete by adolescence, including the prefrontal cortex, the ability of its neuronal networks to communicate and integrate information is still developing, thus making it harder for young people to resist their impulses.

For the Supreme Court case, Luna and ten other researchers wrote that MRI images of young brains indicated that during adolescence the regions associated with executive control are still relatively immature. Studies using diffusion tensor imaging (DTI), a measure of the strength of connections among brain regions, showed that significant development occurs there between the ages of seven and nineteen. The stronger the connections, the better the executive function and impulse control. Other DTI studies made clear that brain regions responsible for the integration of information were still actively developing between ages nine and twenty-three, with the most development occurring between nine and fifteen. Pathways that facilitate the ability to give up immediate rewards to wait for longer-term gains are still developing during this period, as are the behaviors themselves. The letter also cited brain imaging studies that showed adolescents were not as strong as adults in impulse control, decision making, or planning, and that their ability to control behavior improves measurably between the ages of nine and seventeen.

The scientists cautioned against extrapolating all that neuroscientific evidence for use in court, concluding that "we do not, at this time, advocate the use of brain imaging data as evidence regarding an individual adolescent relative to others. Our position is that our converging data shed light on the ways in which adolescents, per se, are still maturing with respect to their capacity for decision-making and self-control."

The Supreme Court justices may or may not have considered the neuroscience; it's not mentioned in the opinion. But they ruled in favor of Terrance Graham: juvenile life without parole for nonhomicide crimes was cruel and unusual punishment. "Terrance Graham's sentence guarantees he will die in prison without any meaningful opportunity to obtain release, no matter what he might do to demonstrate that the bad acts he committed as a teenager are not representative of his true character, even if he spends the next half century attempting to atone for his crimes and learn from his mistakes," Justice Kennedy wrote. "The State has denied him any chance to later demonstrate that he is fit to rejoin society based solely on a non-homicide crime that he committed while he was a child in the eyes of the law. This the Eighth Amendment does not permit."

The same year Terrance Graham was arrested for murder, the sister of Howard Marshall, the man Ronnie Cordell had killed when he was seventeen, started corresponding with Ronnie in prison. Ronnie had written a letter of apology to Virginia Babicki, expressing his guilt, sorrow, and sympathy for her and her family. She visited him and was impressed by how much he had accomplished and how productive he had been. He again told her how sorry he was and that a day did not go by when he didn't think about it.

Babicki didn't believe Ronnie had intended to kill her brother, and she believed he deserved to be punished for it—but not for the rest of his life. He had been just a child, after all, and the more she learned about his abuse and neglect at the hands of his parents and stepmother, the more she believed it was time for him to be released. But he was in for life without the possibility of parole, so none of that mattered.

Two years later, in 2012, neuroscience made another appearance at the Supreme Court, offering Ronnie, and others serving life without parole for murder, hope that they would someday be released.

Evan Miller, like Graham, Cordell, and many other juvenile offenders, had faced plenty of obstacles in life from the start. He grew up under conditions of violent physical abuse, extreme neglect, and severe poverty. The family moved so often that his mother could not recall the name of the different schools he attended. His father beat Evan so frequently that at age five the boy tried to hang himself, according to his mother. He tried killing himself five more times, and by age eight he was using drugs and alcohol and receiving mental health counseling.

When he was ten, the state removed him and his siblings from their home, to protect them from further abuse, and placed them in foster care. His parents divorced, and he was returned to his mom, who was addicted to drugs. Evan soon resumed smoking marijuana, swallowed prescription drugs, and took crystal meth.

The crime that became the center of a Supreme Court case, *Miller v. Alabama,* was convoluted and messy. One night fifty-two-year-old Cole Cannon, visibly drunk, made a drug deal with Evan's mother. Afterward Evan and his friend Colby Smith went with Cannon to his house, where Cannon gave the boys some alcohol and sent them out to buy some marijuana. They came back with the pot, and all three smoked and played drinking games. Evan drank about a fifth of whiskey and took a prescription anxiety medication known to magnify the effects of alcohol, especially disinhibition. Colby later said that he and Evan planned to steal Cannon's wallet.

A fight broke out, the cause unknown. Cannon grabbed Evan's throat. Colby hit him with a baseball bat, and then Evan hit him, too. Evan then took a sheet and placed it over Cannon's head and said, "I am God. I have come to take your life." The boys started a fire in the home, and Cannon's last words to Colby were "Why are y'all doin' this to me?" The boys left, and Cannon died of smoke inhalation.

A week later Evan was picked up by police. After two hours of questioning, he signed a statement implicating himself, which had been written by the investigating officer. Colby was offered a deal. In exchange for testifying against Evan, he would be allowed to plead guilty to felony murder and receive a punishment of life with the possibility of parole. Evan was sentenced to life without parole.

In his Supreme Court appeal, Evan's lawyer cited *Roper v. Graham,* arguing that youth and immaturity have critical roles in determining an adolescent's culpability. "To wholly disregard a fourteen-year-old offender's age and age-related characteristics in sentencing him to be imprisoned for the remainder of his existence makes a mockery of this fundamental precept," Evan's lawyer wrote. "Adolescents are unfinished products, works in progress toward the adult character they have not yet formed. They are flooded by the hormonal surges of puberty; their underdeveloped brain structure and their lack of experience with the world leave them inadequately equipped to cope with the sensation seeking, risk-taking impulses that they experience."

The high court ruled in favor of Evan. As in *Graham,* which ended life without parole for juveniles convicted of crimes other than murder, the court found that sentencing juveniles convicted of murder to life without parole also amounted to cruel and unusual punishment—a violation of the Eighth Amendment. The ruling came from a court divided 5–4. Justice Elena Kagan wrote the majority opinion.

Bryan Stevenson, executive director of the Equal Justice Initiative, the nonprofit law firm in Alabama that represented Evan, believed the ruling would force lower courts to hold resentencing hearings. That meant about two thousand prisoners, some well into adulthood, could look forward to the possibility of getting out someday for crimes they committed as teens. Many states challenged the idea that the Supreme Court's decision should be retroactive, but not the state of Delaware. The legislature amended the law and opened the door for prisoners who had been sentenced to life without parole as juveniles to be resentenced. One of them was Ronnie Cordell.

The public defender's office appointed A. J. Roop, a defense attorney in Delaware who was experienced in capital murder cases, to handle Cordell's resentencing hearing. He knew nothing about Cordell's childhood when he took up the case, but as he read the case reports and accounts of Cordell's life, he knew his circumstances had sabotaged any chance of a normal childhood. "I was appalled," Roop said. "I thought he never had a chance." Roop hired a mitigation expert to interview Cordell's family and people familiar with the case to assemble a sympathetic story for the judge to consider in resentencing. Roop met with Cordell at the James T. Vaughn Correctional Facility in Smyrna, about forty miles south of Wilmington. "He was a real docile, quiet guy, and I could tell he was a little bit guarded," Roop recalls.

Roop arranged to have Cordell evaluated by psychiatrists at the University of Pennsylvania before the resentencing hearing. Dr. John Northrup and Dr. Susan Rushing, attending psychiatrists at the university, spent nearly two hours with Cordell. He told them the murder should never have happened. "I just wanted to get a laugh and watch him stumble," he told them. "I wish it never happened. Wish I was never being an idiot. That was never my intention."

The psychiatrists found a number of significant mitigating factors that could warrant a sentence other than life without parole. The Supreme Court's *Miller v. Alabama* decision, they noted, said that youth "is a time of immaturity, irresponsibility, impetuousness, and recklessness." Even though Cordell had shown a problem with cognitive and emotional development during his early years in prison, and occasionally got into fights, he had aged out of it and demonstrated his growing maturity with his self-improvement, education, and achievements in prison.

B.J. Casey is among the many neuroscientists whose research was submitted to the Supreme Court to support the argument that juveniles' immature brains explain their impetuousness and recklessness. But she also warns against the misuse and misinterpretation of neuroscientific findings about adolescent brain development. Key among her frustrations is the oversimplified claim that adolescents do what they do because their prefrontal cortex isn't developed, when the reality is that younger children, with even less developed brains, don't act as recklessly as adolescents. Moreover, many adolescents, even by twelve to thirteen years of age, can be quite good at making decisions. "So one of the things that I think is an overgeneralization is that they can't think at all. Because they can," says Casey, director of the Sackler Institute at Weill Cornell Medical College in New York City. "This is when we really start to advance what we teach them in school, and there are ways in which you can get them to think about the future, think about the past, and about consequences. But unfortunately, in the heat of the moment, it's hard for them to draw on those capabilities."

Acting in the heat of the moment is key. Casey led a study that sought to determine when young people begin to be able to control themselves in emotionally charged situations. She and her colleagues placed thirteen-to-twenty-five-year-olds into a brain scanner and asked them to do an exercise that required restraint—in this case, pressing a button to identify faces that looked either bored or scared, and not pressing if the face appeared happy. They did this under three separate conditions. In the first, they were told that at any moment they could win one hundred dollars. In the second, they were told they might hear a loud noise. Lastly, they were told nothing at all. The first two conditions were intended to create a sense of heightened emotion, much like that felt by young people who commit crimes in emotionally or socially charged situations. Under the threat of hearing a loud noise, the eighteen-to-twenty-year-olds were less able than the twenty-two-to-twenty-five-year-olds to restrain themselves from pushing the button—a result not much better than that of the thirteen-to-seventeen-year-olds. The brain scans revealed that the youngest group showed reduced activity in the prefrontal cortex, the region that regulates emotion, suggesting that those areas were not yet fully developed, according to Casey.

"Most of the work that's cited in all these briefs is focusing predominantly on decision making in what I would call pretty irrelevant context to the criminal justice system," she says. "Most of the criminal acts that occur in juveniles are actually when they're with peers, and so there's as much excitement as potential threat there." Moreover, Casey believes that the transition from juvenile to adult may not be portrayed accurately. "It's not like we become an adult overnight. The brain just doesn't turn on and off that way. There are a lot of my colleagues who talk about how development is almost magical," she says. "Experience is absolutely essential. . . . The brain has a readiness during this period depending on the experiences it gets."

Bea Luna says she's also cautious about her work, and that of other neuroscientists, being used in legal proceedings. "It's an ethical question that the courts have to deal with," she says. "We have to make sure that as neuroscientists, we're not overstepping the implications."

Translating what happens in the lab to the real world may be a big stretch. "In my studies I have people look at dots and not look at dots. Then try to translate that to a teenager shooting someone," she says. "I have to be very careful. I always refuse to be an expert witness. I don't care how much you pay. I can never tell you anything about an individual."

Ronnie Cordell arrived at New Castle County Superior Court on December 18, 2014. He was forty-nine years old and had been in prison for thirty-two years. His hair was thinner and turning gray. He required glasses to read documents. Judge Jan Jurden offered him an opportunity to speak. Cordell apologized for his actions on that day. "It was a senseless death," he said. "If I had known Mr. Marshall was dying I would have gone to get help . . . After thirty plus years in prison, I've definitely learned my lesson."

Deputy Attorney General John Downs was not going to let the seriousness of the crime go unacknowledged and reminded the judge that it was a "senseless, violent and callous crime and a lengthy prison sentence is appropriate." But he also demonstrated some compassion. He asked Judge Jurden not to resentence Ronnie to life without parole, which was still legal—just not mandatory. Instead, he asked the judge to impose a prison term of forty-four years, eleven months, and eighteen days. That would make Cordell eligible for release immediately, after accounting for credit for good behavior.

Howard Marshall's sister, Virginia Babicki, seventy years old, also addressed the judge. She believed in forgiveness and told the judge she supported his release. Roop, Ronnie's attorney, told the judge that Cordell had matured, citing the GED he earned while in prison and the other trade classes. Cordell said he was very proud of what he had accomplished.

The judge agreed to the recommended sentence, which would set Cordell free. "You have been given, in essence, a second chance—a big second chance," Judge Jurden said. "I hope you make good on that."

CHAPTER 9

The Rich Man's Defense

Assistant New York district attorney Zachary Weiss was the prosecutor on duty on the evening of January 11, 1991. Around six P.M., after most of his colleagues had gone home for the day, he got a call from Detective Frank Connelly, who told him that he had just obtained a confession from a man who admitted to strangling and throwing his wife out the window of their Upper East Side apartment. Connelly filled him in on the rest of the details about Weinstein and his attempt to clean up the crime scene. Weiss figured it would be a simple enough case: a man gets angry during an argument with his wife, kills her, feels guilty, and confesses after a little pressure from the cops.

Weiss arrived at the precinct station and said hello to Herbert Weinstein. "It's Wein*stein*, as in Ein*stein*," the white-haired man said. Weiss assured Weinstein that he'd make a note of it, then asked him whether he was willing to repeat the confession he gave to police on videotape. Weinstein hesitated. What about his right to an attorney? Shouldn't he have a lawyer present? His mind apparently was starting to grasp the enormity and complexity of what he was facing. That was when Weiss felt his hope for a fairly easy case begin to fade. Weinstein told the assistant DA that he did not want to say anything else. He wanted his lawyer.

Murder cases moved slowly through the New York court system, which was choked with them. The city's homicide rate had hit a record high the previous year, when 2,245 people had been killed, including eighty-seven in an arson fire at the Happy Land social club in the Bronx. Prosecutors were at their limits. So Weiss would have plenty of time to assemble the evidence and make a strong case against Weinstein. Even though he had failed to get the confession on videotape, several police officers had heard his confession and written it down in their reports.

But a few months later Weiss realized that the case had become unexpectedly complicated. It kept getting delayed because Weinstein's lawyer, Diarmuid White, said his client required medical evaluation and psychological testing due to the discovery of a cyst in his brain. White also filed papers in court stating that he intended to use an insanity defense. He would present scientific evidence that the cyst had affected his client's behavior the day of the murder, and thus Weinstein was not criminally responsible. Weiss couldn't believe it.

Soon afterward Weiss received a series of medical and psychiatric reports from White. They stated that the cyst was exerting pressure on the left frontal lobe, causing hypometabolism, or a slowing of functions in that area of the brain, thus causing Weinstein to be unable to understand or appreciate what he did. Weiss had never heard of such a thing. He opened up an envelope that contained printouts of brain images taken from a process he had never heard of before either—positron-emission tomography. He was struck by the beauty of these pictures in which seas of blue and gray were punctuated by islands of red, yellow, and white.

The pictures were striking for another reason: there was a large round black space on the left side, as if a chunk of brain were missing. Even to a layperson, this brain looked seriously damaged. Weiss said to himself, "You've got to be fucking joking." He speculated that a judge or jury might consider these pictures as real proof that Weinstein had a mental disease or defect, which would support his claim of insanity. The colorful pictures of a brain with a black hole screamed out that something must be wrong with this guy. Weiss went to see his supervisor in the district attorney's office to discuss the case. The supervisor, a veteran trial attorney, said Weinstein's strategy to bring his brain scans to court was nothing more than a rich man's defense. A jury would find such a claim ridiculous if it ever got that far.

Weiss wasn't going to take a chance and decided that his strategy would be to block the evidence. If the PET scans were thrown out, Weinstein would have nothing. But then Weiss got word that White also planned to bring in evidence from something called skin conductance tests. Weiss was furious. It all sounded preposterous.

Just as White had immersed himself in neuroscience, so now did Weiss. It was all new to him, so he had to move quickly, learning about PET scans, assembling experts, and preparing to counter the claims that Weinstein's brain had made him commit murder. He had to develop an argument that the brain cyst shown in the PET scan images could not explain Weinstein's behavior, and that White was misusing technology that did not belong in court. Weiss searched for legal opinions that might address whether PET scans could be admitted in a criminal trial as evidence for the defense, but he found nothing. He did find instances in which PET scans had been allowed in court to address competency or diminished capacity, but not as part of the guilt phase of a trial. Some defense attorneys had used PET scans in violent murder cases, usually involving the death penalty, in an attempt to show that their clients had brain damage and thus should be spared execution. Lawyers usually presented PET scans to support a diagnosis of severe psychiatric problems, but the scans alone did not prove the existence of a mental disorder. Determined to debunk the brain cyst theory, Weiss looked for experts who could help. He got hold of a neuropsychologist in New York named Daniel Martell, who shared Weiss's skepticism.

Martell was establishing a career in the relatively new field of forensic neuropsychology. He conducted research on violent behavior and testified in criminal cases to assess competency, insanity, or malingering in defendants. He already had seen defense lawyers attempt to bring brain science into the courtroom: when he was a graduate student at the University of Virginia, he had assisted Park Dietz, the government's chief witness against John Hinckley, Jr., during his trial for shooting President Reagan.

Weiss was concerned that the defense was going to argue that Weinstein was volitionally impaired—unable to make a proper decision—and therefore did not know right from wrong, the insanity standard based on the M'Naghten rule. Weiss asked Martell to look at the Weinstein case and analyze the chain of inferences—that is, to examine each piece of evidence, scientific and otherwise, that supposedly led to the conclusion that Weinstein's brain was impaired because of the cyst. Martell would then look for weaknesses in the case that would, he hoped, break the chain.

Martell meticulously analyzed every piece of evidence he could get his hands on, from the crime scene photographs and initial police reports to the brain scans and psychological testing reports. There was no doubt that Weinstein suffered from a neurological abnormality. The question Martell needed to answer was what, if any, effect that abnormality had on his behavior. Martell thought Damasio's somatic marker theory went directly to the issue of volitional impairment, yet strangely Damasio's opinion suggested that Weinstein indeed knew right from wrong but was unable to make the proper choice to control his behavior because of the effects of the cyst on his frontal lobe. Martell believed the defense could easily overwhelm a jury with scientific jargon and wow them with impressive, high-tech pictures of Weinstein's brain while sidestepping the real issues of whether he was sane at the time of the crime.

Martell needed to put all the science aside and look at Weinstein, the person, to try to understand his life. He wanted to know what was going on with his marriage at the time of Barbara's death. What had he been thinking, feeling, and experiencing at the moment the argument began and he strangled her? This might help answer the questions, based on the New York insanity defense standard, of what he knew or appreciated at the time and whether he knew right from wrong.

He interviewed Weinstein himself on two occasions, for a total of seven hours. Diarmuid White was present for both interviews and refused to allow Martell to videotape the sessions. Weinstein told Martell the same story he had told police in his confession. Based on their conversations, Martell thought Weinstein seemed perfectly sane. He believed it was highly unlikely that Weinstein did not understand the gravity or consequences of his actions. Martell wrote down Weinstein's responses to questions about his actions, thoughts, and feelings during each stage of the crime: fighting, strangling, staging the crime scene, destroying evidence, and throwing her body out the window.

Martell wanted to know whether Weinstein had shown evidence of brain impairment at other times. In what other parts of his life, he wondered, had he exhibited aberrant or antisocial or destructive behavior? Or had he exhibited it only on the day he strangled Barbara and threw her out the window? The single act of killing someone in a moment of passion, he thought, was insufficient evidence to prove behavioral impairment on the magnitude that his attorney suggested.

Weinstein had functioned at a very high level for his entire adult life. "This was a man who led a very successful life as an advertising executive, with no overt indications of impairment other than the instant offense," he later wrote in a report.

Martell reached out to Barbara's family, who lived in New Orleans, to find out whether Weinstein had exhibited any unusual behavior. He met with her son and his wife, as well as Barbara's daughter and her husband. They all reported that Weinstein seemed perfectly normal. Barbara's mother told Martell she suspected that Weinstein had a gambling problem but offered no proof.

Martell probed deeper. He obtained a court order compelling Weinstein to provide personal writings, journals, datebooks, calendars, checkbooks, and financial records for the last several years. He obtained Weinstein's datebooks and financial records covering nearly a three-year period, from 1988 to 1991. As he began looking over the material, he found nothing to indicate cognitive impairment or unusual thoughts or behavior. But then he came across some financial records that indicated "substantial" gambling losses in Atlantic City. How much, Martell did not say, but he thought it possible evidence of pathological gambling. (Joni Weinstein later told me that her father's gambling losses were illusory. He often took out markers—lines of credit that he never borrowed from—so that it looked as if he were a big gambler, making him eligible to get comped rooms and meals at hotels and casinos. She described his gambling as "a non-issue.")

Martell also found something disturbing in Weinstein's calendar: an appointment with the Hemlock Society, a group devoted to suicide, about two months before his wife's murder. "I thought this was significant," Martell wrote, "in light of the fact that he staged the crime scene to look like his wife had committed suicide. . . . Some degree of forethought or planning may have been involved." When Martell asked Weinstein about the appointment, Weinstein told him that he believed in the organization's mission and had become involved with it when his first wife was dying of cancer. He had been considering options to ease her pain.

Martell may have uncovered potentially damning evidence, but it would have to wait. Weinstein's next court hearing was going to be a battle of brain experts—neurologists and neuroscientists—whose opinions would determine whether pictures of his brain could be used to prove anything about his behavior the day he killed his wife. This was new territory for most of these scientists. Some of them would testify willingly, others reluctantly, because while their work focused on neurological disorders, they were not professional expert witnesses on the criminal mind. In the decades to follow, however, defense lawyers would seek out a new crop of neuroscientists to assist them in legal battles that raised issues similar to those in the Weinstein case. These scientists were using PET scans and fMRI to research the connections between the brain and criminal behavior.

CHAPTER 10

When Neuroscientists Come to Court

In the fall of 2013, two armed police officers met Adrian Raine as he arrived on the campus of the College of Charleston, a midsize liberal arts school in Charleston, South Carolina, to give a lecture. The officers were assigned to escort him to the auditorium, where he was scheduled to speak on his latest research and his new book, *The Anatomy of Violence: The Biological Roots of Crime.* The college provided Raine with police protection because news of his visit had prompted threats, and a large crowd of protesters was expected.

Raine has dedicated his career to examining the minds of violent criminals. A professor of criminology, psychiatry, and psychology at the University of Pennsylvania, he is considered the father of the discipline known as neurocriminology, which applies neuroscience techniques to investigate causes of and solutions for crime. Raine has spent nearly forty years trying to understand what makes people become violent criminals, investigating the biological and environmental factors that may contribute to antisocial or criminal behavior. A native of England, he is engaging, inquisitive, and charming. Despite the dark nature of his subjects and the ghastly things they have done to their victims, he seems quite cheery. As a world-renowned expert, he is frequently invited to speak about his insights into the criminal mind.

The speaking invitation from Charleston came just as Raine's book was gaining media attention. In the book, he argues that brain impairments, whether acquired or genetic, can predispose some people to violence. Violent behavior, he suggests, has a biological basis just like mental illnesses such as depression or schizophrenia, and his goal is to seek ways to treat it. The talk he was preparing to give at Charleston was similar to dozens of others he had given.

But when word got around Charleston that Raine was going to visit, members of the community were outraged. Twelve years earlier he had testified in a criminal trial on behalf of a man who had raped and murdered a beloved graduate of the college, Peyton Tuthill, in her hometown of Denver, Colorado. In his book Raine explains how he came to analyze the brain of the defendant, Donta Page, whose lawyer had mounted an insanity defense. Raine had not connected the case to his talk at Charleston—it hadn't even occurred to him. But Tuthill's mother and some friends had asked the college to cancel the event.

In the days before Raine's impending visit, the local and college papers published stories about it. *The Post and Courier* in Charlotte quoted the county council vice chairman Elliott Summey, a 1999 graduate of the college, as saying that Raine "has a right to pimp his book somewhere else. But if he's pimping it on the campus where Peyton walked, that's something else." Summey added that that he would no longer vote in favor of requests from the college for financial support.

Thomas Nadelhoffer, the philosophy professor who had invited

Raine to the campus, called to let him know about the protests and said that the college was not planning to back down. Officials would support his visit in the name of academic freedom and in the interest of promoting healthy discourse. Raine hadn't been planning to mention the Tuthill murder case during his talk, but publicity about the event inadvertently opened a wound among those who remembered her brutal murder. People made nasty and threatening comments online. Raine considered canceling—he had nothing to gain by subjecting himself to threats. And he had a wife and two sons. But then he thought, why give in and hide? He decided to go and offered to donate his speaker's fee to a crime victims fund that Tuthill's mother had set up in memory of her daughter.

The night of his lecture, Raine walked through the campus with his two assigned officers. He wasn't sure what to expect as he made his way to the science and mathematics building, where more security staff were stationed. Television crews had assembled. The calls for a boycott may have drawn more people to the event than they kept away: the auditorium was packed with about 150 people, standing room only, and police had to turn more away at the door. Inside, four security guards stood at the ready. Raine found the experience electric, and gave an animated talk about his book, discussing his research and taking questions without incident.

Looking back a few years later, Raine recalls how disturbing the whole experience was. He hadn't really absorbed it at the time. "Oh, it was horrific," he tells me in his second-floor office at the University of Pennsylvania. "I had not connected it all with the Donta Page case. I look back at that and thought, 'Why didn't I put two and two together?' "

What frustrates Raine is that he is not an apologist for criminals—he understands and identifies much more closely with their victims. He could empathize with Tuthill's family because he, too, was once a victim: his throat was slashed during a robbery while he was on vacation in Turkey in 1989. An intruder had slipped into his hotel room late at night, armed with a cheap knife, and Raine was wounded during the struggle. But even if Tuthill's family and friends had known Raine's background and understood that he was a researcher, not a defender of criminals, it likely wouldn't have mattered. It was about perception—that he had the gall to come to campus and dishonor Peyton Tuthill's memory. "They thought this was outrageous. Here was this man who defended this murderer. And he did it for blood money," Raine says. "What they didn't know was that I actually testified pro bono at the trial. I wasn't paid."

The reaction to Raine's visit to Charleston is an indication of a much broader issue: when it comes to trying to explain why someone commits a criminal act, especially one so violent and heartbreaking, not everyone wants to hear it. "I would have liked to think they would want to understand. But also, I can understand their reaction," Raine says. "It was not just me but anger at the institution for inviting me. It was resurrecting old wounds. That must be part of it. There's also a part that some of us cannot forgive."

The Tuthill murder case was one of the few times Raine testified as an expert witness. He tends to avoid doing so, as do many of his fellow neuroscientists and researchers. He sees himself as a scientist who studies the brain and behavior—neither a defender of murderers nor a prosecutor of them. He tells me that if he had an opportunity to speak to Peyton Tuthill's family and friends, he would have explained that his testimony was science based, that he had become interested in the case as a researcher. But as his work, and that of other researchers, finds its way into academic publications and popular media, criminal defense lawyers reach out for his help and expert testimony. "I get a lot of calls from attorneys, and I don't do it," Raine says. "It's very difficult. If you accept the money, you feel you're being biased and tainted by wanting to do well for what you're being paid for. It's a very difficult thing to deal with, and I've always been uncomfortable. And this is something more personal. I think the adversarial system of justice is a game of persuasion, whereas I believe the goal [of science] is understanding the truth. In court, it's a battle; it's about persuasion and getting the slickest expert witness."

Raine studied psychology at Oxford as an undergraduate. In the early 1990s, while doing postgraduate work at the University of Southern California, he got introduced to how brain imaging could provide insight into the minds of murderers. No one else seemed to have done that type of research before. He connected with Monte Buchsbaum at the University of California, Irvine, whose main interest was studying schizophrenia and who had access to PET scanners.

Raine and Buchsbaum designed what would be the first study to examine, through brain scans, the physiology of the brains of killers to determine whether they were different from those of other people. They performed PET scans on twenty-two killers who had pleaded not guilty by reason of insanity, or who had been judged incompetent to stand trial. For comparison, they scanned twenty-two nonmurderers who matched the killers in sex and age. They used the scans to measure metabolic activity and used a continuous performance test to activate the prefrontal cortex. They found that on average the murderers showed significantly lower rates of glucose metabolism in the medial and lateral sections of the prefrontal cortex. Their theory was that poor functioning in the prefrontal cortex predisposes people to violence. Research published prior to their 1994 study had linked prefrontal damage to increased risk taking, irresponsibility, rule breaking, emotional and aggressive outbursts, impulsiveness, and loss of self-control. But Raine and Buchsbaum noted that such dysfunction might only predispose someone toward violence, and that environmental, psychological and social factors can enhance or diminish that predisposition.

A few years after their findings were published, Raine and Buchsbaum sought to strengthen their research by nearly doubling the number of murderers they scanned. They reached out to defense attorneys who had clients on death row and were able to get forty-one participants. The researchers obtained permission to transport inmates to the scanning facility for their tests; the inmates arrived in shackles and under heavy guard. After reading the scans, Raine and Buchsbaum found a "striking" lack of activation in the prefrontal cortex compared to the controls. They also found reduced functioning in the corpus callosum, the band of white nerve fibers that bridges the left and right hemispheres of the brain and that allows the two regions to communicate. Poor connections, they theorized, might mean that the right hemisphere, involved in the creation of negative emotions, was less regulated by the inhibitory processes of the left.

Raine was extremely excited about his findings. The studies were the first to show that the brains of a sample of murderers were functionally different compared to the general population. "It was a honey pot, having all these murderers' brains," Raine recalls. "Having the opportunity to look inside those brains and actually see the cause or causes of their behavior was incredible. This is revolutionary. . . . Their brains are different."

Not long after the second study was published, in 1997, Raine got a call from Denver criminal defense attorney James Castle, who was representing Donta Page, an ex-convict who had confessed to robbing, raping, and stabbing Peyton Tuthill. Page, who only days earlier had been kicked out of a drug and alcohol rehab center, told police that he had intended to burglarize an apartment but was interrupted when Tuthill came home. That was when he lost it and raped and killed her.

Castle told Raine that he intended to mount an insanity defense. Page had suffered from physical and sexual abuse as a child, he explained, including being raped by a neighbor at age ten. When he was just a toddler, his mother had vigorously shaken him to stop him from crying; she had beaten him on the head and body throughout his childhood. State social workers had recommended that Page get psychological counseling, but he never did and began committing burglaries and robberies as a teen. Page was a severely damaged person, Castle told Raine, so mentally and emotionally damaged that he could not have appreciated or controlled what he did. He had been insane at the time of the murder, mentally incapable of forming a deliberate intention to commit the crime. Castle thought Raine might be able to help with a brain-impairment defense.

"We thought that was the route we ought to take," Castle recalls. "There had been some research back in the seventies, eighties, about criminals who committed bizarre, violent offenses. They found there seemed to be a fairly high correlation between two things—one is neurological deficits and the second some horrific childhood issues, sex abuse, physical abuse, neglect—and we had all that in our client's history."

Still, the contest was going to be tough because prosecutors could argue that Page's confession showed that he had known what he was doing and that his actions demonstrated some forethought and understanding. After all, he had wrapped a towel around a beer bottle to hide fingerprints, and after he killed Tuthill, he had washed his bloodstained clothes.

Castle told Raine he was interested in his research and wanted to chat. Raine became intrigued by the case. "I said, 'Look, what would you think about getting on board?'" Castle recalls to me.

Raine felt that Castle wasn't a slick lawyer out to purchase favorable testimony—he seemed genuinely interested in understanding his client and trying to find out why he had committed the rape and murder. And when Castle told him about Page's social background, Raine thought this case offered a great opportunity for him as a researcher, allowing him to investigate the anatomy of violence and test his theories about the biological roots of crime. Raine agreed to work with Castle. Page was transported to the University of California at Irvine to receive a PET scan, at the same facility where Raine had done his groundbreaking scans of murderers with Buchsbaum. The scans showed that Page's brain had reduced functioning in the medial and orbital regions of his prefrontal cortex; Raine would compare that scan to fifty-six normal control subjects to illustrate the distinction.

At the trial, Raine brought the brain scans to the courtroom and testified that the lack of activity in Page's prefrontal cortex suggested he was deficient in his emotional regulation and behavioral control, as well in moral decision making, empathy, and social judgment. Raine believed that Page never planned to rape or murder anyone, but when the unexpected happened, his years of dysfunction, abuse, and anger, along with his inability to control himself, unleashed him to commit a monstrous act.

The prosecution tried to brush all that aside. "A rough childhood is no excuse for what you did—take the life of a truly innocent woman," prosecutor Henry Cooper said during his closing statement to the jury.

Castle's cocounsel, Randy Canney, read the court a letter that Donta Page had written to a staff psychiatrist at a state mental hospital in Pueblo, Colorado. "All they see is a black man that killed a white woman. Nobody took the time to ask why but rather who. I've been asking for help for years. Nobody cares till I hurt someone. . . . I don't see what I really have to live for. I've been asking for help for years. I'm supposed to take medication to keep me alive so they can kill me. I don't think so. If I die, it will be better than dieing [*sic*] by someone else's hand. I'm twenty-four years old. I never had a chance to live. Now it's over."

After two days, the jury came back with its verdict: Page was not insane and was guilty of first-degree murder. Now the question was whether he'd live or die. In a separate sentencing hearing, the lawyers argued their cases before the trial judge and before two other judges assigned to the penalty phase. The judges accepted some mitigating circumstances, allowing that because of brain damage, Page had impaired capacity to appreciate the wrongfulness of his conduct and conform it to law. They also allowed that his emotional state of rage and fear at the time of the crime made him unable to control his impulses.

The panel of three judges spared Page from the death penalty. The brain scans, as well as his social and psychological history, contributed to that ruling. In their sentencing memo, two of the judges noted that "Donta Page endured severe physical and emotional abuse as a child. . . . We conclude that this abuse was a significant factor in the constellation of events and circumstances leading up to the explosive outbreak of violence in the Peyton Tuthill home." But the judges also pointed out that linking Page's past abuse with his acts of violence "cannot be proven to any degree of absolute certainty. . . . We are aware that the 'abuse excuse' may be overused in some cases and often gives rise to justifiable skepticism. In this case, however, we find the proof of abuse and its probable effects to be persuasive."

The judges sentenced Page to life without parole.

Raine tells me that he never thought Page should be excused for what he did, but he hopes that what played out in court, and his own work, had some meaning beyond the case. "I'm for understanding, even if I'm the victim. That gives me some resolution and compassion," he says. "If we have any ounce of humanity in us, it's not to excuse but to understand. I think it behooves us all to gain an understanding because if we don't try to understand, we'll never progress. That's where I come from as a scientist."

During his testimony, Raine revealed something unusual about his own brain. Under cross-examination from the prosecutor, he admitted that a PET scan of his brain looked disturbingly similar to one of an infamous California serial killer, Randy Steven Kraft. "It bears a frightening resemblance to Mr. Kraft's," Raine testified. Those similarities, of course, don't mean that Raine is a serial killer. Rather, he said, they should serve to caution against jumping to conclusions about what brain scans actually mean.

Adrian Raine isn't the only neuroscientist whose brain resembles that of a serial killer. So does the brain of James Fallon, a professor of psychiatry and human behavior at the University of California at Irvine who has studied the brains of violent criminals, psychopaths, and schizophrenics since the 1990s. Fallon has, by his own conclusion, the brain of a psychopath. He made this discovery by accident, when he was a member of the control group for a study of Alzheimer's patients. One of the PET scans that he viewed showed the characteristic pattern of a psychopath's brain—decreased activity in areas of the frontal and temporal lobes—which Fallon says is linked to hallmark deficiencies among psychopaths: empathy, morality, and self-control. The scans did not have the names on them but were coded, and he was curious to find out who this person was. It turned out to be himself. The revelation led him on a journey to better understand himself, which is recounted in his book *The Psychopath Inside: A Neuroscientist's Personal Journey into the Dark Side of the Brain.*

By his own admission, Fallon, a fast talker who barely takes a breath sometimes, has lived much of his life without inhibition. At his home on the campus at Irvine where he teaches and does his research, I asked him why he didn't become a serial killer. "My guess is that I had such a wonderful family," he tells me. "Growing up, I was treated in an unusually good way. I was smart, handsome, and athletic. A lot of things I was just born with gave me resistance to being led astray. My mother and father made sure I did things to keep busy."

Nonetheless Fallon believes that he has classic psychopathic traits, including a very large ego. So while psychopathic killers may have similar brain structures and anomalies, those same patterns are found in others and could be in millions of brains. That's one reason he's not comfortable testifying in court or offering himself as an expert witness.

Fallon's specialty is brain anatomy, and he's been looking at brain pictures for twenty-five years. Several times a week he gets calls and e-mails from lawyers who want him to serve as an expert witness in court. But he doesn't believe that brain scanning translates well to court, where facts and certainty are expected and reasonable doubts can derail a case. "I've looked at all kinds of PET scans, fMRI scans, EEG studies, SPECT [single-photon emission computerized tomography], all that stuff, and I'm really into it. Therefore you might think or guess I'd be really gung-ho about the use of it in court. I'm not. It's not ready for prime time," he says. "Most human beings want categorical answers to things. It hurts their heads to think of anything in any sort of fuzzy way. The legal system is the same way. Jurors want categorical answers—guilty or not guilty. But we scientists tend to love fuzzy thinking, it's all 'what if?' And 'maybe.' . . . Can you look at a brain and say, 'This person is a psychopath or a killer'? The answer is no. You can't determine whether a person is a categorical anything."

Explaining neuroscience to a lay audience is hard enough. "No jury is going to understand this stuff," he says. "Medical students don't even understand it. Then there is the problem of causality. Someone can hand me a scan, and I can say that this person is impulsive or has trouble with moral reasoning because their ventromedial cortex isn't turned off completely. Many of these traits are associated with many disorders and also with the normal population."

What counts, Fallon says—supporting a position shared by many neuroscientists—is the person's behavior. Scans are not magical windows into the mind and soul. If neuroscience is going to be introduced as legal evidence, the courts need neutral parties to analyze it, not hired guns from each side. "I don't go to court. I never accept payment for consultations. It's too easily corrupted. There's just a natural tendency to give people what they want to hear."

Dr. Joseph Wu, a former medical student of Fallon's and now a colleague, has taken a different route. He is director of the Brain Imaging Center at the University of California at Irvine, where Raine and Buchsbaum once did their research. He routinely consults on criminal cases by providing and analyzing PET scans taken at the imaging center and travels around the country to testify.

Monte Buchsbaum recruited Wu to Irvine in the 1980s as he was establishing the Brain Imaging Center. When he started his career, Wu, like Buchsbaum, was interested in studying depression and schizophrenia. Together they published papers and investigated the pathology behind schizophrenia and bipolar disorder using PET scans to show evidence of frontal lobe dysfunction.

Not long after Buchsbaum began consulting with criminal defense lawyers about using PET scans in death penalty cases, including the Randy Kraft case, Wu got interested, too. He now regularly performs and analyzes PET scans for attorneys, mostly in death penalty cases, often with defendants who have documented brain injuries, a history of psychological problems, or psychiatric disorders such as bipolar disorder.

Wu says he believes in his work, that people who suffer from brain dysfunction deserve to be understood. Evidence of frontal lobe damage, as indicated by PET scanning and other neuropsychological tests, can and should serve as a mitigating factor in how the law treats offenders. "It doesn't matter what the cause. If you have damage to frontal lobe function, it can impair your ability to have impulse control," he says. "I like to put it into metaphors. The frontal lobe is like the brake of a car. If you're driving a car and the brake fails, you're going to crash. Is it your fault if the brake fails? If you have a broken frontal lobe, it's like driving with a broken brake. And in certain stressful stimuli, you might have a catastrophic failure in your ability to regulate your aggressive impulses."

Wu insists he's not a hired gun to help criminals beat charges. He's most often hired to present mitigating evidence during the sentencing phase of death penalty cases. He is fighting an uphill battle, he says, because few people want to hear excuses about what drove a killer to kill. But if Wu can show jurors that a defendant was brain damaged through no fault of his own, they might be more willing to show some degree of understanding or mercy.

Wu's testimony is subject to the same criticism that other neuroscientists who present brain scans face: an individual brain scan proves nothing about a specific behavior at a specific time. While studies may suggest that impulsive behavior is localized in the prefrontal cortex, a color-coded picture showing dysfunction in that region cannot be tied directly to a criminal act. Wu admits as much. "You can show there's a greater likelihood of some problem with impulse control under stress," he says, "but I can't make a precise prediction that this person murdered this person on this day."

I asked Wu whether brain scanning has a place in determining a person's guilt or innocence. "I think it does," he replied. "I think our system of justice is based on trying to find the most accurate appraisal of an individual defendant—and their neurological capabilities." Brain scanning "is a development, technologically, that sheds light on an issue that has long been accepted as a significant factor that should be weighed, to determine how harshly a person should be judged."

Wu has been criticized by colleagues who claim that his work can't be validated or replicated and who dismiss his claims as mostly unsupported. The reporter Rex Dalton, in an investigative article in the *Voice of OC,* a paper in Orange County, criticized Wu's frequent use of the university's brain scanners for criminal cases. The article strongly suggested that Wu was earning money for himself and for his lab by scanning criminal defendants and testifying in court. Wu and the Brain Imaging Center, according to the story, had earned a national reputation for dubious use of the technology for forensic diagnoses. Such cases can bring in more than $20,000 each, Dalton wrote, pointing out that Wu had been especially busy in Florida, where he was assisting in mitigation for defendants facing the death penalty.

When I asked Wu about the article, he shrugged it off: "It seemed they had an ax to grind. They seemed to have an agenda. I did not want to go tit for tat with them." He did not discuss the allegations in detail with me but maintained that his work and his reputation were sound and that his motives were certainly not for personal gain. He is especially proud when his work saves a life. In a recent case in Florida, he told me, a jury sentenced Joshua Wayne Davis to death for murdering a young mother. The judge reversed the decision, citing Wu's testimony about Davis's brain damage, and instead sentenced him to life without parole. *That,* Wu says, is why he does it.

Ruben Gur is probably the most sought-after neuroscientist in the country when it comes to testifying in death penalty cases. The demand for his services has become so great that he's had to assemble a team to screen cases before he can even consider taking on another. Gur is director of the Brain Behavior Center at the University of Pennsylvania and has testified in more than thirty trials in which lawyers for convicted killers have asked him to explain what's wrong with their clients' brains. "The overwhelming numbers of cases are about mitigation where they're trying to avoid the death penalty," he tells me.

Like many of his colleagues, Gur came to his role as an expert witness by accident rather than design. A native of Israel, he spent the early part of his career researching the use of brain imaging in the diagnosis and study of people with behavioral disturbances associated with brain dysfunction. He and his colleagues collected hundreds of scans from healthy people, as well as those with an array of clinical problems, including stroke, seizures, head injuries, tumors, and dementia, and those of psychiatric patients with psychosis and mood and behavioral disorders. He assembled what he describes as the largest normative PET database in the country at the time. He was first asked to use his expertise in a criminal case in 1994.

Dr. Frank Wood, a colleague and friend, called Gur because he wanted to compare a PET scan he had obtained against Gur's database of normal scans. It was for a legal case, he said. When Gur looked at the data, he thought there was a mistake. The readings for activity in the man's amygdala were several standard deviations below the control group, indicating severe dysfunction. "Frank said to me, 'Would you mind flying in tomorrow and testifying in court what you just told me?' And that was my first case," Gur says. "It was the want-ad killer in Florida."

The Florida serial killer Bobby Joe Long, who dominated the headlines, was known as the "classified ad rapist." During the 1980s, prosecutors said, Long would answer newspaper ads placed by women selling household goods and then rape and kill them. He already had received twenty-eight life sentences and was facing the death penalty in a case that had been appealed and sent back to trial. Now in 1994 his lawyer was looking for some mitigation. Gur agreed to help Wood and was on a plane the next day headed to Florida.

Upon his arrival, Gur says, he was soon convinced that he was dealing with someone with serious problems. Long was not allowed to remain in the courtroom during his trial because he had been ranting and screaming during the proceedings, and was held in a nearby room. During a break, Gur met Long for the first time and thought his clearly disinhibited behavior indicated frontal lobe damage. While he measured Long's cranium, Gur reported, Long gyrated his hips and said, "Is there anything else you want to measure, doc?" Gur explained his reading of Long's PET scan to the court, testifying that earlier in Long's life a motorcycle accident had resulted in severe damage to his amygdala. The judge agreed that Long had mental impairments, but the aggravating factors outweighed the mitigating ones, and Long was sentenced to death.

Gur's first foray into court did not save a life, but afterward other attorneys contacted him. The team of federal public defenders representing Unabomber Ted Kaczynski called Gur—they suspected Kaczynski had schizophrenia and wanted Gur to examine him. Kaczynski "refused to have any scanning done, and he was adamant against technology and told me so in no uncertain terms," Gur says.

Gur would go on to perform PET studies and testify in a number of murder cases, many of them high profile, over the next few decades. Sometimes he helped save lives, while at other times he could not. In 2013, for example, Gur's testimony helped save a killer named John McCluskey from death row. McCluskey escaped from an Arizona prison in 2010 and, along with two accomplices, carjacked a couple in their sixties who were vacationing from Oklahoma. McCluskey shot Linda and Gary Haas inside their camping trailer and set it ablaze with their bodies inside. Gur testified that MRI scans showed McCluskey had unusually small superior lobes, which could interfere with his ability to control his own behavior, especially when he was under emotional stress. A PET scan showed abnormalities in his frontal lobes and amygdala. Gur said the frontal lobes were broken, allowing "primitive emotional impulses emanating from the amygdala" to go unchecked.

Gur also testified on behalf of Steven Dale Green, one of four U.S. soldiers convicted of murder, rape, and obstruction of justice in connection with a 2006 attack on an Iraqi family south of Baghdad. The jury found Green guilty of raping a fourteen-year-old girl, killing her, and setting her body on fire to destroy the evidence. He was also found guilty of killing the girl's parents and her six-year-old sister. Gur concluded that Green was brain damaged. He testified that he compared Green's brain to those of forty-one normal controls and found evidence of head injuries and dysfunction, making Green prone to acting inappropriately in chaotic situations. After jurors were unable to reach a unanimous decision, the judge sentenced Green to life without parole. Five years later he hanged himself in his Arizona prison cell.

Prosecutors, of course, challenge Gur's interpretations of brain scans and bring their own experts to counter his claims. "The data I provide is solid from a scientific perspective," he says. "The next question is how you apply it to a case. And there is where you get tremendous resistance—especially from the prosecution. . . . They will bring in a radiologist or a neuroradiologist, and they'll say 'I looked at the PET scan and I looked at the MRI and they're normal.'" Gur is adamant that brain science has value in explaining what makes people act. The brain controls behavior, and behavior informs culpability. Neuroscience offers a level of explanation for behavior, he argues, which is part of the question in culpability and mitigation. His work in court is presented as a piece of mitigating evidence, along with testimony from friends and family, to try to save a life.

If someone is spared death, Gur feels relief, pleased that he had something to do with it. But that's not the end of the story, he tells me. Brain-damaged prisoners and the mentally ill are unlikely to receive help or treatment behind bars.

Earning money as an expert witness, he says, is not his motivation. When lawyers pay him to testify, he reinvests that money into researching the brain processes that relate to violent behavior. Because his schedule is so packed, however, he's planning to cut back on testifying in court. He wants to wind down. "I stopped taking any cases other than death penalty," he says. "And with death penalty cases I feel okay. We shouldn't be killing people with brain damage."

Gur, Wu, Buchsbaum, and other neuroscientists hired by defense lawyers to testify in capital cases have often faced off with their colleagues. One of their biggest nemeses is Helen Mayberg, a professor of psychology, neurology, and radiology at Emory University School of Medicine in Atlanta. Mayberg was drawn into courtroom battles over neuroscience by happenstance, she tells me. She had once worked closely with Joseph Wu researching depression but later found herself on the other side of the courtroom, criticizing his work and that of his mentor Monte Buchsbaum. In 1992 she was at the University of Texas using PET scans to study epilepsy, Alzheimer's disease, and stroke when she got a call from a frantic prosecutor in California who needed an expert witness—fast. "At the time, neuroscientists didn't have the time or experience to testify in cases like this," she says.

The prosecutor told Mayberg that he needed her in two days. The defendant was Gregory Scott Smith, a former day care aide who had pleaded guilty to kidnapping, raping, and strangling an eight-year-old boy and then burning his body in a field near Simi Valley, California. Monte Buchsbaum had testified that a PET scan showed Smith's brain was abnormal. The prosecutor wanted Mayberg to contradict Buchsbaum. He sent her the case files, including Buchsbaum's brain studies. "I get reams of papers, get on a plane, show up, and was not even prepped," she recalls. During the flight, she studied Buchsbaum's report of finding ten abnormalities in Smith's brain through the scan, which showed reduced glucose metabolism in the frontal and temporal lobes.

Mayberg was unimpressed, seeing methodological problems in Buchsbaum's work. "Even if we accepted the findings were true, the reduced metabolism, linking it to a particular behavior was impossible. How could you do that?" she says, looking back. "The idea that you could go from this scan taken two or three years after the crime to then understanding what he was like at the time of the crime, that he had was something wrong with his brain at the time of the crime? That is easy to rebut."

Buchsbaum's PET scan turned out to be of no help to Smith. The jury voted to sentence him to death.

Since then Mayberg has testified in about sixty cases and has seen a pattern emerge. Desperate defense lawyers will order brain scans, which often add nothing to a case in which a person's mental state is in question. "People will screen and find experts who will support their point of view. Their job is to have a vigorous defense for their client. The truth doesn't matter," she says. "Neuroscience is not objective. Two people can analyze the same data differently. There are failures to replicate. Scientists can tweak experiments."

Mayberg has found that judges and jurors, when weighing the evidence, are unlikely to ask the right questions, such as finding out what condition the person was in during the scanning procedure, whether they were nervous or on medication or had their eyes open or closed. "All those things can affect metabolism so you need context," she says. And if a lawyer attempts to use a scan to show brain dysfunction, Mayberg says, it's vital to find out what kind of control group the person's scan is being compared to. "Are they paid volunteers or a guy in prison in solitary confinement?" It's also vital to look at how a particular dysfunction is being defined. "How are you defining low metabolism in the frontal lobe?" she says. "Does different [metabolism] mean abnormal? If it's low, what does it tell me about this guy? Zero."

While she is critical of the misuse of neuroscience in court, Mayberg tells me she doesn't relish criticizing her colleagues or questioning them in court. It doesn't feel good. "What I do puts me in the gutter," she says. "I've worked for nothing. I don't want to be paid for this—it's devil money. But then you realize how much time it takes. You need something. Everyone needs to be paid for their time."

Mayberg revealed that back in 1991 Herbert Weinstein's attorney, Diarmuid White, had called her while he was preparing the case, and asked whether she thought using PET scan evidence was a good idea. She told him she didn't think so because it would invite an evidentiary hearing and only complicate matters. Keep it simple, she said. "He didn't follow my advice."

CHAPTER 11

The Brain Science Battle

More than a year had passed since the New York City police had arrested Herbert Weinstein. He still had the cyst in his head and, by all accounts, had been on good behavior while out on bail. He was allowed to move back into the apartment he shared with Barbara, which some of his neighbors regarded as strange and unseemly. But Weinstein didn't care. He passed the time playing bridge with old friends, reading, and going out to dinner with a woman he was dating. He told people he met her after answering a personal ad in *New York* magazine.

By the spring of 1992, Diarmuid White was ready to test his newly acquired expertise in neuroscience. He had all his scientific evidence lined up—the PET scans of Weinstein's brain, the reports from Antonio Damasio's skin conductance tests, various studies about the connection between violence and frontal lobe damage, and doctors ready to testify about Weinstein's neurological and psychological states. White believed that collectively it would support his contention that

Weinstein had been insane at the time he killed his wife and thus was not criminally responsible. It was a big gamble.

Zach Weiss had a plan, too. His first move would be to try to block much of the scientific evidence that White wanted to introduce. He filed a motion asking the judge to keep it out, arguing that it was neither valid nor generally accepted in the scientific community. PET and SCR technology were not considered reliable as diagnostic devices to test for brain abnormalities, he argued, and had no place in a criminal trial in which they might be used to account for criminal behavior. Without that evidence, Weinstein would have nothing.

The judge presiding over the case was Richard D. Carruthers, a former prosecutor who had been on the bench for nearly ten years in the criminal courts division. Carruthers scheduled a special hearing, called a Frye hearing, to consider the scientific evidence. It was named after James Alphonso Frye, a defendant in a 1923 murder trial in Washington, D.C., who had initially confessed to killing a prominent physician, then later changed his mind and said he hadn't committed the murder. In an unusual move, his lawyer tried to admit polygraph-like evidence to show that his client was being truthful this time when he retracted his confession. Frye subjected himself to a crude predecessor of the lie detector test called the "systolic blood pressure deception test." The theory was that changes in emotions influence blood pressure and that nervous impulses cause the systolic blood pressure to rise. A person who is consciously trying to deceive the police or conceal facts of a crime will be fearful of detection while being questioned, and his systolic blood pressure will rise.

The judge was not impressed by the test and refused to admit the results. Frye was convicted. His lawyer appealed, arguing that the judge should not have excluded relevant scientific evidence. But the circuit court of appeals upheld the conviction, concluding that the trial judge's decision to exclude the evidence had been correct because the systolic blood pressure deception test had not gained general acceptance among authorities in the fields of physiology and psychology. "Just when a scientific principle or discovery crosses the line between the experimental and demonstrable stages is difficult to define," the opinion noted. "Somewhere in this twilight zone the evidential force of the principle must be recognized, and while courts will go a long way in admitting expert testimony deduced from a well-recognized scientific principle or discovery, the thing from which the deduction is made must be sufficiently established to have gained general acceptance in the particular field in which it belongs."

"General acceptance" became the most common standard for the admission of scientific evidence at trial in U.S. courts, and it would be applied in the Weinstein case as determined by the Frye hearing. If Judge Carruthers found the PET and SCR evidence to be generally accepted, then experts could testify as to whether that evidence supported a diagnosis of brain dysfunction and offer their opinions about whether it might explain Weinstein's conduct. The Frye hearing would also give each side a preview of what the other was planning for the trial and which witnesses they planned to call. Both lawyers had ventured into new territory, studying the complexities not only of neuroscience but also of the machinery used to read and diagnose brain disorders.

The Frye hearing began in May 1992 in an antiseptic courtroom at 80 Centre Street, next door to the main New York Supreme Courthouse. The hearing was sparsely attended. Even though the Weinstein case had received front-page coverage in the New York tabloids and had been on local television news after the murder, there was no press to be seen. Reporters may have not realized the significance of this part of the proceedings.

Diarmuid White called his witnesses to the stand first, beginning with Dr. Norman Relkin, the neurologist who had examined Weinstein after his arrest. Relkin, coordinator of the Neurobehavior Evaluation Program at Cornell University, was not a hired expert but rather a working physician. His initial examination of Weinstein had been to determine what, if any, treatment he would need for the growth over his brain. Relkin said he found that the direct pressure from the cyst was altering blood flow to areas of Weinstein's brain and was cause for concern, which he had shared with his colleagues at the medical center.

"Doctor, did you and the Neurobehavior Evaluation group ultimately conclude in the case of Mr. Weinstein that the arachnoid cyst was contributing to his brain dysfunction?" White asked.

"Yes, we did." Relkin explained that in most cases, these kinds of cysts remain the same size throughout a person's life and are unlikely to cause sudden, aberrant behavior, such as Weinstein's attack on his wife. But Weinstein's cyst had become enlarged, the doctor said, and might very well have contributed to his brain dysfunction.

White asked Relkin to explain the results of Weinstein's PET scan and how reduced glucose metabolism might affect brain function and behavior.

"In some cases, it may not manifest at all in behavior," Relkin said. "Because it is not a one-to-one relationship between what we see on a PET scan and what a person does in the course of his day-to-day behavior."

Relkin said that in his medical practice he routinely ordered PET scans for patients, as did other physicians at North Shore Hospital, where he worked. The scans were used, for example, to measure metabolic changes in patients with dementia or epilepsy. In addition to the PET scan Weinstein had had at North Shore Hospital, Relkin testified, a second scan had been done at a higher resolution. It showed a similar pattern of decreased metabolic activity and dysfunction. Interestingly, the images also indicated decreased metabolism in the cerebellum on the *opposite* side of Weinstein's brain. This was significant because in cases of frontal lobe dysfunction, a phenomenon called diaschisis, or transsynaptic effects, is often present as well, in which the cerebellum on the opposite side also shows decreased function. The structures of the brain are interconnected and form functional networks. When one portion of a network breaks down, other components of that network may also stop functioning normally, multiplying the effects of a brain injury thought to be limited to one side.

White moved on to ask Relkin about the SCR testing. Relkin, who had accompanied Weinstein to Damasio's laboratory in Iowa, said skin conductance tests were routine and generally accepted in the neurological community to study various neurological functions. But these tests, he noted, did not provide *direct* evidence of brain dysfunction.

White asked Relkin to explain the significance of Weinstein's test results.

"Mr. Weinstein's responses on that test were the most dramatic example of the pattern that was seen in other cases of orbital frontal dysfunction," he said. He likened Weinstein's results to those recorded in a study by Damasio and his colleagues of patients who exhibited behavioral changes after suffering from brain injuries. Weinstein's responses were nearly identical to those of the once high-functioning, successful patient known as Elliot.

Prosecutor Zach Weiss finally got his chance to cross-examine Relkin. He began by asking the doctor to explain the many possible symptoms that people with frontal lobe disorder might exhibit. Those symptoms included trouble with movement, awkward gaits, loss of ability to distinguish smells, incontinence, diminished libido, unusual eating habits, and disrupted sleeping patterns. Personality changes were possible, as well, and Weinstein certainly seemed to exhibit those.

Relkin said that Weinstein's behavior at times seemed odd, and his sense of humor seemed inappropriate considering the gravity of his situation and the recent death of his wife. "In the interactions that he had with the various physicians at the University of Iowa and in some of my interactions with him," Relkin testified, "he does have at times a somewhat inappropriate jocularity as though he didn't fully appreciate the import or consequences of what is going on."

Weiss asked if that might be a result of frontal lobe disorder.

Relkin couldn't say with medical certainty; his demeanor very well might have been part of Weinstein's long-standing personality.

Weiss wanted to know whether Weinstein's personality had changed as the cyst grew inside his head.

"The only indication that I have is the patient's own report that he was quite perturbable as a youngster and cried easily, was easily upset when he was teased and taunted about being overweight, et cetera," Relkin said. "And when he reached maturity, he believes that he consciously changed that."

Weiss got to the heart of the matter: "In your report, you never concluded that the defendant's frontal lobe dysfunction was linked to the killing of his wife, did you?"

"I did not use those explicit terms, no." Relkin explained that he had never been asked to link Weinstein's decision to kill his wife to his frontal lobe injury.

"Just because a person has a frontal lobe dysfunction, that doesn't mean they will engage in violent crime, does it?" Weiss asked.

"Violence is one of, again, those many possible symptoms that can attend frontal lobe dysfunction. It does not necessarily follow from frontal lobe dysfunction, but it can."

"Just because a person has frontal lobe dysfunction, that doesn't mean they will kill people, does it?" Weiss said.

"No," Relkin responded.

Weiss moved on to ask Relkin whether other researchers used skin conductance tests similar to those performed by Antonio Damasio.

Relkin said several laboratories across the country were using SCR tests to investigate the effects of emotional stimuli, but Damasio was at the forefront of using it to research frontal lobe dysfunction.

Weiss asked whether he agreed with Damasio's conclusion that Weinstein did not know the "appropriate response option" when he killed his wife and whether he believed Weinstein had known right from wrong at the time.

"Under the circumstances which are described, I think he lacked capability," Relkin said. "My belief, based upon the findings of significant brain dysfunction in Mr. Weinstein, is that his ability to know under the circumstances in which he killed his wife was impaired."

"In the report that you wrote, you never made that finding, did you?" Weiss said.

"That's not a finding, sir. That's my opinion. You just asked me for my opinion."

"Do you hold that opinion to a reasonable degree of medical certainty?"

"I'm going to say that that is my belief within the bounds of medical certainty." Relkin explained that neurological tests and brain scans were not the only evidence he had used to reach the conclusion that Weinstein was impaired. Other observations had led him to suspect that Weinstein suffered from frontal lobe dysfunction, including the odd behavior previously described. "As an example, the patient returned to the apartment in which the killing of his wife occurred, and continues to live there to this day. I find that somewhat unusual and, again, my colleagues shared in that opinion," Relkin said. "It is the kind of thing, again, that we would not expect in a patient who had a past history of violence, committed an act of violence, and then was returned to the site that the event occurred."

When Weiss finished questioning Relkin, White took one more turn with the neurologist. "Let me ask you this, doctor," White said. "Is it generally accepted in the neurological community that reduced levels of cerebral glucose metabolism can cause cognitive dysfunction in the brain?"

"It is."

"I have no further questions."

Zach Weiss continued to try to dismantle the PET scan evidence, both in legal motions and in the courtroom. He spent considerable time arguing that the PET scan of Weinstein's brain was subject to technical imperfections, possibly creating an inaccurate representation that, in turn, could lead to a misinterpretation of the evidence. The images were of such low resolution that their usefulness was in question. The scans could have been marred by "artifacts," readings that were incidental or caused by movement or other activities.

To address these concerns, White agreed to find someone to perform a second PET scan to prove that the first one was not an anomaly. He landed one of the best possible people to do it: Abass Alavi, a world-renowned physician and research scientist from the University of Pennsylvania who was a pioneer in developing PET scanning technology. Alavi introduced the process of fluorodeoxyglucose PET scanning in the mid-1970s, which revolutionized brain imaging and its use in diagnoses.

During a break in the proceedings, Weinstein was allowed to fly to Philadelphia to undergo the second scan. The images came back with even better resolution, and they mirrored the results of the first scan in detecting reduced glucose metabolism in the same brain regions. Alavi said the scan clearly indicated that Weinstein had brain dysfunction in those areas, adding that any artifacts would not have been strong enough to account for the hypometabolism detected even in areas distant from the cyst.

White called Alavi to testify. The doctor not only shared his observations but also stated that PET scanning was far from a novel technique and was, in fact, widely used as a research and diagnostic tool in clinical settings. PET already had been subject to careful review in major medical publications, he told the judge, and was widely accepted in the scientific community. Under cross-examination from Weiss, on the other hand, he testified that the complex mathematical models used to quantify the results of the PET data had not gained general acceptance, a distinction the judge would have to consider.

Alavi concluded that "with high probability" the cerebral dysfunction detected by the PET scan was related to the cyst in Weinstein's brain. It was clear, he said, that the areas of Weinstein's brain that were pressed against the cyst showed problems. "Here you've got a situation that is not different in doing a chest X-ray and seeing a nodule in someone's lung and saying this person may have lung cancer," he said.

White concluded his witnesses with Dr. David Eidelberg, the chief of neurological PET scanning at North Shore Hospital and assistant professor at Cornell Medical College who had performed the first PET scan on Weinstein. Eidelberg came to the hearing as a reluctant witness. His primary interest in examining Weinstein, he explained, was as a treating physician—to determine whether the cyst could be harmful, whether it was affecting Weinstein's mental state, and whether surgery was needed to remove or drain it.

White's main objective in calling Eidelberg to the stand was to show that the doctor was adamant about the accuracy and reliability of his imaging studies and that his opinion could be trusted. Eidelberg explained his technique in great detail—how he used the PET scan not just to create an image but to measure absolute metabolism using numeric analysis. His conclusion: Weinstein showed significant reduction in glucose metabolism, which was evidence of frontal lobe impairment.

When it was Weiss's turn to question Eidelberg, the prosecutor drilled down to a simple question: "Do we know what this metabolism corresponds to in terms of his thought processes over what's going on in his brain?"

"No," Eidelberg replied. "We don't know what he's thinking about. These studies would not tell you his thoughts."

Now it was the prosecution's turn. Zach Weiss had only two witnesses to call, and he felt they were strong enough to discredit White's claims altogether. He began with Dan Martell, the neuropsychologist who months earlier had examined and interviewed Weinstein extensively and uncovered the evidence that Weinstein might have had a gambling problem and that he had an association with the Hemlock Society. But as much as Weiss was eager to make that information known, it was not relevant to this Frye hearing. He could save it for the trial.

Weiss wanted Martell to debunk the theory that PET scan images could identify specific areas of brain dysfunction and be used to explain behavioral problems. Under questioning from Weiss, Martell explained that neuropsychologists like himself were much better at observing the behavioral symptoms associated with frontal lobe damage than at pinpointing the exact locations in the brain that caused them. It was an imperfect science in which cause and effect were not easily linked, especially by images of brain activity.

Weiss asked whether Martell knew of evidence that linked arachnoid cysts with other physical or mental problems.

"I think it's sort of inconclusive whether the cyst causes the problems or whether the patient has both—has two independent problems," Martell said.

Weiss moved on. "Frontal lobe damage can lead to dramatic alterations of personality, is that true?"

"I'm not sure I'd use the term *dramatic,* but it can lead to alterations in personality, yes," Martell said.

"At the same time, though, it can leave cognitive and motor functions relatively intact, isn't that true?" Weiss asked.

"It depends. We're talking about a large area of the brain, so depending on the location of the lesion, it could have very different effects on personality or behavior." Frontal lobe damage, Martell noted, could lead to a wide range of behavioral changes. Some people with prefrontal lesions could become profane, slovenly, facetious, irresponsible, grandiose, or irrational. Some could lose spontaneity, a sense of security, or initiative; or develop apathy, even suffer from the erosion of judgment, insight, and foresight. "Some show a mix of all of that," he said.

"And some lose the ability to delay gratification and the capacity for remorse?" Weiss asked.

"That may be more controversial," Martell replied.

Controversial or not, Weiss wanted to make sure the judge understood that the list of possible symptoms resulting from frontal lobe damage was drawn not from evidence of reduced glucose metabolism as recorded on a PET scan, but from medical literature that described patients with frontal lobe dysfunction caused by lesions, surgery, or neurological disease such as Alzheimer's disease.

Weiss had one more witness who he hoped would debunk what he considered scientific speculation. Dr. Jonathan Brodie, a professor of psychiatry at New York University Medical Center, had done extensive research on PET scanning. He studied biochemical functioning in the brains of people with various psychiatric disorders, had done hundreds of PET scans himself, and reviewed thousands of others. Brodie used PET scans not to diagnose psychiatric disorders but to study them.

Weiss's strategy was to have Brodie serve as the voice of reason, to urge caution about concluding what reduced glucose metabolism in the brain really meant. Brodie did just what Weiss wanted him to do and in terms easily understood. He explained that glucose metabolism was simply a measure of energy use, not necessarily an indicator of a specific dysfunction in the brain. "It's like one can think of a car," he testified. "The glucose is the fuel. How fast the car runs is not merely a function of how much fuel there is in the tank."

Brodie said a brain's performance could be measured by many functions. It was difficult to distinguish the effects of Weinstein's cyst from others who might also have such cysts, he explained, because there was no control group to compare. But his main point was that a biochemical process—glucose metabolism—is simply a brain function, not an indicator of behavior. "And so the question of what the relationship is of chemistry to behavior is not a direct one in a sense. Energy utilization is the final common path of all energy processes in the brain. And behavior is the output of brain activity. And there is no one-to-one correspondence."

"In your considered opinion," Weiss asked the doctor, "does an abnormal PET image such as the one you observed, which was made from defendant Weinstein's brain, mean that he has a dysfunctional brain?"

"Not to me," Brodie said, then clarified. "If one means that, that an abnormality in glucose metabolism translates into an abnormality of behavior, I would have to say no, that has never been proven, to my knowledge, using PET."

Brodie went on to say studies had shown that brain functions do not necessarily localize to any particular region—that they can be diffusely organized. Different parts of the brain can make up for deficiencies, even loss of brain tissue, in other areas. Moreover, glucose metabolism is not an exact indicator of anything. "The brain is a paradigm of highly interconnected networks, and everything you do affects every other part of the brain," he said.

Finally, Weiss asked Brodie about the study that suggested a group of patients who exhibited violent behavior showed abnormal readings for frontal lobe metabolism.

"I think it's of some potential interest," Brodie offered. "But it's like so many of the PET studies, that we see behaviors and we ask the question, can we find anything biologically that correlates with the behavior or a group of behaviors? And this is one of many studies which have said, 'Gee, we find something different without necessarily knowing what to make of it.'"

"Do you think that the study definitively establishes that people with relatively low levels of regional glucose metabolism are likely to commit violent acts?" Weiss asked.

"Absolutely not."

"Is it generally accepted in the community of PET researchers, of which you're part, that relatively low levels of regional glucose metabolism are associated with acts of physical violence?"

"No."

Brodie was the last witness to testify in the Frye hearing. The rest of the arguments came from the lawyers.

For Weiss, it all came down to this: the scientific evidence that Weinstein's lawyer intended to present simply did not belong in court. It was not generally accepted by the scientific community and proved nothing about the state of Weinstein's brain or why he had strangled his wife and thrown her out the window. PET scanning was an unreliable technology that was a mere sixteen years old. The fifty or sixty PET scanners in the United States were not standardized in any way, operated with different types of hardware and software, and often yielded inconsistent readings. At best, they produced similar, though not identical, results to show levels of glucose metabolism. Accurately developing a PET scan image and reliably evaluating it, he argued, was a complex process riddled with the potential for error.

Weiss pointed out that there were discrepancies between the PET scans taken at North Shore Hospital and at Pennsylvania, and that the experts differed as to why. Even if the technology was reliable, Weiss still argued that it was not generally accepted in the scientific community that it could reveal frontal lobe dysfunction.

Weiss also took issue with a study in the *British Journal of Psychiatry* that supposedly linked low glucose metabolism in the frontal lobes with frontal lobe dysfunction and violent behavior. Three of the four patients studied, he noted, had histories of alcohol or substance abuse, as well as diagnosed mental disorders. Even the study's authors cautioned against attributing the violence to brain abnormalities alone. "Most of the violent behavior seen in patients probably represents complex interactions between neural systems, neurotransmitters, hormones, environmental stimulus and learned responses," the study concluded. Weiss also explained that arachnoid cysts were found in 0.5 to 1 percent of the population, so that in a city such as New York with eight million people, about forty thousand would have these structures in their brains. They certainly were not all homicidal or suffering from frontal lobe damage.

He went on to try to discredit Damasio's skin conductance study, suggesting that it was flawed because the population sample was small and because the results might be skewed due to lack of controls for age and sex. "There is no way of stating with any confidence that the data in the study would be at all representative of the larger population," Weiss said.

In Weiss's view, the absence of peer-reviewed scientific literature supporting the defense theories about frontal lobe dysfunction spoke volumes. He could not find a single study reporting a "significant statistical association" between arachnoid cysts and frontal lobe dysfunction. Nothing proved that hypometabolism could definitively diagnose frontal lobe dysfunction. Nor had any scientist replicated Damasio's SCR study results. This all proved, Weiss argued, that White's claims carried no weight with neuroscience community.

Finally, Weiss concluded, if a brain defect could indeed cause an otherwise normal person to acquire an impulsive, violent-prone personality, where else in Weinstein's life was there violence? There was none, of course. So how could a PET scan prove that a brain defect caused a single act of violence in a man who had never done anything violent before? If Weinstein's brain was compromised, and his condition was worsening so much that it caused him to kill his wife, wouldn't his condition cause him to commit further acts of violence? Because he had done no such thing, Weiss said, Weinstein was living disproof of the very theories he sought to assert.

Nonsense, responded Diarmuid White. Weiss was attempting to try the case rather than discuss the admissibility of evidence. White accused him of quoting selectively from the literature when he stated that PET scanning was "in its infancy" and that its results were not accepted as reliable and diagnostically significant. In fact, White pointed out, PET scanning was developed in 1972, and the technique had been continually refined and had become quite reliable for medical diagnostics. A month earlier in the *New York Times,* a researcher from the National Institute of Mental Health had been quoted saying, "The information you can get from this technique is unbeatable. It has just opened up a window to the brain that we did not dream of ten or fifteen years ago." Neither newness nor lack absolute certainty was enough to render a test inadmissible. Moreover, White dismissed the contention that skin conductance was not scientifically valid—its diagnostic usefulness had been reported in countless texts and medical journals.

Finally, and perhaps most important to the defense, White argued that PET scans were quite capable of showing regional glucose metabolism. Metabolism or lack thereof, he agreed, was not a direct measure of behavior, but a psychologist or neurologist could reasonably use that information to form an opinion about his client's sanity. The PET scans and Damasio's SCR tests could be used to support, not replace, an expert opinion about Weinstein's cognitive faculties, which White said were so impaired that he could not distinguish right from wrong nor appreciate the consequences of his actions when he killed his wife.

As White and Weiss concluded their arguments, the time came for Judge Carruthers to sort through mounds of complex science and conflicting opinions over the value of PET scans in assessing brain dysfunction and to decide whether a jury should be allowed to evaluate that evidence. It was Weinstein's only hope.

As Judge Carruthers waded through the testimony, read the scientific studies, and pondered the evidence, he could find no precedent-setting cases or high court rulings that addressed the admission of PET scans in a criminal trial. His colleagues on the bench in New York had no experience in this area, either. He was entering uncharted waters, and his decision could have profound implications.

While the New York courts had yet to grapple with the admissibility of PET scan evidence, lawyers in California had already been presenting scans during the sentencing phase of murder trials for some time. During sentencing hearings, the rules of evidence are not as ironclad as they are during the guilt phase of a trial, which opened the door for lawyers to bring in scans unchallenged. One of the first reported cases involved a thirty-six-year-old electronics technician and air force veteran named Barry Wayne McNamara. On the night of January 5, 1985, McNamara walked into his parents' ranch home outside Santa Barbara carrying a hunting rifle. He shot his father in the head, then walked down the hall to a bedroom and shot his four-year-old niece and his sister. He then used a stone to crush his mother's skull. When police arrived, McNamara calmly denied that he had killed his family members and told the officers that his family might have been Soviet spies. He told his attorney that he had been instructed to kill his family by voices broadcast from the television set, later adding that he thought he was the illegitimate son of Queen Elizabeth. McNamara claimed, in his own words, to have "flipped out" that night.

McNamara's defense lawyer, Michael McGrath, told the court that his client had schizophrenia. He clearly had not known what he was doing when he killed his family. How could he have? McGrath put on an insanity defense, hoping that despite the horrific nature of the crime, a jury and judge might spare McNamara from the death penalty, given his mental incapacities.

During the trial, several mental health experts testified that McNamara was indeed a paranoid schizophrenic who had suffered from crippling emotional problems for years. Two psychiatrists testified that he was insane and could not distinguish right from wrong.

Prosecutors said that was simply not true. Dr. Donald Patterson, a psychiatrist who examined McNamara immediately after the killings, testified that in his opinion McNamara was not disturbed enough to be unaware of what he was doing.

The jurors deliberated for two days and found McNamara guilty of killing his parents, his sister, and her daughter—that is, they decided that he was sane. McGrath still needed to push the insanity argument to show them that his client was a very sick man and did not deserve to die. Monte Buchsbaum, from the University of California at Irvine, was willing to help. Buchsbaum's expertise in the use of PET scans to study mental illness, particularly schizophrenia, could help boost the argument that McNamara was insane and thus serve as mitigation in his sentencing hearing. Buchsbaum believed that the disease was based in the frontal lobe, and that a PET scan could show whether there was a low glucose metabolism in the frontal lobes, which could indicate schizophrenia.

Buchsbaum performed a PET scan on McNamara and told McGrath that he found signs of hypoactivity, or low glucose metabolism, in the prefrontal cortex, which would be consistent with schizophrenia. The images were allowed as evidence during McNamara's sentencing hearing, where Buchsbaum testified that the results were consistent with the diagnosis that two other psychiatrists gave. The PET scan evidence clearly had an impact on the jury, which deliberated just two hours before deciding to spare McNamara's life. In later interviews, jurors said the neuroimaging evidence played a significant role in their decision.

Other lawyers who had clients facing the death penalty began calling Buchsbaum for his services, and he obliged. Among the most notorious cases was that of the serial killer Randy Steven Kraft, who was accused of killing as many as forty-five young men in southern California, Oregon, and Michigan. Most of the victims were between eighteen and twenty-five years old and had been sexually abused and sexually mutilated. Their bodies were usually dumped along freeway ramps or in remote areas. After a jury voted to convict Kraft of killing sixteen people, his lawyer, C. Thomas McDonald, brought in Buchsbaum for the sentencing phase to try to save his client's life. Buchsbaum testified that Kraft suffered from an abnormality that could affect "emotional, impulsive, and sexual behavior," basing that diagnosis in part on PET images showing damage to the frontal lobes. In most areas, Buchsbaum told the jurors, Kraft's brain was normal, but the frontal lobes were significantly different from those of twenty-four controls.

On cross-examination, Buchsbaum acknowledged that some leading authorities believed that PET scans were too experimental for use in criminal cases. He was probably the only PET scan expert involved in such cases at the time. The technology was still relatively new, with only about two dozen PET scan centers across the country, including three in California.

Buchsbaum said Kraft's psychological problems could have stemmed from a head injury that he suffered when he was a year old. "If the jury's position is [that] Randy is guilty, we can at least show them it wasn't because he is an evil person," Buchsbaum later told the *Los Angeles Times*. "It's something organic he can't do anything about." Neither the PET scans nor Buchsbaum's testimony helped. On August 11, 1989, the jury recommended the death penalty; three months later the judge sentenced Kraft to death.

In all these early cases, lawyers did not use neuroscience to try to absolve their clients of responsibility. Rather, they presented it to try to lessen their sentences by offering an explanation for a violent disposition. Blaming the brain rather than the person for committing a crime did not appear to be a promising tactic. Weinstein's novel argument—that a brain cyst could be responsible for criminal behavior—had yet to be tested in a criminal trial.

CHAPTER 12

Deadly Tumor

Herbert Weinstein had been living a comfortable middle class life in New Milford, New Jersey, during the summer of 1966. His advertising career was thriving. His marriage was good. He had a nice three-bedroom house with a backyard where he and his wife entertained and had parties for their children, Nelson, seven, and Joni, five. And he seemed to be in pretty good health, unaware of the cyst that was growing inside his skull and squeezing into his brain.

On July 31, some seventeen hundred miles away, Charles Whitman, a twenty-five-year-old student at the University of Texas at Austin, sat down at a typewriter and began composing a suicide note. "I don't quite understand what it is that compels me to type this letter," he wrote. "Perhaps it is to leave some vague reason for the actions I have recently performed. I don't really understand myself these days." He didn't understand his growing disaffection with life, his aggressive impulses, and his desire to kill his wife, his mother, a group of strangers, and finally himself. He suspected something was going wrong inside his head.

"I am supposed to be an average reasonable and intelligent young man," his letter continued. "However, lately (I can't recall when it started) I have been a victim of many unusual and irrational thoughts. These thoughts constantly recur, and it requires a tremendous mental effort to concentrate on useful and progressive tasks."

Whitman's psychological problems had worsened, he wrote, when his parents separated, which caused him a great deal of stress. He visited a doctor at the university's health center and asked him to recommend a psychiatric consultation. "I talked with a Doctor once for about two hours and tried to convey to him my fears that I felt overwhelming violent impulses. After one session I never saw the Doctor again, and since then I have been fighting my mental turmoil alone, and seemingly to no avail."

Around midnight Whitman drove to his mother's apartment, where she was expecting him to visit. Once inside, he choked, beat, and stabbed her, plunging a hunting knife into her chest. He then returned home, quietly crept into his bedroom, and stabbed his sleeping wife to death. In the morning, he got a military footlocker and loaded it with knives, a machete, various tools, cans of food, water, a container of gasoline, rope, and other items, including an ammunition box. He then went shopping, building an arsenal that included three rifles, a shotgun, two pistols, a revolver, a hunting knife, and about seven hundred rounds of ammunition. He hauled it into his car and drove to the University of Texas campus on one of the hottest days of the summer, when the temperature reached the nineties before noon.

When he arrived, he wheeled his footlocker on a dolly to the Texas Clock Tower and took an elevator to the twenty-seventh floor, where he encountered a receptionist. He killed her by crushing her skull with the butt of a rifle. He then went out onto the observation deck with his weapons and began to fire shots down below. He killed sixteen people and wounded thirty-one others before a police officer shot him dead about an hour and half later.

The suicide letter that police found at his apartment ended with an unusual request: "After my death I wish that an autopsy would be performed on me to see if there is any visible physical disorder. I have had some tremendous headaches in the past and have consumed two large bottles of Excedrin in the past three months."

Two days after the shootings, Texas pathologist Dr. Coleman de Chenar opened Whitman's skull and removed his brain. In the middle part, he discovered a small grayish yellow tumor, about the size of a pecan. The growth was nestled beneath the thalamus, which relays sensory and motor information and regulates sleep, and it was pressing on the amygdala, which helps regulate emotions and behavior. The doctor didn't think the tumor was related to Whitman's psychiatric complaints or headaches and certainly not to his homicidal rampage. But many of Whitman's surviving family members and friends wanted to believe that the tumor was somehow responsible for his actions. Whitman's father said his son was clearly sick. Democratic senator Robert F. Kennedy from New York suggested that had Whitman been taken alive and tried in court, he would have been acquitted for the crime because he "was so clearly insane." The priest at Whitman's funeral said he trusted that "God in his mercy does not hold him responsible for these last actions."

It's easy to see why people would grasp for an explanation for such an otherwise inexplicable, evil, inhuman act. Whitman's story has been retold and dissected over the years, yet there's still no consensus on what drove him to kill that day. He was a smart and friendly but often troubled young man who was an Eagle Scout and served in the marines. He also had a volatile personality, abused amphetamines, and spoke of hating his father and being unloved by his mother. He suffered from mental anguish, physically abused his wife, and had a fondness for guns. In hindsight, the architectural engineering student seemed inevitably bound for some type of explosive outburst.

The Texas pathologist's conclusion that Whitman's tumor had nothing to do with his violent behavior was not the last word on the matter. Public officials still wanted to understand what had happened and why. A Texas state commission of inquiry, called by Governor John Connally, reviewed the case. A team of medical experts, including pathologists, psychiatrists, psychologists, and neurosurgeons, examined brain tissue and tissue from the tumor. They identified the tumor as a glioblastoma multiforme, a malignant growth with widespread necrosis, or deadening of cells and tissue around it.

In its report, the commission left open the possibility that the tumor played some part in Whitman's murder spree: "Abnormal aggressive behavior may be a manifestation of organic brain disease," the commissioners wrote. While "the highly malignant brain tumor conceivably could have contributed to his inability to control his emotions and actions," they could not establish, with any clarity, a *causal* relationship between the tumor and Whitman's actions.

After Whitman was shot to death by police, a grand jury was called to investigate. In 1986 authorities in Travis County, Texas, finally released the report, which had been kept secret until then. It stated that Whitman's tumor "undoubtedly caused him much mental pain and possibly contributed to his insane actions." It urged a complete medical-legal case study so that such tragedies might be prevented in the future. After that report was released, Thomas Blackwell, the prosecutor who had led that grand jury probe (he had since became a judge), dismissed that statement, telling the *Dallas Morning News* that if Whitman had put on an insanity defense, he as a judge would have put it down. "He wasn't a blithering idiot," Blackwell told the paper. "He planned it. He was aware of the circumstances that he was probably going to lose his life when he got on that tower. I could have won." Author Gary Lavergne, in *A Sniper in the Tower,* wrote that "nearly all the physicians and criminologists who have made themselves familiar with the case have pronounced the tumor 'innocent.'"

The Texas Tower massacre raised a debate over whether brain tumors can cause criminal behavior. In 1967, a year after the killings, the San Francisco physician Nathan Malamud reviewed the case files of eighteen patients who had been diagnosed with or treated for depression, anxiety, or schizophrenia. Each of them also had a brain tumor within some part of the limbic system, the brain structure associated with basic emotions, such as fear and anger, and with primitive drives such as hunger, sex and aggression. Many of these patients also experienced small, barely detectible seizures, known as petit mal or absence seizures. One of them, a nineteen-year-old man, had begun showing behavioral disturbances when he was eight years old, disturbances that worsened as he got older and turned into criminal behavior, including assaults, sexual assaults, and burglary. Barely noticeable seizures often accompanied his aggressive behavior. At thirteen he was admitted to a state mental hospital. His physical and neurological examinations were uneventful, and he scored an IQ of 86, considered normal. Doctors thought his bad behavior and mental disorder were the result of a broken home, and he was treated with psychotherapy. At seventeen he had a more serious seizure and was sent for an angiogram, which revealed a tumor on the left hippocampal region of his brain. His condition deteriorated, though he never underwent surgery to remove the tumor. He was diagnosed as schizophrenic with epilepsy and died of complications from his condition at nineteen. Malamud suggested a "direct causal relationship" between the brain tumor and this patient's psychiatric symptoms.

In 1982 Dr. Frank A. Elliott, a neurologist and emeritus professor of neurology at the University of Pennsylvania, noted that most studies about the causes of aggressive behavior focus on social and psychological factors, "with little more than lip service being paid to the neurological part of the equation." Elliott suspected brain injuries played a significant role as well.

He reviewed 286 cases of patients who had had episodes of "unprovoked rage" since early childhood or after sustaining a physical brain injury later in life. Ninety-four percent of these patients had developed or acquired brain defects caused by stroke, a TBI, a brain tumor, or other neurological trauma. About a third of them were described as stable until they had such a "brain insult." Of the 286, fifty-one had suffered a head injury, forty-seven had some type of epilepsy, and thirteen had a brain tumor or cyst, like the one in Herbert Weinstein's brain. Elliott said that the study strongly suggested links between these types of brain damage and aggressive behavior but said more studies were needed.

In 2003 a dramatic case linking a brain tumor to criminal behavior became public knowledge. A forty-year-old married schoolteacher from Virginia inexplicably began to have a sexual interest in children. Unbeknownst to his wife, he surreptitiously collected child pornography and regularly viewed it on the Internet. His desires grew to the point that he solicited prostitution services from adults in a so-called massage parlor and later made subtle, unwanted sexual advances toward his prepubescent stepdaughter. The girl told her mother, who discovered her husband's secret porn stash and called the police. He was charged with child molestation. He was convicted, and the judge gave him a choice: either enter a twelve-step program for sexual addiction or go to prison. He chose the program, but at the facility his sexually inappropriate behavior seemed to worsen. He tried to solicit sexual favors from staff and clients and was kicked out of the program. He had to go back to court and face the judge for a prison sentence. But the night before sentencing, he complained of horrible headaches and was taken to the University of Virginia Hospital in Charlottesville for examination.

At the hospital, he talked about committing suicide. He made sexual advances toward the nursing staff and spoke of raping his landlady. He had trouble with balance. During the neurological exam, he had trouble writing legibly and drawing simple pictures. His brain seemed to be progressively malfunctioning. He explained to the staff that he had no family history of psychiatric illness and had never experienced anything like the problems he was having. He also told them he never had taken part in any deviant sexual behavior until his recent urges began.

The schoolteacher explained to his examiners that he had previously worked as a corrections officer and had completed a master's degree in education in 1998. He was in his second marriage, which had been stable for two years until he began having his unusual sexual urges. While he was articulating this personal history in a seemingly unremarkable fashion, his condition suddenly deteriorated. During the exam he made sexual remarks to female staff and urinated on himself, seeming unconcerned about it.

A doctor ordered a brain scan. The MRI revealed that the schoolteacher had a large orbitofrontal tumor on the right side of his brain. After surgeons removed it, his pedophilic urges disappeared. Authorities were convinced that he was no longer a threat, and he was allowed to complete the sexual rehabilitation program. He eventually moved back home with his wife and stepdaughter, and everything seemed fine. But a year later he began getting headaches and once again began to amass pornography. He went to the hospital to get an MRI, which revealed that the tumor had grown back. It was surgically removed. His sexually deviant behavior disappeared once again.

The study's authors theorized that the teacher's tumor may have heightened a previous interest in pornography and likely transformed him into a criminal pedophile by interrupting the brain signals that control his impulses. The story seemed like a clear case of cause and effect between brain tumors and criminal behavior. As a case study, it has been frequently discussed as an example of how a person might know the difference between right and wrong but lack impulse control due to a biological impairment.

Curious about it, I reached out to Dr. Russell Swerdlow, one of the neurologists who treated the teacher at the hospital in Virginia and authored a paper on the case. Swerdlow had since moved on to become a professor at the University of Kansas. He told me that he had never seen anything like that case, though such radical behavioral changes caused by a tumor were not surprising, given the abundance of literature on the subject. "But it was the first case in which the bad behavior was pedophilia," he said. "What was so striking about this was his inability to act on his knowledge of what was right or wrong."

In his paper, Swerdlow pointed out that research on orbitofrontal lesions showed that sociopathic behavior often resulted from a loss of impulse control rather than a loss of moral knowledge. Referring to Antonio Damasio's somatic marker hypothesis, he suggested that those with frontal lobe lesions have impaired autonomic responses. Swerdlow explained to me that when pathways between the orbitofrontal lobe and the amygdala are broken, the result can be impulsive behavior. "You don't get the feedback that controls your decisions. You don't have the brakes on your behavior," he said.

When Swerdlow's paper was published in 2003, Dr. Daniel Tranel, the neurology researcher who had worked with Damasio at the University of Iowa in studies of frontal lobe lesions, said in a news interview that he had seen people with brain tumors lie, damage property, and in extremely rare cases, commit murder. "The individual simply loses the ability to control impulses or anticipate the consequences of choices," he said. Dr. Stuart C. Yudofsky, a psychiatrist at the Baylor College of Medicine, reported seeing similar effects from brain tumors. "This tells us something about being human, doesn't it?" he said. "Does it mean we have less free will than we think?"

I asked Stephen Morse, the leading neuroskeptic and a professor of psychology and law in psychiatry at the University of Pennsylvania, about the case, which he frequently refers to in his papers and lectures. Morse told me that while the teacher might have deserved some mitigation in sentencing because of his ailment, it is not clear whether he lacked the ability to control his impulses or simply *chose* not to. "People want to say his tumor made him do it. He made him do it. There is always a reason people do it," Morse says. "We don't give a pass to the other pedophiles. He felt an urge, which he understood and did not resist, but acted on it."

Yet Swerdlow's theory seems plausible. If the pathways between the orbitofrontal lobe and the amygdala were broken or interrupted, an otherwise reasonable person who understood right from wrong might not be able to control impulses, whereas most others could. In fact, two neuroscientists from the University of Wisconsin at Madison, in a review of the literature, came to similar conclusions: that when there are abnormalities in the structure or functions of the orbitofrontal cortex, the amygdala, and the anterior cingulate cortex, emotional regulation can be inhibited. Compromising the pathways or circuitry among them can increase a person's propensity for impulsive, aggressive behavior.

Charles Whitman rightly suspected that something unusual was going on inside his brain. Whether his tumor was to blame for his deadly shooting spree remains open to debate. In a moment of lucidity, he suggested someone try to find out why he was going to do what he was about to do. Near the end of his suicide letter, he left instructions to settle his affairs after his death: "If my life insurance policy is valid, please see that all the worthless checks I wrote this weekend are made good. Please pay off my debts. I am twenty-five years old and have been financially independent. Donate the rest anonymously to a mental health foundation. Maybe research can prevent further tragedies of this type."

CHAPTER 13

What's a Picture Worth?

On October 8, 1992, Judge Richard Carruthers signed and released his decision on the Frye hearing and had his office send copies to prosecutor Zachary Weiss and to defense attorney Diarmuid White. It looked good for Weinstein.

Carruthers decided to allow Weinstein's PET scans and readings to be admitted as evidence. He sided with White that these diagnostic procedures had been generally accepted by the scientific community. But there was a catch. He would not allow experts to testify that the readings could explain or account for specific behavior. In other words, jurors would see the colorful pictures of Weinstein's brain with the big black hole, but they couldn't hear testimony that his arachnoid cyst, or the reduced glucose metabolism in his frontal lobe, had *caused* him to kill his wife. Such extrapolation was beyond what was generally accepted as valid in the fields of psychiatry, psychology, and neurology. The judge further said that the notion that an arachnoid cyst or reduced glucose metabolism could directly cause violence was not an accepted theory, nor was the idea that impairments of the brain directly caused violence. Thus, these arguments could not be introduced at trial.

As for Antonio Damasio's somatic marker theory, Carruthers wrote that as interesting as it sounded, it was not yet generally accepted in the scientific community and had no place in the trial. He acknowledged that cognitive problems might render a person unable to choose a proper behavioral response in moments of stress, but he was unconvinced that experts accepted the theory that aberrant behavior could be the product of a person's history of reward and punishment responses, which were supposedly encoded in the autonomic nervous system. "Rather, Doctor Damasio appears to have first proposed this theory in his research report as a 'possible' explanation of the phenomena that his team observed during reported SCR studies," Carruthers wrote.

Prosecutor Weiss had successfully shot down the possibility that experts could testify that Weinstein's brain damage caused him to be violent, but he still had serious concerns about the jury seeing the dramatic PET images. The last thing he wanted was for Weinstein's lawyer to flash them in front of an impressionable jury in the absence of a more sophisticated discussion about what they meant. He wondered if a jury was capable of seeing beyond them and following the more important testimony and evidence that Weinstein was not insane—not even temporarily insane—but simply had gotten angry and killed his wife.

Weiss felt strongly that Weinstein had to be held responsible for his crime. He might indeed have lost control of himself during the fight with his wife and strangled her, making it a crime of passion and perhaps a case of manslaughter. Weiss saw those kinds of cases all the time. The law took into account whether a murder was premeditated or not.

But something else was gnawing at Weiss. The medical examiner suggested the possibility that Barbara Weinstein had not died after her husband squeezed her throat but had been unconscious. She might very well have been alive when Herbert threw her out the window and then died from the impact of the fall. Those two distinct acts, one of passion and one of forethought, made the murder feel all the more sinister to Weiss.

But the prospect of a full-blown trial was daunting. The Frye hearing gave both lawyers a sense of the complexity of the case and of the cost of hiring experts to testify. Weiss weighed his options. Would a jury be swayed by the pictures of Weinstein's brain and excuse him, or would it see through such theatrics, as Weiss considered them? Weinstein, if convicted, faced twenty-five years to life. He was now sixty-seven years old. Even if the judge sentenced him to the minimum, it would be effectively a life sentence.

On the other hand, Weiss thought, there might be another way to get Weinstein a life sentence without a trial. What if he could work out a deal and offer manslaughter instead of murder? That would still guarantee that Weinstein would serve until he was a very old man, maybe even until his death. Weiss had good reason to believe a deal was possible because Diarmuid White had hinted that Weinstein might not be able to afford to go through with a full trial. In an earlier court filing, White had suggested that his client was running out of money to hire multiple expert witnesses to navigate mounds of complex scientific evidence. White asked Carruthers to consider releasing state funds so he could keep up with Weiss who, White argued, had access to vast resources at the district attorney's office. White described himself to the judge as an average person with little formal education in or aptitude for scientific matters. He certainly wasn't schooled in neuropsychology, psychiatry, neurology, or nuclear medicine and needed expert help. Although Weinstein had been paying for his legal services to this point, he had not been employed since his arrest and lacked significant assets. He had been able to make bail only because he borrowed money from his brother. He never anticipated the kind of defense that arose after the discovery of a cyst in his skull.

The district attorney's office had already spent about seventy thousand dollars on the case, and they hadn't even gone to trial. Weiss thought this was a good time to talk and reached out to White to discuss a deal. White said he was open to a negotiation and went back to Weinstein to discuss it. At the same time, Weiss reached out to Barbara's family to see how they would feel about a deal. Kim Goldberg, Barbara's daughter, felt that putting her grandmother through a full trial might be more than she could bear. If Weinstein agreed to substantial prison time, that would be enough for them.

It didn't take much to convince Weinstein. The expense of a trial and the risk of a lengthy prison sentence if he lost were enough to induce him to give in. He told his attorney to accept the offer for manslaughter, which carried the possibility of a seven- to twenty-one-year prison sentence.

On the morning of October 19, 1992, when jury selection was supposed to take place, Weiss and White brought their plea agreement to Judge Carruthers. Weinstein stood next to his attorney, ready to make some concessions.

Carruthers asked Weinstein whether he understood the plea agreement and its possible consequences. Weinstein said yes, he did.

Weiss explained to the judge that he had agreed to negotiate a plea agreement to bring finality to the case and to help the victim's family move on. He told Carruthers that he had spoken with Barbara's mother, Alice Shapiro, who was eighty years old and had attended every hearing. "She's indicated to me that every day this matter is not resolved is another day of agony for her. I don't know that this guilty plea will ever make up for the loss of her child," Weiss said. "I think it will help her and the rest of Barbara's family close a chapter on their life and get on with their life."

Weiss told the judge that he felt manslaughter was appropriate since there was no indication that Weinstein's crime was premeditated. It wasn't the kind of crime that Weinstein was likely to commit again, and the man was not a threat to society. Weiss said he felt justice would be served. "Seven years by some may not be considered to be a fairly significant sentence," he told the judge. "However, given the defendant's age and given the fact that the years at the end of your life are in many ways more precious than the beginning, the People feel this is a sentence that satisfies the state's interest in having the defendant pay for the consequences of his deed."

White told the judge that he agreed the deal was in his client's best interest. Given the grim nature of the crime, and the possibility that a jury might not have sympathy for Weinstein, White said he felt this was the best option.

Judge Carruthers complimented both attorneys for their work. "You've handled this very difficult case in a highly professional way," he said.

Before sentencing Weinstein, the judge reviewed a presentencing report, prepared by a probation officer, that indicated that Weinstein was by all accounts a good citizen, a nonviolent person who had led a productive, crime-free life until the day he killed his wife. But there was another side. Probation officer Rhoda Bation interviewed members of Barbara's family to prepare a victim impact statement for the judge to consider before final sentencing. Alice Shapiro told Bation she hadn't stopped crying for two years since her daughter was killed, that she felt heartbroken, betrayed, and desolate. Barbara's daughter, Kim, spoke of the nightmares she'd had, thinking of the torture her mother suffered before her death. Kim used to call Barbara daily and was reminded of that loss every day.

Nelson and Joni Weinstein also had their say. Joni, thirty-one, said her father was kind and gentle, the least likely person to do anything violent. She described life with her parents as "a storybook upbringing" and recounted how her father stayed by her mother's side until her death from cancer. Nelson said, "There was no better father or husband. People generally act within their nature, and this was an act totally out of his nature for reasons we will never understand."

Herbert Weinstein had his own story, which he told the probation officer. He called himself an extremely mild-mannered individual, quiet and nonaggressive, who had reacted in self-defense when his wife scratched his face. "I was the last person on earth who anyone who knew me would believe capable of hitting anyone, let alone killing them." He said he believed his cyst had impaired his judgment. He deeply felt the loss of his wife, a woman he very much loved, and he deeply regretted what he had done and the pain he had caused.

The presentencing report brought up the medical examiner's theory that Barbara had been alive when Weinstein threw her out the window. Bation wrote that while she thought Weinstein was indeed amiable, gentle, mild-mannered, and nonviolent, "the defendant admittedly committed a most abominable act when he viciously beat and choked his wife into unconsciousness, attempted to clear the scene of physical evidence and then threw her body out the twelve-story window, without knowing whether she was alive or dead." Finally, when Weinstein first spoke to the police, he had fabricated a story, in an attempt to remove himself from suspicion. "His behavior immediately thereafter was cool, calculating, self-serving and remorseless."

On December 14, 1992, nearly two years after he killed his wife, Weinstein appeared before Judge Carruthers to be sentenced. Assistant district attorney Zach Weiss made the opening statement. "One thing I learned from this case is the victim's pain never forgets," he said. "When the defendant killed Barbara Weinstein, he killed a part of everyone who loved her."

Weiss said that Barbara's family had endured two years without resolution, a source of continual frustration for them. "Today marks the end of that long wait. I do not think that whatever the sentence the defendant receives could eradicate the pain and suffering of Barbara's family," he said.

When it was White's turn, he told Carruthers that before proceeding, he had two major points to make. First, he strongly disagreed with Weiss's assertion that Barbara had been alive when she was pushed out the window. "We were prepared at a hearing to present the testimony of two former chief medical examiners of the City of New York contesting that conclusion," he said. Second, White denied allegations that Weinstein had outstanding gambling debts.

When the judge asked Weinstein whether he had anything to say before being sentenced, Weinstein said he did not and deferred to his attorney.

"Mr. Weinstein has asked me to convey to the court, and to everyone in the court, that he has a deep and abiding sense of guilt about what he did, combined with anger at himself for what he has done, and he as much as anyone deeply regrets the suffering he has caused Barbara's family and to his own family," White said. "And he hopes that the conclusion of this case today has some therapeutic value and he hopes the fact that this case [is] being ended by a guilty plea rather than a trial will spare Barbara's family and his own family any additional pain."

White then said something surprising. "Your honor, when somebody has died, nothing really good can come of it. But Mr. Weinstein would like the court to know that he has agreed at the request of New

York Hospital, Cornell Medical Center, to donate his brain and spinal cord for further research, as well as his organs for possible transplant."

After news of Weinstein's plea agreement hit the local papers, White told the judge, he had received, unsolicited, a letter, which he read aloud: "Dear Mr. White, kindly give the enclosed letter to Mr. Herbert Weinstein. Tell him it's from Beatrice Rabinowitz from days at Taft High School. He was a sweet, gentle boy, and a wonderful friend. Thankfully, sincerely, Beatrice Rabinowitz."

White summed up by reminding the judge that back on the day of Weinstein's arraignment, many had described him as gentle. "I would simply remark that those who would condemn him too harshly might reflect on this: But for the grace of God go I. Thank you, your honor."

Carruthers asked Weinstein if he had anything to say.

"I requested Mr. White speak for me, and he has. I have nothing more to say," Weinstein said.

Carruthers took a moment. "Just a word to the mother of the deceased, the family of the deceased, and also to the family of the defendant. I deeply sympathize with all of you," he said. "Your lives have been irrevocably changed by this tragic incident, and I deeply feel some of that tragedy although, of course, I cannot share the same level of pain that all of you do share."

The judge explained that the deal Weiss and White made was a fair one, and he turned to Weinstein: "You are to serve an indeterminate term of imprisonment, the minimum term shall be seven years, the maximum shall be twenty-one years."

News of the plea agreement spread beyond the city due to the unusual nature of Weinstein's defense. *USA Today* labeled the story in its national digest column with the headline "WIFE KILLER" and reported that the case came down to Weinstein "blaming a brain cyst for causing him to strangle his wife."

That's how many looked at it. The details of the case, the scientific evidence, the brain scans, and the testimony went largely unnoticed and remained out of public view.

Just weeks after Weinstein was sentenced, Dr. David Eidelberg, the neurologist who performed the first PET scan on Weinstein and appeared reluctantly as a witness for the defense at the Frye hearing, offered a more sophisticated analysis—and shared his fears that lawyers would abuse the technology. "This decision opens a new era for nuclear medicine. It's a Pandora's box that's been opened," he said. Eidelberg said that lawyers should be dissuaded from using PET evidence because there is such a large variability among the brains of normal individuals. "One abnormal brain region does not make a case."

Joni Weinstein was in San Francisco when she heard the news. She had been getting periodic reports about the case from Nelson. She knew about her father's brain cyst, though she never saw his PET scan or heard anything about his glucose metabolism or how it might have affected his behavior. She was reluctant to accept the brain blame theory that her father's lawyer had put forth. She had trouble believing that the cyst could have caused his actions. She loved her father but was not sympathetic to him for what he had done. She thought he deserved to go to prison.

In the brief conversations Joni had with her father before he was transported upstate to begin serving his sentence, she came away puzzled as to why he seemed unconcerned about going to prison. He never spoke of being remorseful. He was always so neutral and acted as if this whole affair hadn't happened. When she spoke to him on the phone, she thought he sounded Zen-like. He seemed preoccupied with the relationship with his new wife, who had moved in with him. Joni became increasingly angry at her father—an anger fueled by his indifference, the deliberate way in which he was going on with his life without feeling the weight of what he had done. Joni felt awful that her father was a killer and that she had to live with that fact and with the world knowing it. Worse than that, Barbara's two children had to live with the fact that their mother had been murdered. Joni felt their loss.

When it came time for Weinstein to go to prison, there were no dramatic farewells or tearful good-byes. Joni remained in San Francisco, declining to fly in to see him one last time. Weinstein simply got on a bus and rode north to the Walkill Correctional Facility, a medium-security prison about eighty miles from Manhattan. He didn't complain or cry. He never spoke of being scared. He acted as if it were just a ride into the country. He would not be eligible for his first parole hearing until seven years later.

The Weinstein name soon disappeared from the newspapers, and the "high-rise horror" story was largely forgotten. But the case had sparked a particular interest among neuroscientists and legal scholars, who began to analyze it in greater depth. That's when Herbert Weinstein became Spyder Cystkopf.

That was the pseudonym a group of neuroscientists and lawyers gave Weinstein in a 1996 journal article that explored his case and medical history. It allowed them to freely share details about the case without violating Weinstein's medical or legal confidentiality, even though anyone familiar with the case would recognize who Cystkopf was. The name was inspired by the weblike structure in which the arachnoid cyst resides.

A neurologist named Richard Restak was hired to be the guest editor for the June 1996 issue of the journal *Seminars in Clinical Neuro-*

psychiatry. The special issue, called "Brain Damage and Legal Responsibility," contained seven articles that addressed the Weinstein case and the medical, legal, and moral issues that accompanied it. Among those who contributed articles were prosecutor Zach Weiss, neuropsychologist Dan Martell, neurologist Norman Relkin, neurologist and research scientist Helen Mayberg, and legal scholar Stephen Morse. Most of the authors argued that PET scanning was premature for the courtroom, highly prejudicial, and of no value in determining legal responsibility.

But Relkin and a group of colleagues who wrote the lead article painted a rather sympathetic picture of Weinstein, making the case that his cyst most definitely caused dysfunction in the frontal lobe and should be considered in making sense of his murderous deed. "In our opinion," they wrote, "Cystkopf's isolated episode of violent behavior and his constricted emotionality are most consistent with damage to the prefrontal cortex." Moreover, it was consistent with a predisposition toward stimulus-bound aggression. The novel threat of his wife's scratching suggests it forced him to have an immediate stimulus-bound aggression that he could not stop. He did not have the opportunity to "develop the alternative response strategies." His actions were an extreme and unfortunate example of what could happen when prefrontal mechanisms are damaged.

Daniel Martell, who had spent significant time with Weinstein doing testing and interviews, provided a more skeptical view in his article. He started with the idea that Cystkopf's insanity defense was based on the claim that his cyst was affecting the normal function of the left side of his brain and that it had grown over time. If that were the case, Cystkopf might show impairments in organization, planning, control of his behavior, and memory and language function. None of that came to pass. However, Martell said his records showed evidence of gambling losses at Atlantic City casinos, which supported a possible diagnosis of pathological gambling. Martell also noted Weinstein's appointments with the Hemlock Society. "These findings began to suggest a possible motive for the crime other than an uncontrollable organic rage attack, as well as providing evidence that some degree of forethought or planning may have been involved," Martell wrote.

After reviewing all the evidence, Martell concluded: "The picture of Mr. Cystkopf that began to emerge was very different from the defense's portrait of a tragic character with a brain disorder that caused him to kill the only person that he really loved." He said he was prepared to testify at trial that Weinstein's thinking and behavior simply were not affected by his cyst.

Zach Weiss's article served as a warning signal about the future of using neuroscience, particularly PET scans, in court. PET scans might be viewed like grisly crime scene photos, which are often barred from view of juries because of their prejudicial nature. A medical examiner can testify about the victims and achieve the same fact-finding purpose as the scans. Weiss also pointed out that PET scans weren't fully accurate shots of a working brain but rather colorized pictures that were meaningless unless compared to others. "It could be argued that in the case of a PET image, a picture is not worth 1,000 words. Seeing is not believing. The image can be highly misleading unless placed in a proper context."

From experience, Weiss knew that juries tended to believe what they saw, not what they heard, and would fixate on the picture, not on the experts. "Many lawyers would like nothing more than to exploit this tendency in front of juries," he wrote.

Looking into the future, he wondered what would happen if lawyers began offering PET scans as evidence in insanity cases. By the rules of discovery, prosecutors would want to get their own scans, a highly invasive procedure that involves injecting radioactive material into a person's brain. "No court of which I am aware, except for Courts of Inquisition in medieval Spain, would issue such an order."

But Weiss's most prescient observation was this: "If I were forced to hazard a prediction, I think the age of scanning has dawned in our courtrooms. This is not a technological genie we are going to be able to put back in the bottle. It will be the rare judge in a murder case who will limit a defendant's use of this kind of evidence no matter how unreliable," he wrote. "Defense lawyers with visions of acquittal swimming in their head are unlikely to exercise any principled restraint."

CHAPTER 14

Not One Healthy Brain

On a steamy July afternoon in Florida's Panhandle in 2014, a thunderstorm is moving in fast—the air thick, the clouds turning black. Stephen Cobb, a criminal defense attorney, pulls his rented white SUV into the parking lot of the Okaloosa County Courthouse in Fort Walton Beach and dashes inside just before the storm releases its fury. He has just a few minutes before a court appearance and heads up to the third floor, where he takes a seat on a bench in the hallway and flips open his laptop. He clicks on a file that displays color-coded brain images of his client, who is due in court for a sentencing hearing. He's a young man who was in the air force and has been charged with soliciting sex with a minor over the Internet.

Cobb is reviewing images that were taken using SPECT, or single-photon emission computerized tomography. It's similar to a PET scan in that it shows brain functioning using a radioactive substance and a camera to create 3-D pictures. Cobb holds up his laptop to show the image to his cocounsel, then turns to me. "Reasonable brains do reasonable things," he says. "Unreasonable brains do unreasonable things. He has an unreasonable image."

When he gets his chance, Cobb will explain to the judge what he means by an unreasonable image. As we speak, his client walks in, a tall man in a navy suit with short-cropped blond hair. He's with his parents and girlfriend, along with some other supporters from Eglin Air Force Base, just up the road. They walk into the courtroom as another proceeding is wrapping up.

In this largely military town, many of those who go through the civilian legal system have connections to the base. The courthouse halls are decorated with photos and paintings of aircraft, ships, and notable veterans, including Col. George Bud Day, the most decorated American war veteran of all time, whose name is on a plaque alongside paintings of jet aircraft.

Cobb takes a seat in the public section of the courtroom as a man in an orange jumpsuit stands before the judge. He's up for violation of probation because he failed to report his whereabouts to his probation officer. The man pleads for a break, telling the judge he suffers from PTSD, that he has a special needs child, that he was wounded and in a VA hospital and didn't have the time to check in with his probation officer.

"That's a conscious decision you make every day—not to own up to your past," the judge says.

Every day in court, it's about weighing conscious choices—or what we think are conscious choices. Did the accused mean to do it? Did he do it willingly? It goes back to the fundamental concept of *mens rea*—a guilty mind. That's what court is all about. This is where decisions are evaluated and deconstructed to their essence. The judge doesn't budge. The man should have known better.

Cobb is ready for his turn. Before today's proceeding, Cobb's client, Bryan N.,* who is twenty-nine years old, agreed to plead guilty and is now facing sentencing—and the possibility of prison. Cobb's plan is to present a package of evidence, including brain scans, that he contends shows that his client suffers from brain dysfunctions that, with treatment, might well dissipate. Not long after he was arrested, Bryan tried to kill himself by cutting his wrists. He was hospitalized and received mental health counseling and a prescription for Prozac. Cobb is seeking probation for his client, along with treatment, as an alternative to prison. To support his case, Cobb has a thick three-ring binder prepared by the Amen Clinics, where his client was scanned and underwent a full psychiatric examination. The Amen Clinics specialize in SPECT imaging and the treatment of various mental health disorders.

Cobb begins his remarks to the judge with a variation of what he said to me in the hallway, that "Bryan does not have, in effect, a normal brain image. He has an abnormal brain scan. Conscious decisions made by someone with an abnormal brain are not the same as conscious decisions made by someone with a fully functional brain."

Cobb is ready to call his first witness, a psychiatrist who will explain what's wrong with his client's brain.

It's been twenty years since Zach Weiss predicted the dawn of brain scanning in America's courtrooms, and Cobb represents just how far it has come. Cobb may be the only lawyer in the country who asks every one of his clients—whether they're arrested for murder or charged with DUI—to undergo a brain scan. He's been doing this

*The real name of Cobb's client is being withheld to protect his privacy because he agreed to share confidential medical information.

since 2006, and what he's seen, he tells me, is shocking. "Not a single healthy, normal range, patient-defendant brain image in over seven years," he says. "Not one."

Healthy and *normal range* are relative terms, of course, and open to interpretation, but Cobb says that what these images show, and what he confirms with professional medical diagnosis, is evidence of mental health problems—frequently worsened by drug and alcohol abuse. Cobb asks clients to get brain scans not because he thinks they'll absolve them from criminal responsibility or help get them not-guilty verdicts. He orders them because he believes the images and accompanying reports will convince his clients—and judges—that his clients need treatment and should receive compassionate sentences that take into account their brain dysfunction. "The real issue is what the hell do we do with people when it comes to sentencing," Cobb says. "This is where brain imaging and neuroscience become vital."

Cobb doesn't pretend to be a scientific expert—he hires others for that. He thinks like a lawyer. And what lawyers do, as he readily explains, is prepare a defense and, at the same time, prepare for mitigation in case their client is found guilty or decides to make a plea agreement. Most of his clients would not meet the criteria for insanity, so he doesn't waste his time going down that legal avenue. He tries to get them help because of their broken brains.

Cobb became a student of the broken brain in 2006, when he came across the book *Change Your Brain, Change Your Life,* by Dr. Daniel Amen, a psychiatrist, clinical neuroscientist, and popular television personality who touts good brain health. Amen's best-selling book bills itself as "The Breakthrough Program for Conquering Anxiety, Depression, Obsessiveness, Anger, and Impulsiveness." It includes case studies, brain images, and a prescription for improving brain health through natural remedies, which are available through his clinics and Web site.

"I read this book and saw all these images of brains. I see healthy brains and I see problem brains, and the visual effect is clear," Cobb says. So, he thought, why not get similar images for his clients who seemed to have mental health deficiencies? Medical experts could then create customized psychiatric reports with specific diagnostic and supporting material to help his clients, whom he refers to as patient-defendants.

"When I first started doing this, I thought I might find slight brain problems. But I found they were so all out of the ballpark, they were amazing," he says. "Now, the imaging is not some magical thing. It's a tool like anything else. But it's important to use it."

Here's one example of how Cobb uses SPECT brain scans as a tool. James, a thirty-one-year-old party promoter, was caught with a large amount of drugs and faced prison time if convicted. A friend told him about Stephen Cobb, and James gave him a call. He was soon sitting in Cobb's office. "I want to inform you about something that might be going on in your brain," Cobb told his client.

Cobb explained that having his brain scanned not only could help his case but might help him with his mental health problems if he agreed to a treatment plan based on his diagnosis. The money would have to come out of James's own pocket—about three thousand dollars.

Two months later, James was at the Amen Clinics in Atlanta for his scan. He also underwent psychological testing. The tests lasted two days.

James was a bit nervous. He had played football in high school and suffered two concussions. He'd also drunk a lot of beer and smoked marijuana. Then he got the results. "My brain wasn't as damaged as I thought it was," he says. "But you could still see the damage."

The damage, he was told, was mostly from drinking and smoking pot and was not irrevocable. The plan, if he was convicted on drug charges, was for him to seek treatment as part of the sentencing. "It wasn't like I wasn't playing with a full deck," James told me. In the end, the scans didn't matter. The charges against James were dismissed because of an improper search. "I guess [Cobb] had that in his back pocket, just in case," James says. "But it got me to thinking about my life. It changed me."

At the Okaloosa County Courthouse, Cobb calls his first witness so that he can build his case that Bryan solicited sex with a minor because he has a brain dysfunction. The witness, Dr. Jay Faber, is a psychiatrist for the Amen Clinics in Atlanta. Faber was unable to make it to Fort Walton Beach on this day, so the judge agreed to allow him to testify via speakerphone, which is broadcast into the courtroom.

Faber explains that Bryan came to the clinic for a typical psychiatric evaluation, as well as a SPECT scan "to functionally understand how the brain is working." In general, he says, images that show more "holes" on the brain indicate less blood flow and thus less brain activity. Bumps on the brain suggest head trauma.

"Did you notice any abnormalities in the resting scan?" Cobb asks, referring to Bryan's image.

"There's a lot of bumps throughout. We call that scalloping," Faber says, adding that this pattern gave him cause for concern about head trauma and exposure to toxins or drugs and alcohol. And on the top third of Bryan's lower frontal lobe, Faber saw holes. "That area should look very smooth, especially for someone Bryan's age. When we see this, our impulse control may not be as good as we'd like."

Cobb moves onto another image taken during Bryan's active scanning. "Do you notice anything unusual about the cingulate gyrus?"

Faber says he noticed some abnormalities there, explaining that the cingulate gyrus is like a gear shifter. "If it's too active, we tend to see people getting stuck on thoughts," he says. "People with addictions get stuck on addictive thoughts." Faber says he also sees problems in Bryan's thalamus, indicating depression and a feeling of being unloved. Bryan also has active basal ganglia, which can suggest anxiety and nervousness. Faber concludes that Bryan is a lonely guy seeking love. And when you're looking for "ways to seek love," he tells the court, "you're more apt not to think through your decisions."

Cobb asks Faber whether Bryan's afflictions, and his poor decision making, are treatable.

"They are treatable as long as the person is willing to commit and rehabilitate their brain."

"Would a period of incarceration be positive or negative to Bryan's brain health?" Cobb asks.

"If he doesn't seek the treatment recommendation, I don't see that as positive," Faber says. "Bryan understands the pictures and how his brain was affecting his behavior."

Faber's final diagnosis is that Bryan is compulsive, anxious, and depressed and suffers from a mood disorder "otherwise not specified." He's currently on Prozac but would benefit from other treatments for his brain health, including a seven-supplement formula for his basal ganglia, his thalamus, and other areas of the brain where he needs more blood flow to the cortex. (Amen Clinics sells the supplement formula under the name NeuroLink.) Bryan should see a cognitive therapist, Faber recommends, as well as consider exercise, yoga, and meditation. He recommends that Bryan read Amen's book, *Change Your Brain, Change Your Life*.

"What does exercise do?" Cobb asks.

"It increases blood flow to the cortex. It actually makes your cortex smoother and helps calm you down."

Prosecutor Jennifer Lieber lets the SPECT scans and their meaning go unchallenged. She says she has just a couple of questions. One is whether the so-called treatment Faber recommended can be obtained in prison rather than through the Amen Clinics. Faber said yes, it can.

Dr. Daniel Amen has built a multimillion-dollar business through his best-selling books and six clinics, which treat people with mood and behavioral disorders. A cornerstone of his treatment is SPECT scanning. "In 1991 I started ordering scans," he says, for which he has drawn controversy and criticism. "I got no end of grief from my colleagues." But "How do you know unless you look?" is his motto.

The clinics were not created to serve lawyers seeking brain scans for their clients. That just sort of happened. "I really don't like lawyers and fighting because that's a competitive thing," Amen tells me. "My intention is to help people get well."

Amen is a longtime critic of traditional psychiatric medicine, which he says hasn't changed in sixty years. During my conversation with him at his office in Costa Mesa, California, he explains that psychiatrists rarely, if ever, look inside the brain. Instead, they make their diagnosis based on clinical exams and observed symptoms. What SPECT scanning does, according to Amen, is evaluate areas of the brain that work well, areas that work too hard, and areas that do not work hard enough. Amen's clinical staff analyzes information from the scans, along with a detailed clinical history, and try to identify underlying brain patterns associated with patients' problems. This information, Amen says, helps them decide on the proper treatment to balance brain function.

It was in 1995 that he first got interested in the possibility that criminal behavior could be linked to brain dysfunction. His sister-in-law called to tell him that her nine-year-old son, Andrew, had attacked a little girl for no apparent reason. He offered to have his nephew's brain scanned and found the boy had a cyst, about the size of a golf ball, pressing into his left front temporal lobe, which Amen suspected was causing him to be unusually aggressive. "And he's homicidal and suicidal. He's Columbine, Aurora, and Sandy Hook waiting to happen," Amen says, referring to the notorious mass fatal shootings. "He had a structural problem that, when they fixed it, his behavior went back to normal, and eighteen years later he's a great kid."

Since that case, Amen says, he has examined forty-three patients with cysts in their brains. "One boy sat on that couch and wanted to cut his mother up into little pieces, and I'm like, 'Huh?' He had a cyst the size of a tennis ball. He had a normal neurological exam." The cyst, in the frontal temporal lobe, was pushing on the amygdala. "It's just a little unfair to just punish him because his brain's not right."

Amen has continued probing possible links between brain dysfunction, as observed on SPECT scans, and criminal behavior. He says he has found some common patterns among those who exhibit aggressive behavior. The scans show either increased or decreased activity in the left temporal lobe, increased activity in the anterior cingulate gyrus, and decreased activity in the prefrontal cortex, leading to poor judgment and impulse control.

Amen may not be fond of lawyers and fighting, but he has testified in court dozens of times using his SPECT scans of criminal defendants. In one of the most high-profile cases, he testified in 2004 on behalf of Peter Chiesa, a sixty-five-year-old man on trial for shooting to death two of his neighbors over a property dispute. Minutes before the shootings, Chiesa had dialed 911 and told the dispatcher, "I'm going to shoot these motherfuckers." That he killed the women was not in doubt: it was the degree of his culpability and how much prison time he would face that was at issue. His attorney wanted manslaughter and decided to mount a "diminished actuality" defense, meaning he actually lacked intent, not just the ability to form intent. Amen testified that Chiesa's prefrontal cortex and other areas of his brain were grossly underactive. The jury convicted Chiesa of second-degree murder, and he was sentenced to eighty years. Amen tells me he feels good about helping brain-damaged defendants avoid the death penalty in such cases. Their crimes, he says, are not entirely their fault.

One of the victims' friends later wrote the judge. "Brain damage? I don't think so. He was just an old, irritable man with a good lawyer."

Lynn "Kelly" Beck is a psychotherapist and mental health counselor in Fort Walton Beach. Before Bryan's court hearing, Stephen Cobb hired her to examine him, and she has come prepared to testify that Bryan suffers from depressive disorder, anxiety disorder, and acute distress disorder. When she takes the witness stand, she describes Bryan as a high-functioning person but with Asperger's symptoms, which may account for his social awkwardness. "People with Asperger's spend a lot of time on the Internet because they lack social skills," Beck tells the judge.

Beck did not rely solely on the SPECT images for her diagnosis, she says, but consulted them as one tool. Under questioning from Cobb's cocounsel, Beck says that Bryan's condition is treatable, though she does not believe he would receive proper treatment in prison. She says she talked with Bryan about responsibility and control. "He is a good patient and highly motivated," she testifies. "I believe he is not a threat and can be rehabilitated. This is not so much a sexual issue as poor impulse control and social anxiety."

She says Bryan is highly remorseful and unlikely to reoffend. "He doesn't fit the usual profile of sexual offender," she says. "This was about poor social skills."

Stephen Cobb gets up to make his final argument in support of

Bryan's brain defense. "We're not asking you to give Bryan a pass here," he tells the judge. "He's going to suffer for what happened in this case." But what his client needs is help, not prison: "The state is asking you to embark on a failure path." Cobb asks the judge to consider sentencing Bryan to five years of probation, under supervision, with proof that he complies with a treatment plan through the Amen Clinics.

Prosecutor Jennifer Lieber says Bryan suffers not from a mental deficiency but from a sexual social disorder. She reminds the judge that he conducted explicit sexual conversations with minors over the Internet. "The primary goal for this should be punishment," she says. "If he needs treatment, he can get it in prison."

"He will be punished," Cobb says. "One thing is very clear. He has a medical condition. He has an abnormal brain scan. It's pretty clear, even to a layperson. We're looking at brain images that should be smooth that aren't smooth."

A half hour later Judge John T. Brown asks Cobb to clarify the diagnosis.

"When someone has reduced function in the prefrontal cortex, when someone's judgment is impaired, they won't do the same things a reasonable person would do," Cobb explains.

The judge sentences Bryan to four years of probation and six months of community control, during which his movements will be monitored. He will have to register as a sex offender, see a psychiatrist, and receive sex offender counseling.

Bryan embraces his girlfriend and parents and shakes Cobb's hand. He hustles out with his family into the steamy Florida afternoon.

Cobb is buoyant after the hearing and suggests we meet at a nearby TGI Friday's for a bite. "We're obsessed with assigning blame or not blaming," he says over dinner. "In courtrooms across America I see lawyers who are not productive."

Productivity, to Cobb, means making a difference in his clients' lives—by keeping them out of jail, placing them in rehab, getting them mental health treatment, and getting their brains healthy. It's a philosophy that seems to fit the trajectory of his career. He started out as a public defender in Pensacola and handled hundreds of cases for down-and-out clients who had a host of mental health problems. He began to see a pattern among them, especially the repeat offenders. "I said, 'Holy hell, these people are getting arrested because of mental health problems,'" he says. "I think we need to make proper psychological and psychiatric evaluations in all criminal cases."

He left his job as a public defender to start his solo criminal defense practice in Fort Walton Beach, where he grew up. His cases were very much like those he handled as a public defender—drug offenses, robberies, murders. Then in 1998 a judge appointed him to represent Jeffrey Glenn Hutchinson, a Gulf War veteran who was accused of murdering his girlfriend and her three children ages four, seven, and nine. Hutchinson claimed that he suffered from Gulf War syndrome, the broad category of mental health afflictions suffered by veterans of the 1990–91 Gulf War. Cobb never doubted that Hutchinson committed the crime, but he believes his client had problems beyond his control.

"The two years that he had been complaining about Gulf War syndrome had been a cry for help," Cobb says. "I think if his brain had been imaged, there would be plenty of mitigating circumstances. He was a soldier, he was injured. I wish we had learned more about brain injuries when I was working on that case. I would have been jumping up and down that he should be scanned." Hutchinson, who was found guilty and sentenced to death, has appealed his conviction.

Cobb says his life's work became clear in 2005 when, at forty-five, he was diagnosed with prostate cancer. His doctor told him that he should prepare for dying. But Cobb refused to accept the grim prognosis and found a surgeon in Alabama who performed a successful robotic prostatectomy. "After cancer I was given a new lease on life, and I was given a mission." And so, having read *Change Your Brain, Change Your Life,* he began suggesting to all his clients that they consider having their brains scanned. "It's hard to get everyone to do it," he says. "But many of them already have gotten into the spiral of death."

The spiral of death, according to Cobb, is drug and alcohol abuse. One of the first things he asks clients is whether they've had drug or alcohol counseling. "Most of the court-ordered ones fail. Rehab fails. I see it all the time." So he lays it out there. "I tell my clients, 'You're at a fork in the road. It's going to go one way or the other. This is an investment in never having to pay a legal fee again.' "

A set of SPECT scans costs about three thousand dollars and requires traveling to Atlanta for two days. Cobb says people can raise the money if they want to, because many often raise money needed for bond. Once again he emphasizes that he does not use brain scans in an attempt to get his clients acquitted or to excuse them from culpability. "I don't think brain imaging rises to the level of a defense," he says. "I use it for mitigation."

That's what has happened in court this afternoon with Bryan—some understanding and some treatment for his client. It's the kind of result Cobb seeks in every case. While pleased that he saved his client from prison today, Cobb says Bryan will pay a steep price nonetheless. "His military career is over. He has a felony record. He has sex offender registration."

I ask Cobb about the prosecutor's suggestion that Amen Clinics benefit by recommending treatment with supplements they sell. "I've seen that tactic before. I don't care if they get the supplements from them or from GNC," he says. "I just want him to get better. Doctors who have their own proprietary products are always going to catch flak for that."

Being a lawyer with such unconventional methods in a conservative place can be tough. "One of the things about my practice is that it's so lonely," he says. "None of my colleagues do this. But it will be mainstream someday. This is not Miami. It's more like rural Alabama. The legal culture is not at the cutting edge."

He sees a stronger future for neuroscience in the courtroom. "The technology will only get better, and there is always more to learn. Yes, some claim it is junk science. Yet we can already use what we have to solve the problem of crime, one patient-defendant at a time," he says. "The bottom line is that we can take control of our brains."

Though Daniel Amen has stayed away from the courts recently, he tells me that he sees Cobb's work as worthwhile. "Stephen's using it in the most creative way. He's getting people treatment instead of jail time, and I've never seen anybody doing anything like that before," he says. "When I met him I really felt . . . his motives for doing this really felt genuine."

CHAPTER 15

The Death Penalty Attorney and the Broken Brain

Terry Lenamon, a Florida death penalty attorney, has represented some of the state's most vicious and notorious killers, and he will do just about anything he can to save their lives. In his twenty-year career, his clients have included people who have drowned their infants; stomped toddlers; robbed, raped, and killed women; and beaten, bludgeoned, and shot their friends, relatives, and strangers.

Most of his clients unquestionably committed the crimes for which they've been charged. Lenamon's job first and foremost, he says, is to save them from the electric chair—Florida's method of execution. Many were addicted to drugs and alcohol and suffered from mental illness or brain trauma. Lenamon digs into their personal histories to create a narrative. "You know, it's all about storytelling, really," he says, explaining his approach to me during a visit to his home outside Fort Lauderdale. "When you get into capital litigation issues, you're telling a story of a damaged client."

To save his clients' lives, Lenamon must convince judges and juries that they deserve mercy, that they suffered from some type of trauma or circumstance that has affected their brains and their judgment. In short, he looks to prove they have broken brains.

Lenamon, who started out as a public defender, says he does this work because he wants to understand his clients—not seek to absolve them of guilt or responsibility—and to save their lives. His legal strategy is to investigate what led them to the fatal moments when all reasoning and logic seemed to fail. He sometimes will use an insanity defense, even though he knows the likelihood of it succeeding is slim. But by pursuing this line of defense, he's setting up his case for what's going to come up later if he loses. "From the very beginning you're saying your client did it. You're admitting that he did this horrible crime, but you're also front-loading all the things about his mental health, mental illness, brain damage, whatever it is," he says. "So if the jury doesn't acquit him on an insanity defense, which they rarely will, you're going to flow right into the penalty phase, where you're still talking about all the things you talked about already in the first part of the case."

But some clients don't want to pursue an insanity defense, even if they might have broken brains. One was Grady Nelson, a former social worker and convicted rapist. In 2005 the state appointed Lenamon to represent Nelson, who had been charged with the stabbing death of his mentally handicapped wife, Angela Martinez, as well as stabbing his eleven-year-old mentally handicapped stepdaughter and thirteen-year-old stepson. It was among the most disturbing crimes and difficult cases that Lenamon, a father himself, had ever seen.

The bloody attack occurred hours after Nelson had been released from the Miami-Dade County Correctional Center, where he had been held on charges of sexually assaulting his stepdaughter. He was set free because conflicting and inconsistent testimony from the mother and the daughter forced the prosecutor to drop the charges. Though the charges did not stick, Nelson's wife had requested a domestic violence injunction against her husband, stating that he was a violent crack cocaine addict who beat her, stomped on her abdomen, pulled her by the hair, and locked her in a closet. She said she was "in great fear for her safety and that of her family" and needed an order of protection. Her petition was granted on the same day Nelson was released. But he was already on his way home.

By the time police officers arrived at the home on January 7, 2004, Nelson had locked himself inside. As officers looked through the front window, they saw him hiding knives under sofa cushions. When police forced their way in, they noticed that his hands were splattered with blood. His wife, Angela, was lying on the floor. She had been stabbed repeatedly and her throat had been sliced so long and deep that she was nearly decapitated. A knife protruded from her head. As police searched the house, they found Nelson's thirteen-year-old stepson, also mentally disabled, hiding in a bathroom. He had stab wounds all over his upper body. Officers found Nelson's stepdaughter, eleven, hiding under the sheets of a bed. She was naked and bleeding from deep stab wounds. A four-year-old boy, the only child they had together, was asleep on the floor unharmed.

Officers took Nelson to the police station, where he confessed. He said that after being released from jail that morning, he had shown up at the family home and later in the afternoon sexually assaulted both stepchildren. Afterward he took them to Pollo Tropical for a chicken dinner. After coming home from dinner, he said, he stabbed his wife as his stepson watched. He then attacked his two stepchildren as they pleaded for their lives. He told police he had taken cocaine that day and wanted to kill himself.

Nelson soon changed his mind about taking responsibility for the crimes and demanded a trial to prove his innocence. Lenamon and attorney David S. Markus decided to argue that Nelson's videotaped confession had been coerced by Miami-Dade police. Nelson, they would contend, had not murdered his wife or stabbed the children. He had stumbled upon the crime scene when he returned home and gave a false confession under duress. Knowing that a verdict of not guilty was a long shot, Lenamon would also set the stage during trial to show jurors that Nelson was a damaged person who suffered from paranoia and impaired thinking and had been triggered into a cocaine-induced rage.

So Lenamon and his colleagues prepared for Nelson's sentencing hearing at the same time as they prepared for the guilt phase of the trial. In the sentencing phase of a death penalty case, lawyers present what are known as aggravating and mitigating circumstances for the jurors and the judge to weigh in deciding whether to impose death. Aggravating factors are those that would support a harsher sentence, such as previous convictions or committing a crime with particular cruelty. Mitigating factors, as we have seen, are those that would lessen the severity of a sentence, such as a defendant's upbringing, history of mental illness, or intellectual disability. Lawyers are permitted wide latitude with respect to the factors they're allowed to present. The U.S. Supreme Court spells out clearly that defendants can present "any aspect" of their character, record, or personal history when seeking a life sentence instead of death.

Still, it didn't look good for Nelson. The state would have several key aggravating factors on its side. In 1990 he had been charged with three counts of sexual battery of a seven-year-old neighbor, accused of dragging the girl by her hair into his apartment and raping her. But the girl had been too afraid to testify. His lawyer struck a plea deal that gave Nelson ten years of probation and mandatory sex offender treatment. But within a year Nelson was charged with cocaine possession and was sentenced to eight years in prison for violating his probation. And worse, the current rape and murder charges against him were categorized as HAC—heinous, atrocious, or cruel—indicating crimes designed to inflict a high degree of pain with utter indifference to, or even enjoyment of, the suffering of others. Lenamon didn't have much to work with, considering Nelson's criminal history. "You had to explain why would somebody do something like that," Lenamon says. Drugs clearly had an influence on Nelson's behavior, he says, but when someone with a damaged brain takes drugs, the effects can be amplified and trigger even worse behavior.

Lenamon reasoned that to save Nelson from the electric chair, the best he might do would be to persuade a jury that he had committed the crimes under the influence of an emotional disturbance so profound that he could not appreciate the criminality of his actions. The defense team could also present other mitigating factors, such as his dysfunctional family history—a common strategy in death penalty cases. But there was a problem. Nelson wasn't very cooperative with his lawyers, usually refusing to answer their questions in detail. "Grady Nelson was very suspicious, and our relationship, at times, was volatile," Lenamon says. "He was mistrustful."

Lenamon hired a mitigation specialist, a professional whose job is to dig into a client's past to create a narrative that explains how he came to be the person he is. Cynthia O'Shea began visiting Nelson in the county jail to build trust, a process that took time. Nelson eventually told her that he had grown up in the small, racially segregated rural town of Hawkinsville, Georgia, in the 1950s and '60s. When she went there to visit, she learned that most of his family had died or could not be found. She finally located a cousin who was able to remember Nelson and his family.

The cousin told O'Shea that Nelson had grown up without a

father; his mother was a prostitute and alcoholic who drank through her pregnancies. When police arrested his mother for prostitution, they would bring the young Nelson to his mother's jail cell because there was no one to feed or house him. O'Shea also learned that Nelson had a sister who was raped by three white carnival workers. He had witnessed the rape as he hid behind a wall, afraid for his life. His sister was so badly hurt from the attack that she died. Nelson later revealed that he had been sexually abused by a pastor but never reported it to anyone. His mother, realizing she was unfit to raise him, sent him to live with her sister.

In later conversations with O'Shea, Nelson told her that as he grew into his teens, he abused drugs and alcohol. He enlisted in the army and later received a general discharge because of unresolved anger issues. He had been knocked unconscious several times during fights. He had a scar on his head from another incident, though there were no records of any of these injuries. He stumbled through life, using cocaine, getting arrested on drug charges, and serving time in prison. He said he had been briefly employed in Miami as an outreach counselor helping to feed and find housing for homeless people, but he was still addicted to drugs and could not hang on to his job.

Lenamon and his defense team thought Nelson's story might help explain his struggles with anger and violence, but they were not strong enough as mitigating factors to make an argument for life over death. Lots of defendants had troubled childhoods and drug and alcohol addictions. The lawyers felt they needed some solid neurological evidence pointing to a brain disorder and hired psychologists and neuropsychologists to examine and interview Nelson. They found he had a history of childhood abuse and suspected he suffered from some closed head injuries, but none of it was documented in medical records. Everything was reported by Nelson himself and not corroborated in any way.

This is where neuroscience came in.

"It's a horrible case. I knew that it was an uphill battle, and I needed any help I could get," Lenamon says. "It becomes the lawyer's responsibility to find the tools to first understand the client, and then to be able to persuade the trier of fact, the jury or the judge or both, that those deficits come into play in some form or fashion."

Heather Holmes, a psychologist hired for the defense team, told Lenamon about a technology called quantitative electroencephalography (QEEG) that might help. The EEG had been around for decades: a tool that measures electrical activity in the brain, most often to help diagnose or monitor brain disorders from seizures, tumors, Alzheimer's disease, or other conditions. The QEEG used computer technology to amplify and mathematically transform the data into 3-D images—color-coded, topographical representations of brain wave activity, a sort of brain mapping. Whereas PET measures glucose metabolism and fMRI measures blood flow inside the brain, QEEG measures electrical activity. QEEG readings are compared to readings from a large sample of normal subjects to determine whether there's damage. The quantitative technology was developed by Dr. Robert W. Thatcher, a nationally known neuroscientist and pioneer in QEEG analysis. He initially used the procedure to examine traumatic brain injuries in accident victims, veterans, and active military personnel. Thatcher created a company called Applied Neuroscience, which provides patented software to perform three-dimensional imaging of the brain using computerized EEG data.

Lenamon arranged to have Dr. Gerald Gluck, a marriage and family therapist and one of the founders of the International Society for Neurofeedback and Research, go to the Miami-Dade Correctional Center to perform a QEEG scan on Nelson. Gluck and an assistant arrived at the jail with a Deymed head box, electrodes, wires, a laptop computer, gauze, alcohol swabs, and conductive paste. They were led to a room with desks and tables and left alone without guards, who were stationed just outside the door.

Gluck explained to Nelson why they were there and what they were doing. Nelson was cooperative but not very talkative. Gluck began by asking Nelson a few questions for a mini-neuropsychiataric evaluation, which showed that Nelson had a few deficits. For example, he didn't know the season of the year and had difficulty paying attention and doing simple mathematical calculations. His memory also was mildly impaired.

The assistant cleaned Nelson's scalp and affixed the electrodes, while he seemed irritated and complained that the wires and leads hurt. They measured Nelson's electrical brain activity in five different states for about twenty minutes at a time: while he was staring at a spot on the wall, sitting with his eyes closed, listening to the assistant read, reading to himself, and being induced to hyperventilate, a technique that slows brain waves and enhances the EEG readings. Everything was recorded and later digitized, using a program called Thatcher's Tru-Scan Acquisition software, and cleaned of irrelevant signals caused by eye or muscle movements.

After the readings were run through the computer program, Gluck read the results, which indicated Nelson had frontal lobe damage. In addition, his brain wave activity suggested prenatal alcohol exposure, loss of cognitive function due to TBI, and early childhood abuse. Prenatal alcohol exposure, Gluck noted in his report, was often related to increased aggression and to decreased inhibition and judgment. The results would surely strengthen their case that Nelson's broken brain contributed to his criminal behavior.

"There's no question this guy is damaged," Gluck told Lenamon, who was ready to bring this information to trial. But the test results never made it to court. After nearly four months of the guilt phase, during which the jury had been hearing evidence, the judge declared a mistrial. A detective had let slip during his testimony that Nelson had a prior conviction for molesting a child, a fact that the jury was not supposed to hear because of its prejudicial nature. The jurors were dismissed. Lenamon saw two jurors shake Nelson's hand and wish him good luck. Another juror, a woman, turned to Lenamon and Markus and said, "You all are pieces of shit."

In the new trial, Lenamon and Markus once again argued that Nelson's confession had been coerced and that he had come upon the murder scene when he arrived home. After nearly eleven hours of deliberation, the jurors came back with a guilty verdict. Lenamon's next job would be to save Nelson from the electric chair. Here he could use the QEEG evidence to show that his client had brain damage.

Prosecutor Abbe Rifkin had not been aware that Lenamon was going to introduce this evidence at the sentencing hearing and strongly objected. During the guilt phase, the judge had allowed Lenamon to keep the QEEG information private, along with other information he had been preparing for mitigation. Lenamon had requested the order because the information might be damaging to his client. That meant it was not subject to the rules of evidentiary discovery, which require both parties to turn over evidence they plan to use in court during the guilt phase.

Just as Zachary Weiss had challenged the use of PET scans in the case of Herbert Weinstein, Rifkin argued that QEEG had been excluded in other court proceedings because it was new, was not generally accepted in the scientific community, and was considered unreliable. In 1997 the American Academy of Neurology and the American Clinical Neurophysiology Society had published (and republished in 2006) a recommendation against the use of QEEG evidence in legal proceedings: "On the basis of clinical and scientific evidence, opinions of most experts, and the technical and methodological shortcomings, QEEG is not recommended for use in civil or criminal trials." Dr. Gluck, however, dismissed the report, saying it was "quite flawed" and "based on rumors."

The judge ordered a Frye hearing to determine whether the scientific principles and theories behind the procedure were generally accepted in the scientific community. Lenamon was able to secure the testimony of Dr. Robert Thatcher, the QEEG pioneer. The state tried to exclude Thatcher's testimony in part because Thatcher admitted that his sole source of income for the past nine years had been his role as president and owner of Applied Neuroscience, Inc., which develops, manufactures, and distributes the software that Dr. Gluck had used to evaluate Nelson.

Lenamon countered that QEEG was not novel and could aid in the diagnosis of psychological or neurological dysfunctions much as how CT scans and MRIs were used to supplement other tools in diagnosis and treatment. The FDA had approved it to assist in the diagnosis of mild TBI, and the Defense and Veterans Head Injury Program used it as well, supporting the idea that it wasn't novel science. Lenamon pointed out that QEEG was not the sole method of diagnosis but was an adjunct to the expert opinions of other mental health experts who examined Nelson.

Circuit court judge Jacqueline Hogan Scola decided to allow it, saying that based on everything she had heard, "the methodologies are sound, the techniques are sound, the science is sound." However, she added, "there's not unanimous acceptance. There are clearly detractors and dissenters . . . I feel comfortable that the average juror can figure out what they believe and disbelieve, just like any battle of experts, and that's what it's going to come down to."

Lenamon brought in Dr. Thatcher to prepare the jurors for understanding the QEEG findings. Thatcher gave them a lesson on brain imaging and diagnosis using a computer slide show, replete with colorful graphics of the brain and explanations of the effects of frontal lobe damage.

Prosecutor Rifkin brought in her own experts, who dismissed QEEG as junk science. She called QEEG an "electronic Ouija board" and tried to ridicule and discredit it. The hearing became a battle of expert witnesses, and jury members had to figure it all out for themselves.

In his closing argument at the sentencing hearing, Lenamon reminded jurors that his client had indeed committed horrific acts but was a damaged man. "See, understanding who he is doesn't mean we have to accept it or excuse it," he said. "And in levels of culpability, that means that we have a responsibility to look below the surface."

After only an hour of deliberations, the jury came back deadlocked at 6–6, which, by law, meant Nelson would receive an automatic life sentence. Afterward juror Delores Cannon, a hospital secretary, told the *Miami Herald* that she had been leaning toward sentencing Nelson to death. "But then when it came in, the facts about the QEEG, some of us changed our mind," she said. Juror John Howard, an airport fleet services worker, said he, too, had been ready to recommend death, but "the technology really swayed me. . . . After seeing the brain scans, I was convinced this guy had some sort of brain problem." Another juror, a retired mailman, said he had voted for a life sentence not because he believed the QEEG scan proved anything but because he wanted Nelson to rot in prison with the stigma of being a child rapist. "All that testimony, that was a waste of taxpayer money. That's phony," he said. "There's nothing wrong with that guy's brain."

Lenamon later spoke to the press. "The moment this crime occurred, Grady had a broken brain," he said. "I think this is a huge step forward in explaining why people are broken—not excusing it. This is going to go a long way in mitigating death penalty sentences." He also made a prediction: "QEEG brain mapping is the future. QEEG technology will have a huge impact around the country in a wide variety of legal cases, civil and criminal, as well as in all kinds of medical issues."

"It was a lot of hocus pocus and bells and whistles, and it amounted to nothing," Abbe Rifkin told the *Miami Herald.* "When you look at the facts of the case, there was nothing impulsive about this murder."

Ten years after the trial, I ask Rifkin what happened. She says she was caught off guard when Lenamon introduced QEEG. "It's pretty much like getting in a fistfight with one hand tied behind your back and a blindfold on," she tells me. Had she known before trial that he intended to use QEEG evidence, she would have questioned potential jurors about their beliefs in the value of technology and in brain science in particular. Many potential jurors, she explains, are influenced by the "CSI effect." In the popular television series *CSI: Crime Scene Investigation,* police use high-tech forensic science to solve crimes. Jurors who have seen the series are often wowed by scientific evidence and may overvalue its real-life applications. "We need to know whether they think it's voodoo science or whether they think it's absolutely valid," Rifkin says.

I ask Rifkin whether there's a place for this type of science in the courtroom. She says yes, but in the proper context. "It would be helpful if it was science that was based on scientific principles and not based upon computer programs that are being commercially sold for profit," she says. "I have to tell you, juries like scientific tests. They like to believe themselves as kind of investigators. They like to put it together."

Looking back, Lenamon tells me he had his doubts about whether the jury would spare his client. "You're never quite sure if you do or say all the right things," he says. "I felt pretty confident in the powerful display we put on with the QEEG and with the experts that we had. But I was surprised. I mean, it was a horrific, horrible murder that involved children, and I just was surprised that the jury was able to understand the importance of the imaging that we had presented that showed the damage to the brain. And I'm grateful that they did."

After the Nelson case, lawyers speculated that a new wave of death penalty litigation would employ expensive technology to explain or excuse violent behavior. Defendants would expect, even demand, such tests for themselves. For those already on death row, a failure to perform brain scans could become a postconviction issue. *Why,* the condemned could ask, *wasn't my brain scanned?* An increasing number of inmates are asking that very question.

Deborah W. Denno, a professor at Fordham University School of Law, analyzed eight hundred criminal cases in which neuroscientific evidence was mentioned, most of them involving capital murder. She found that in death penalty cases, lawyers are now all but expected to bring neuroscience to the table. "Courts not only expect attorneys to investigate and use available neuroscience evidence in their cases when it is appropriate," she declared in her 2015 paper, "but they penalize attorneys who neglect this obligation." She found that defendants were increasingly filing ineffective assistance of counsel claims, arguing that their lawyers should have presented neuroscientific evidence on their behalf. Appellate court judges have been paying attention, because in seventy-four cases, the defendants won appeals based on arguments that their lawyers mishandled or omitted neuroscience evidence. "That means the courts are taking this seriously,"

Denno tells me during an interview. "A lot of courts don't have a problem allowing the evidence in."

A popular theory has it that while the use of neuroscientific evidence may help exonerate defendants, it could backfire by unfairly marking them as a future danger to society by showing their brains aren't working properly. In her paper Denno rebuts that theory, finding that such evidence is rarely used to invoke or predict a defendant's future dangerousness.

While her paper doesn't explicitly support bringing neuroscience into the courtroom, Denno makes her position clear to me. If the science appears to be helpful to the criminal justice system, she says, why not use it? For example, it could support a psychiatric diagnosis that's based on an expert's examination and opinion. "Brain scans can answer questions that a psychiatrist can't. I think if the evidence is used well, and if it's used in the right way, that's a good thing," she says. And in sentencing hearings, she believes, the argument for inclusion of neuroscience is even stronger. "If you can allow evidence in that his mother loves him or that he's religious or he's a good father, why wouldn't you let in evidence of an MRI and what it shows?"

Terry Lenamon has continued to bring QEEG into the courtroom, with mixed success. Judges have been inconsistent in accepting it. Juries that hear too often that defendants suffered from bad childhoods, poverty, and abuse and may view such stories as cliché, he feels. But seeing scientific evidence of psychological damage may make them more comfortable about considering those factors. "When you're able to show a jury, with specificity, the damage, it makes it easier for them to remove some of that personal responsibility and to give way to the mitigation," Lenamon says. "I think it's the responsibility of the lawyers to push as far as they can possibly push in presenting these items in an admissible context in court so that the jurors and the judge can ultimately use these as tools in deciding the appropriate punishment or outcome."

Sometimes whether QEEG is admitted depends on which judge is assigned to a case, according to Lenamon. The judge in the Grady Nelson case had some science education in her background, showing she was familiar with head injury issues. When a judge does not admit QEEG, Lenamon will request that they allow a PET scan instead. Though PET scanning is widely accepted, it's also more expensive and requires prisoners to be transported, with security, to a facility that has a PET scanner. For a case in the summer of 2015, Lenamon was able to do just that. The judge said he was worried that if he excluded the scan, a higher court could toss out the sentence on appeal. The accused, a man who had murdered a beloved teacher, got his scan and was sentenced to life instead of death.

I asked Lenamon whether he goes home satisfied after cases like this, saying to himself that he saved a life today. "Absolutely. That's what my whole motivation is: saving a life. Because it's rare that I'm going to win a case, especially with the cases I have, so absolutely," he says. "It's not about excusing. This is about explaining and giving the jury the opportunity to understand that their ultimate decision here is that you're not going to release this person on the street—this person is never going to get released. The question is, you know, do we stick this person in a prison and they spend the rest of their life there because they did something that wasn't completely their fault, or are we a society that wants to kill these people?"

Prosecutor Abbe Rifkin understands that Lenamon's role is to try to save his clients' lives, and she also appreciates the challenge jurors face in deciding whether to recommend killing someone, no matter how horrible the crime. She believes jurors tend to lean on scientific evidence to help them feel comfortable making an uncomfortable decision. "It's one thing for somebody to say, 'If I were on the jury, I would vote for death,'" she says. "It's another thing when you're actually on the jury and it's your turn to raise your hand."

The Nelson case was certainly difficult for Lenamon—his client was an unlikable person who had committed a despicable crime. But Lenamon still tried to see some humanity in Nelson and take into account what he believed was his broken brain. Nelson is now in a place where he cannot harm anyone on the outside again.

CHAPTER 16

"What Possible Harm Can I Be?"

Herbert Weinstein, not one to sit idly, decided to make the best of his prison time, whether he was going to be behind bars for the minimum seven years or the whole stretch of twenty-one. He knew he had to build a record of good behavior if he had any hope of being paroled. So not long after he had settled into the Walkill prison in upstate New York, he enrolled in educational programs to help curb his apparent violent impulses and lack of impulse control. He started off with a program called "Aggression Replacement Training," which offered tips on preparing for stressful conversations and strategies for responding to anger and avoiding fights. During his first few years of incarceration, Weinstein completed more than thirty hours of anger management courses. A prison official noted that he performed exceptionally well, leading insightful discussions about moral reasoning and conflict resolution. "Mr.

Weinstein not only possessed a very positive attitude, but he showed exceptional leadership qualities," the official wrote.

But prison was lonely, and Weinstein longed for good conversation. Visits from his wife and from Morton and Cecile Wagner, his closest friends, boosted his spirits. His son, Nelson, visited from time to time, but daughter Joni did not. She lived in San Francisco, had a demanding career, and just didn't want to see her father in a prison environment. Weinstein found things to do in prison; reading and playing cards were among his favorite pastimes. He also was active in a veterans' therapy group and earned certificates in classes about post-traumatic stress disorder. Among his proudest achievements, he would later say, was volunteering to tutor other inmates in adult basic education courses.

Weinstein was doing all the right things to set the stage for his first parole hearing, which was scheduled for the fall of 1999, at the seven-year mark of his incarceration. His children, friends, and other family members sent letters of support to the parole board.

Joni Weinstein had spent those seven years wrestling with what her father had done. She also was busy building her career in marketing. She was featured in *Fast Company* magazine for her innovative approaches to engaging people online, at a time when online marketing was still nascent. She also made art, creating colorful mosaics and abstract resin paintings, which she showed in Bay Area art shows and galleries. Through it all, she remembered her father's encouragement of her artistic expression and his enthusiasm for whatever she did. Still, it was not easy for her to forgive him. In her letter to the parole board, she explained that when she learned about her father's cyst and its possible effects on his brain, she began to think differently. "My father has never been a violent man, nor has he been one to get upset easily," she wrote. "There were definitely factors at work in this incident that were beyond his control."

Nelson also wrote a letter, explaining that the murder of Barbara was a single, uncharacteristic episode of violence in his father's otherwise peaceful life. There was no reason, he told the board, to believe that his father would commit another crime. "I have spent much time trying to understand how this could have happened and have never found a reason with which I could be comfortable," he wrote. Nelson acknowledged that his father should pay a price for what he had done, and he hoped he would try to rebuild what was left of his life. Given his father's advanced age and deteriorating health, Nelson wrote, he believed his father already had paid that price. More prison time would amount to a life sentence, which was not the judge's order. "My father's 'Life Sentence' is that he will have to live with what he did for the rest of his life."

Morton and Cecile Wagner also sent letters to the parole board. Cecile described Weinstein as caring, responsible, well respected, and trusted. "I have never met a kinder, or more considerate person," she wrote. "I have never seen him lose his sensibility or his temper," Morton wrote. "He certainly does not represent any threat to any community in any form and most assuredly would not be a burden to any society."

On November 4, 1999, Weinstein appeared before the parole board, which was made up of two members: Commissioners Lawrence C. Scott and Marietta S. Gailor. Kim Glazer Goldberg, Barbara's daughter, sat in the hearing room with her grandmother. They had told the parole commissioners in advance that they strongly objected to allowing Weinstein to be released.

Scott began the proceedings by describing Weinstein's crime in a way that Weinstein had continually challenged—that Barbara was still alive when he tossed her out the window. "You had an argument with your wife which resulted in her being repeatedly struck and strangled to the point of unconsciousness, dragged her over to the window, and dumped her body out a twelve-story—" Scott began.

Weinstein interrupted. "Well, excuse me. That record is a reflection of the district attorney's version of the case."

"This is the official record, I might add," Scott said.

"Yeah, it is the official record," Weinstein answered.

"Okay, so tell us—give us your version."

"Well, I killed my wife. That I did."

"How did you kill her?"

"By strangulation."

Weinstein told the story of how a seemingly mundane argument had escalated into murder. He and Barbara had been talking about the inconsistent communication between Barbara and her daughter, Kim, and the conversation got testy. They hadn't heard from Kim in a long time and were debating whether to call her or wait for her to call them. "I'm a pragmatic type," Weinstein told the commissioners. "I said, 'Look, if you really want to communicate with her, call her.' I mentioned the fact that she's a spoiled brat, which is something we agreed upon for years in advance."

The spoiled brat comment, Weinstein continued, triggered a retort from Barbara about Nelson's weight, a sensitive topic. "And she kept going on and on," Weinstein said. "By nature, I'm a very soft spoken, quiet individual, and I felt that, to respond to her anger, would just be throwing coals on the fire. So I just didn't say a word."

The silence only fueled the tension. "At one point she became so enraged that she said, 'Goddamn it! Don't you have anything to say?' and reached out."

That's when the physical fight began. Weinstein said he struck out at her, and she kept scratching him as he kept hitting her. "She fell to the ground. I put my hand on her throat, and in an effort to protect my face, I turned my head away, but at the same time I put a lot of pressure on her throat, and there was a point where I was, I mean, convinced that she was dead . . . and it was panic, it was stress. It was unbelievable and I . . ."

"Why did you throw her body out the window?" Commissioner Scott asked.

"Well, I made an irrational attempt to make this whole thing go away."

The commissioner asked what he told the police.

"I foolishly attempted to absolve myself of this violent crime, but it . . . it was a matter of minutes before I just said, 'Look, I killed my wife.' "

The commissioner asked Weinstein what he would do if he were paroled. He said he would live in Tuxedo, New York, with the woman he met ten months after Barbara's death and had married before he went to prison, and he had an offer of full-time employment. The commissioner asked if he had anything else to say.

"If you're interested in the, well, evolution of my feelings—at the time of the crime, I was totally at a loss for anything that was happening," Weinstein said. "I've never had an opportunity—even as a child or even as a Merchant Marine officer during World War II—I was never involved in or even exposed to violence, and I just, I couldn't believe what was happening—"

The commissioner interrupted, "I can imagine she couldn't, either."

Weinstein mentioned the possible influence of his cyst on his behavior. "For a while, I attributed what I did—I found an excuse for what I did. I have this condition and some foremost neurologists and neuroscientists said, as a result of that, my cognitive functions were impaired, and I resorted to what they referred to as the primitive brain for my actions."

Weinstein offered a bit of contrition. "But while I was incarcerated, I said, 'It very well may have been that—that it was the primitive brain, but in the end, I did it.' I broke the laws of man and God, and I have been in a position of regretting it ever since."

It didn't take long for the commissioners to make their decision: "Your violent conduct reveals a total disregard for human life and leads the panel to conclude your release to the community is not in the best interests of society."

By claiming that the cyst in his brain had had something to do with causing him to kill his wife, Weinstein might have hurt his chances for parole. It gave the commission good reason to conclude that Weinstein was still a potential danger to society. After all, if he had been unable to control his impulses due to a brain dysfunction, what would he do if another person angered him? Could his condition spark another attack?

Not long after the parole hearing, Weinstein was transferred to another minimum-security facility in upstate New York. He was crushed to learn that he had to give up his job as a tutor because the tutoring positions at the new prison were filled. His days became even more monotonous. As the years crept along, he slowed down physically, as age took its inevitable toll on his body.

Still hungry for good company and conversation, he was fortunate to develop a friendship with Rabbi Irving H. Goodman, a prison chaplain. He happily chatted with Weinstein and engaged in the kind of intellectual discourse that he so much wanted. Goodman got to know Weinstein well during the last six years of his incarceration and found him to be especially intelligent and thoughtful compared to the other inmates at the facility. By the time Weinstein's next parole hearing came up in 2001, the good rabbi was willing to vouch for him and wrote a letter to the parole board. In his forty-three years as a prison chaplain, Goodman wrote, he hadn't met anyone with Weinstein's intellect or his easy rapport with and reverence for others. "In addition to his intellect, Mr. Weinstein possesses high moral and religious values which will serve him well once he is released," Goodman wrote.

At his second parole hearing, Weinstein complained that he'd been feeling devalued in prison. Once he had made good use of his time by tutoring other inmates, but now "what I do here all day is a total waste of a human being," he said. "I am a porter." He spent mornings dusting windowsills and evenings sweeping floors. Each job paid him ten cents. He asked several times to serve as a GED math tutor but was told there were no openings. "They've reassured me that I will be a porter," Weinstein said. "My evaluations as a porter are uniformly excellent. I happen to be someone who does whatever it is, I do it to the best of my ability, even if it's sweeping the floor."

Weinstein concluded, "Well, I think deep in your heart you know that a seventy-five-year-old man is not a threat to the community."

That's not how the commissioners saw it. "This offense demonstrates a propensity for extreme violence and a depraved indifference for human life," they stated. "Your release is incompatible with the public welfare."

Weinstein tried again at his next parole hearing two years later. To prepare, he carefully typed an eleven-page statement laying out his case. What distinguished this statement was the depth of his contrition. He was now seventy-seven, and his health was continuing to decline. "My chronic ailments have worsened, and my posture has deteriorated," he wrote. He described his feelings of regret and responsibility for Barbara's death. "My remorse for her loss, as well as that for her family, particularly since it was occasioned at my hands, will remain unrequited until my very last breath. I am and will forever remain haunted by my inexcusable actions." He continued to insist that his wife had not been alive when he threw her out the window, and he said he would have called 911 had he seen any signs of life. He also wanted to put to rest any speculation about his marriage to another woman within a year of Barbara's death. "I was lonely and needed companionship to help me deal with my loss."

He pleaded for compassion. "I have been sufficiently punished. . . . It would be a strain in the quality of mercy not to afford me the privilege of spending the few remaining years of my life with my loved ones and friends," he wrote. "I will forever live with the unhealed scars wrought by my criminal behavior."

He explained that his effort to make Barbara's death appear to be a suicide was a product of extreme emotional distress and utter panic. "How did I permit the situation to get so out of control that it resulted in her death? How did I do this to someone I loved?" he wrote. "My initial thought was that it was an accident. I did not mean for it to happen. Yet, I did it." He was tortured by his inability to figure out why. "In reflecting on my actions over the years of my incarceration, irrespective of the existence of the cyst and the implication it might have in accounting for my strange behavior, I nonetheless ascribe full responsibility for my wife's demise to my actions," he wrote. "It would be easy to assess sole culpability for my conduct on the cyst, but in my final analysis it was my deed that was the vehicle that occasioned her death."

Weinstein assured the parole board that he was incapable of doing such a thing again. "I do not constitute a threat to the safety of the community," he concluded. "What possible harm can I be?"

The parole board received Weinstein's statement before his hearing on October 14, 2003. It took no pity on the ailing old man and once again denied parole: "This panel concludes there is reasonable probability that you would not live and remain at liberty without violating the law. Your release is thus not presently compatible with the public safety and welfare." The statement did not elaborate why the commissioners believed Weinstein was likely to break the law again or how his release might jeopardize public safety.

He had served eleven years by then, four years above the minimum sentence. He would have to wait two more years for his case to be considered again.

How could the parole board suggest, Weinstein wondered, that he was likely to break the law again, that the public safety would be in peril if he were released? It seemed preposterous. He decided he must take legal action. He researched case law and wrote up a *pro se* appeal, which he would send to the New York Department of Corrections. *Pro se* appeals were, and continue to be, common among prisoners with plenty of time, and the help of law books, to draft their own legal documents without a lawyer. In the appeal, Weinstein cited his exemplary prison record, his completion of therapeutic programs for aggressive behavior, and all his other accomplishments and certificates. He suggested that public pressure and politics had played a role; Governor George Pataki had sought to curtail parole for violent felons and announced that he wanted to end parole altogether for criminals. He argued that the parole board had failed to explain its decision or make a persuasive case that he was a dangerous person likely to break the law again. It was an impressive document for a nonlawyer and included citations for case law. To boost his case, Weinstein referred to a 2001 report that found that the median time served by violent felons, including those convicted of manslaughter and first-degree murder, was 63.6 months. Weinstein already had served 132 months, more than twice the average. "With but a few years statistically left to his life," his appeal said, "what possible harm could appellant be to anyone?"

The corrections department lawyers denied Weinstein's appeal, citing their own case law.

Weinstein decided to go to a higher authority and filed another appeal, this time with the Supreme Court of New York. Justice Shirley Werner Kornreich read it. In April 2005 she ordered another parole hearing, saying that the board failed to follow the law as well as its own guidelines. It had flat-out ignored the many programs and therapy sessions that Weinstein had successfully completed, disregarded his work tutoring and teaching fellow inmates, and failed to consider his release plans. And just as Weinstein had argued, it had neglected to give detailed reasons for denying parole. At the plea proceedings, the district attorney, she noted, had made clear that its office believed the seven-year minimum was sufficient punishment.

"Nothing in the more than fourteen years since his weaponless crime of passion, points to any violent behavior, danger or shortness of temper," Kornreich wrote. "Rather, the facts before the Board speak of a kind, temperate and insightful individual who worked hard while in prison to understand the violence of his offense and reign [*sic*] in whatever instincts or physical disability precipitated the crime." She took issue with the board's unfounded conclusion that there was a reasonable probability that Weinstein would again violate the law and that his release would be incompatible with the public safety and welfare. She called such speculation an empty recitation and the board's finding "irrational bordering on impropriety."

Four months later, Weinstein was back before the board.

"How are you feeling today?" a commissioner asked.

"As best as an old man can with arthritis," Weinstein said.

"How old are you?"

"Seventy-nine."

"Seventy-nine. Well, you don't look like you're in terrible shape. You're walking?"

"I'm not in terrible shape. I walk with the aid of a cane."

And with that, the hearing went just as the others had. Weinstein was asked to tell the story of killing Barbara, and he again insisted that she appeared dead when he dragged her body to the window and threw her out. This time he told the board he had put his head to her heart to listen, and there were no signs of life.

The commissioner asked Weinstein a question no one had asked before: "How do you feel about taking someone's life, especially about someone you knew, you loved?"

"If you've never done it, you can never understand the pain that I go through daily. There is remorse, there is regret, there is the constant 'How could you possibly do such a thing?' Every single day I am haunted by that."

Weinstein's remorse, clean record, advanced age, and failing health didn't matter. The board determined once again that there was reasonable probability that Weinstein would violate the law and that his release "would be incompatible with the welfare and safety of the community." This time the board laid out its reasoning, stating that despite Weinstein's claim to the contrary, he had thrown Barbara out the window while she was still alive and had tried to minimize his culpability by saying he had been defending himself in an argument. The board noted his positive accomplishments in prison as well, but they didn't count for much. He was going back to prison.

Weinstein never had another parole hearing. In December 2006 he became eligible for conditional release, which allowed him to go free as long as he had a place to live and regularly checked in with a parole officer. He was instructed that he could not leave the state without permission. He was prohibited from owning a weapon and was not allowed to consume alcoholic beverages.

Weinstein lived out his remaining years in an assisted living facility in Tuxedo Park, New York, a suburb about forty miles northwest of Manhattan. Though his health was in decline and he was feeling weaker as he aged, he was relatively happy. He had his own room and regularly played poker with other residents. He wasn't able to walk around easily, and in the spring of 2009, the staff suggested he move to a nursing home, which could offer more hands-on care when he needed help. Weinstein said no, despite urging from his son and daughter. Joni flew in from San Francisco to visit him in early June and saw how weak he had become. He died just a few weeks later, on June 24, 2009, at eighty-three. Joni was unable to travel back for his funeral, a modest service attended by about a dozen people including Nelson, the Wagners, and a few other friends. He was interred next to his first wife, Belle, in a mausoleum in a Jewish cemetery in Paramus, New Jersey.

No one took up Weinstein's offer to remove his brain for study, and so it went, along with the arachnoid cyst, to his final resting place. But pictures of his brain would be examined around the world.

One evening not long after her father died, Joni Weinstein decided to Google his name. The top hits that flashed onto the screen referred to news articles, journal articles, and blogposts, many of which included images from his PET scans. For the first time, she saw the color images of his brain, the images that had been used during the Frye hearing to determine their admissibility. She had no idea that her father had been studied, discussed, and referenced in scores of journal articles and neuroscience and law books under the pseudonym Spyder Cystkopf. The articles gave her a deeper understanding of how the cyst on her father's brain might have had a role in his inability to stop himself from killing Barbara.

"When I saw that image of my father's brain scan, that crystallized everything for me. I knew immediately why the prosecutor didn't want the jury to see that," she tells me. "You couldn't look at somebody's brain and see so large of a space and not think it wasn't functioning right." But Joni tells me that she's always believed, and continues to believe, that her father bears responsibility for what he did and deserved prison time. "I was not sympathetic to my father in the least," she says. "I thought he should go to prison, possibly get the death penalty. He did something heinous."

Prosecutor Zach Weiss left the New York district attorney's office after the Weinstein case and became an administrative law judge, specializing in Social Security disability claims. The case remains embedded in his memory not only because of its groundbreaking nature but because it evolved from a chance MRI that revealed something that could have remained unknown for the rest of Weinstein's life. What should have been a simple murder case, he tells me, took on a life of its own. "If he hadn't been scanned, none of this would have ever happened," Weiss says. "Look, a guy got mad at his wife and he killed her. It was a crime of passion. I've seen a lot of cases in which well-meaning people have cracked. People's judgment gets clouded by their emotions. Weinstein thought he was smarter than everyone. I think there were aspects of this case that went beyond a bad brain."

Weiss recalls how he spent hundreds of hours enveloped in neuroscience to prepare for the case, but he thinks all that brain science really didn't matter. "The way the current legal doctrine is, it has no real value. In the end, it will always be debated," he says. "The mystery of consciousness is always something people will be interested in. People want an explanation. Maybe it just happened. It wasn't just Herbert Weinstein's brain. It was everything he brought to that moment in his life."

Daniel Schwartz, once New York's most famous forensic psychiatrist, who had examined and interviewed Weinstein twenty-five years earlier, is retired and living in a senior citizens' home in Hewlett, New York, just east of Brooklyn. In the card room, he's brought with him a manila folder that contains a few documents he's kept from the case, along with some newspaper clippings. He remembers being struck by how erudite and intelligent Weinstein was when they met. "He's the only person I know who applied to be on *Jeopardy!*," Schwartz says. He remembers being taken aback when attorney Diarmuid White shared information about Weinstein's cyst and the possibility that it had contributed to Weinstein killing his wife. "I don't know how much [the murder] had to do with his tumor or how much it had to do with his personality," Schwartz tells me. "This was something that was out of character."

Even without seeing Weinstein's cyst or PET scan results, he says, he concluded that his behavior, flat affect, and indifference, and the results of other neuropsychological tests, were consistent with some type of organic brain disorder. Still, Schwartz believes it was unlikely that Weinstein had a dangerous lack of impulse control that might cause him to commit another crime. "He was so upset about his wife's behavior that he became so angry and he lost control, and that's it," he says. Like Weiss, Schwartz believes it was a simple crime of passion, a onetime deal: "If the victim is your wife, I don't think the average person is in danger."

Antonio Damasio was never called to testify at Weinstein's hearing by either the defense or the prosecution. I wanted to get his take on the case, but given his demanding schedule, he was very difficult to reach. In January 2014 Joni Weinstein called to tell me that Damasio was scheduled to give a talk in San Francisco. I flew out to meet with Joni, go to the lecture, and hopefully, speak with Damasio. She, too, was eager to meet the world-famous neuroscientist who had examined her father.

Joni was ill the night of the lecture, so I went by myself to a packed house of thirteen hundred people at the Nourse Theater. "It says something about the popularity of neuroscience that a neuroscientist can pack an auditorium orchestra and balcony, with young and old, in a setting befitting a play or a symphony," Damasio said as he settled in for his talk. He started out with the story of Phineas Gage, then launched into a discussion of emotions and his study of moral behavior.

He agreed to meet me the next morning at the Four Seasons. Our time was limited, so I asked him the most pressing question: Did he think Weinstein's cyst somehow influenced his behavior when he killed his wife? Damasio said, "Yes, I believe it had compromised his brain function." Then he left to catch a plane, but later he elaborated by e-mail.

Weinstein's cyst affected his frontal lobe function, Damasio explained, because such growths displace tissue and often compress brain structures in their vicinity. The pressure can injure neural tissue and restrict the blood supply. However, he seemed cautious about stating the cyst had actually *caused* Weinstein to lose control and kill his wife. "We have no way of knowing," he wrote. "Not every lesion of the frontal lobe is associated with behavioral changes . . . or associated with violent behavior." Violent behavior can be triggered by many factors: biological, social, cultural, and situational. Perhaps, he suggested, it was a combination of those factors and Weinstein's cyst that steered him to kill his wife.

In the years following the murder of her mother, Kim Glazer Goldberg raised two children, worked various jobs, and became president of a philanthropic foundation bearing her late father's name. She's done her best to move on from that day on the Upper East Side in 1991, she tells me, and has returned to New Orleans, where she grew up. When she thinks of her mom, it's not about how she died but about how much she misses her, how beautiful she was, and how close they were. Kim and Barbara were best friends, shared secrets, and had the kind of special relationship that only mothers and daughters can understand.

When Kim first heard Weinstein's claim that brain damage caused him to kill her mother, she thought it was ridiculous. "This thing with having a cyst, I didn't buy it," she says. "Of course you're crazy when you do something like that. You're insane at that moment. For him to use that as an excuse? He had the money to pay a good lawyer. I suppose I'd do the same thing if I made that kind of mistake."

Kim believes Weinstein was telling the truth when he said he thought her mother was dead before he hoisted her out the window. "I think he overpowered her, strangled her or whatever . . . and it appeared she was dead and he got scared and just tossed her out the window," she says. "I think he flipped for the moment. Anyone who would do such a horrific thing is crazy for that moment. . . . I didn't think he would do it again. But I still think he should have been punished. . . . Do I think he would have been a serial killer? No. People snap all the time."

Time and distance have helped the memories fade and softened her anger over her mother's death, but the deeper wound remains in her heart. "I worked out my anger a long time ago about this, so I'm really not angry," Kim says. "Sad? Yes. Angry? No. Did Herbert deserve a second chance? No, he did not."

As for Joni, she has not forgotten that Weinstein's killing of Barbara that winter afternoon left many people deeply hurt. "I didn't think Barbara deserved to die the way she did. I didn't think her children needed to live their lives knowing how she died," she says. She believes her father loved Barbara and just lost it that day. "I believe that the incident would never have been even a remote possibility if he had not had the giant frontal lobe cyst that interfered with his thinking and impulses," she says. "It took me years of researching the brain angle before I truly understood what had happened and was able to forgive my father."

CHAPTER 17

Defending America's Defenders

Not long after Kris Parson returned home from the war in Iraq, his girlfriend began calling the police to their house in Coon Rapids, Minnesota, a suburb about fifteen miles north of Minneapolis. She'd dial 911 to report that she and Kris were fighting and that she was afraid he was going to hurt her. Every time police came to the house, on at least a dozen occasions, things would calm down and the officers would leave. The police found no evidence that Kris, who served as a combat engineer with the Minnesota National Guard, had physically hurt his girlfriend in any way, and he hadn't done anything to warrant an arrest.

Then one night she called the police again. This time she said Kris had put his hands around her throat and tried to strangle her. The police arrested Kris on felony charges of domestic violence. While he was being booked at the jail, Kris knew just whom to call. There was this lawyer over in Minneapolis who handled lots of cases for veterans and had once represented Kris on a drunk driving charge. The guy understood veterans and how the war had messed them up. He knew what was going on in their brains and could help. His name was Brock Hunter.

Hunter has developed a specialty in representing veterans charged with crimes outside the military justice system. He and his colleagues in this area offer a version of the brain defense, an approach that considers the possible influence of post-traumatic stress disorder, depression, and TBI caused by their military experience on their clients' criminal behavior and seeks understanding and treatment instead of prison and, in some cases, mercy instead of execution. Hunter is a veteran himself, having served four years in the army, mostly as a sniper scout in the tension-filled DMZ of Korea during the late 1980s. When he returned, he spent a few years in college not knowing what he wanted to do, went to law school, and joined a corporate firm. He hated it. Big button-down firms were a terrible fit for a freewheeling, spirited man with a passion for social justice.

After leaving his job, Hunter took on criminal cases and worked for the local public defender's office. He soon began to see lots of veterans in the system, including Vietnam vets. Many were homeless and addicted to drugs and alcohol and seemed deeply wounded psychologically. In the years following the 9/11 terrorist attacks, he saw veterans in court who had come home from the wars in Afghanistan and Iraq, and his attachment to them grew stronger.

On a kayaking trip around Lake Superior's Apostle Islands, Hunter stopped at the nearby town of Ashland, Wisconsin, and browsed in a used-book store. There he happened to see a copy of *Achilles in Vietnam: Combat Trauma and the Undoing of Character.* The book, by psychiatrist Jonathan Shay, draws comparisons between the experiences of modern combat veterans and those in Homer's *Iliad* and *Odyssey.* The warriors three thousand years ago, Shay observes, suffered the same kinds of psychological wounds as their modern counterparts. In the *Iliad,* Achilles experiences profound grief after losing a friend in battle, goes berserk, and mutilates enemies. In the *Odyssey,* after the Trojan War, Odysseus and his men pillage a city and get addicted to drugs. When he finally comes home, Odysseus murders men who had been courting his wife while he was at war. He lost his mind.

Something in Hunter clicked while he was reading Shay's book, and he couldn't stop turning the pages as he stood in the bookstore. "It changed everything," Hunter says. "That was a turning point for me."

The psychological toll of combat is well documented. Killing others, being shot at, watching comrades die, being sleep deprived, and feeling constantly stressed have a profound impact on the psyche that can lead to impulsive and destructive behavior. Post-traumatic stress disorder, while not named as such or understood back in Homer's day, is as old as war itself. Hunter decided that he had found a special niche and a mission as a lawyer. He immersed himself in research and literature about veterans, looking closely at how PTSD and TBIs affect them. He decided to dedicate his practice to helping veterans navigate the criminal justice system and receive treatment rather than prison time. He believes his fellow citizens should place high value on the nation's military personnel for their service—regardless of the politics of war—and be willing to give them a few breaks because of their sacrifices for the country.

Kris Parson can be an intimidating figure. Muscular and lean, he stands about six feet tall, with a square jaw and intense brown eyes. His voice is deep, probably thickened by the cigarettes he chain-smokes. His speech is hesitant at times, as if his words are a few beats behind his thoughts. He was diagnosed with a TBI after surviving a harrowing attack by insurgents against U.S. and Iraqi government troops in Sadr City.

I'm talking to Kris in his home in Coon Rapids, the shades drawn and most of the lights off. During the attack, he was hunkered down in a concrete building. "I remember nine blasts. I felt this huge wave. I didn't hear anything—you just feel it. Things started coming through the wall. I didn't know if I was alive or dead. I had an out-of-body experience." His head felt as if someone were stomping on it or striking it with bowling ball. Then came a feeling of euphoria. *Is this real?* he wondered.

The blasts stopped. "I remember getting up and saying, 'Awesome, man!' 'Cause that's what you do," Kris tells me. "Life got really weird after that."

Blast injuries like those Kris suffered are signature wounds of the wars in Iraq and Afghanistan, primarily because of the prevalence of improvised explosive devices (IEDs). According to one estimate, more than 50 percent of injuries sustained during the conflicts in Iraq and Afghanistan were the result of explosives—that includes bombs, grenades, landmines, mortar and artillery shells, and IEDs. The most common cause of injury among American soldiers at Walter Reed Army Medical Center is blast injuries, according to the Defense and Veterans Brain Injury Center. By 2008, an estimated four hundred thousand troops in Afghanistan and Iraq had experienced mild to severe TBIs. Many were never diagnosed.

Multiple blast injuries can feel like being hit by a wave and then being pulled back into the surf. The explosion triggers an intense rise in atmospheric pressure, which has the force to push organs within the body and then release them when the pressure falls again. Kris may seem to have emerged physically unscathed because he had no penetrating head wounds or blunt trauma to the outside of his skull. But with a blast injury, the sudden movement causes hidden injuries inside. A sudden jerk of the head, along with the blast pressure, can cause shearing within the brain, tearing arteries, veins, connective tissue, and nerve fibers. It gets even more complicated inside the brain's gray and white matter: its variations in weight, density, and structure cause it to move at different speeds than the blast, damaging the dense layers of neurons throughout the cerebral cortex. The long, microscopic axons, the conduits that communicate information throughout the brain, are stretched, pulled, and twisted, resulting in what's called a diffuse axonal injury.

A heavy blast can result in more damage to a brain than a penetrating wound from a bullet or shrapnel. Multiple blast injuries like Kris's, in which his head went back and forth and shook from side to side, can compound the damage and cause a variety of physical, emotional, cognitive, and behavioral symptoms. And many of these symptoms emerge with other conditions such as depression or PTSD. Microscopic damage at the neuron level, often caused by TBI, is not always as evident as a penetrating brain injury might be, and among combat veterans in Iraq and Afghanistan it became known as the invisible injury. The effects of TBI suggested its presence. Studies have shown that people with TBI have greater impulsivity and a greater propensity to aberrant behavior. Soldiers with TBI often sense that something is not quite right but can't figure out what or why. Their relationships suffer, they lose concentration, or they become distracted on the job. The incidence of substance abuse is high among those with TBI. That's exactly what happened to Kris.

It's not clear how TBI and PTSD intertwine or whether those who suffer from one or both are more likely to commit crimes and acts of extreme violence than others. The studies can't make that leap into cause and effect. Many veterans who suffered through combat and are afflicted with TBI and PTSD have never committed crimes or hurt others. They feel hurt and resentful when people assume they're capable of violence or homicidal rage. The stigma may even prevent them from seeking treatment, and those who suffer from PTSD are more likely to harm themselves.

In 2007 Hunter helped draft a Minnesota law that permits judges to consider the option of sending veterans to treatment programs instead of prison if they suffer from combat-related mental health disorders. The law requires courts to ask if a criminal defendant is a veteran and allows their lawyers to order psychological evaluations. If a defendant is diagnosed with a mental health disorder, the court can work with the Department of Veterans Affairs on a treatment plan as part of the sentencing.

About a year after Hunter helped create the Minnesota law, a special veterans treatment court was established. Robert Russell, an associate judge for the city court of Buffalo, New York, had noticed more veterans showing up in his drug and mental health treatment courts. His idea was to create a court especially for veterans. Since then, more than 220 such courts have been established across the country to take into account that those who return from war often turn to drugs or alcohol to alleviate suffering from physical, mental, and emotional damage. These courts help veterans receive the government-provided services they are entitled to but may not be aware of or have ignored. Veterans who stay clean and out of trouble can have their criminal charges dismissed and records wiped clean.

In 2009 Hunter won a landmark case that resulted in the kind of collaboration he'd sought to get veterans help instead of prison. His client, Arthur Torgeson, was a Vietnam vet who suffered from severe PTSD and had a history of depression and alcoholism. He was charged with second-degree murder and arson for stabbing his wife, Sherrill Harnden, and setting their home on fire. By common legal standards, he would not qualify as insane because he was aware of his actions at the time of the crime and understood that what he did was wrong.

His confession suggested he had carefully thought through his plan. He was stressed about a recent cancer diagnosis and financial trouble and had decided to kill himself. Even though he'd been with his wife for twenty-five years, they'd been married for just a year. Torgeson said in his confession that he was afraid she wouldn't receive his military benefits after he died. Rather than let her suffer and go broke, he decided to take her life and then his own. After he stabbed her, he drank wine, called relatives to say good-bye, doused himself with gasoline, and set the house on fire. He fled the burning home but was badly injured.

Hunter suggested to the judge that Torgeson receive mental health treatment rather than prison time. At Hunter's request, the Anoka County prosecutor, Bob Johnson, consulted with Sherrill's family about a plea agreement that would allow Torgeson to go directly to a mental health facility. The family felt it was the right thing to do.

Hunter started getting national press attention for his work; the *New York Times* quoted him in a series about veterans charged with murder. Demand for his services grew. In hometowns across the country veterans were getting arrested for domestic violence, drunken driving, fights, and other crimes.

High-profile cases drew even more attention. In Fort Carson, Colorado, returning soldiers were arrested for fighting, beatings, rapes, DUIs, drug deals, domestic violence, shootings, stabbings, kidnapping, and murder. The violence prompted the army to commission a study called the *Epidemiologic Consultation* to examine why veteran violence was increasing. It found that the murder rate at the base had doubled, and the number of rape arrests tripled. From 2005 to 2008, thirteen soldiers at Fort Carson were charged with homicide. Soldiers from one particular unit, known as the Lethal Warriors, were charged with most of the murders. Members of that unit, which by reputation had served in the most violent battlefields in Iraq, also had a rate of PTSD three times that of other units. The report found "a possible association between increasing levels of combat exposure and risk for negative behavioral outcomes." However, it also cited other risk factors among the soldiers, such as criminal histories and experiences of drug and alcohol abuse. The report was careful to note that "overall, most soldiers are doing well." Many, it pointed out, had seen heavy combat and had risk factors for violence yet committed no crimes.

Then in 2012 Army Staff Sgt. Robert Bales was charged with killing sixteen unarmed Afghan civilians inside their homes—the worst murder spree by a single solider. Bales had sneaked out of his base in southern Afghanistan and into a walled compound, where he inexplicably beat and kicked a group of civilians, shot them, and set several bodies on fire. His lawyer suggested that Bales was a good soldier who had had a mental breakdown due to PTSD and a TBI that he had suffered during his four deployments. Bales eventually pleaded guilty. At his sentencing hearing, he tearfully apologized to the families of his victims but gave no explanation. He did say that after returning from tours in Iraq, he felt angry, weak, and fearful and quit counseling because he saw no improvement. His prosecutors characterized him as a frustrated man with financial and marital problems, prone to drinking and violent outbursts.

While Hunter has been able to negotiate treatment instead of prison for veterans, the cases he takes on don't always end favorably. In 2006 he was hired by Anthony Klecker, who had killed sixteen-year-old Deanna Casey in a car crash while driving drunk. Hunter was able to get Klecker a one-year jail sentence with the promise that he undergo treatment. But Klecker was kicked out of a VA program for pushing a friend during an argument, engaging in a verbal altercation with another patient, and admitting to carrying a small pocket knife onto the premises. In 2011 he was arrested again for drunk driving, though no one was hurt this time. A judge sentenced him to four years in prison.

In the weeks and months after Kris Parson survived the blast attacks in Iraq, he came to realize that he was damaged in ways he hadn't expected. His scratches and cuts had healed, but he felt strange. "I couldn't speak a whole sentence after that," he said. "People would say to me, 'Are you drunk?' "

When Kris finally came home to Minnesota, he had trouble making the transition to civilian life. He was unable to find work and felt lost. His difficulty in speaking was a liability in job interviews. He suspected his wife was having an affair, and their marriage ended soon afterward. He started drinking every day. He had haunted dreams, reliving some of the attacks, the explosions, and the sounds of people getting wounded. "There was a lot of screaming," he recalls. "One of the worst things to hear is another man screaming."

Kris spent many of his days at the VA for speech therapy and treatment, and the rest of the time drinking. "For four or five years, I didn't feel like I was alive," he says. "I still feel like that sometimes. A lot of things don't make sense to me anymore." He loved to read but couldn't remember what he read or would remember only much later. He felt volatile but did not realize the extent of his simmering anger. "You don't really understand until you scare the living shit out of someone," he says. "Everything bothered me. Everything made me mad. I was pumped with adrenaline."

That first year home was the worst. "I was really needy," he says. "I drank every single day. I planned to hang myself."

One night Kris did try to kill himself, but not by hanging. He crushed a handful of sleeping pills and mixed the powder with beer to make it go down easier and absorb faster. Then he drank four beers. He must have passed out. He heard pounding on his front door, and then someone kicked in the door. It burst open, and men in black stormed in. Kris's military mind and combat experience took over—people in the dark were the ones who attacked him in Iraq. He went wild, swinging and hitting cops—he hurled one cop into a wall. They finally subdued him. In an act of mercy, rather than arrest him, they took him to a VA mental health facility. He's not sure who called the cops that night, but that person saved his life.

Kris says he was not himself in those days. "I can get violent," he recalls. "But it's not on purpose. It's my natural reaction. I'm surprised they didn't shoot me." He says he used to sleep with a knife but for some reason did not that night. "Thank God I didn't."

Kris first encountered Brock Hunter by accident. He'd been arrested for drunk driving and had searched the Internet for a local attorney. Hunter seemed like a good candidate, though Kris didn't know that he was a veteran. When they spoke on the phone for the first time, Hunter intuitively asked whether Kris was in the military. Kris told him about his experience. "You were in Sadr City?" Hunter asked. Then he knew Kris likely had some postcombat problems.

Kris is typical of the veterans Hunter represents. High-profile murder cases receive national and international attention, but most veterans charged with crimes are not accused of murder. More likely they're arrested for domestic violence, fighting, drugs, or drinking. Many have TBI, and their anger is easily triggered, even by someone they perceive is looking at them the wrong way. Drinking is the favored way to self-medicate, as it was for Kris, whose girlfriend liked to drink, too, he says. After his marriage ended, Kris met his girlfriend at the gym, and soon afterward she moved into his house with her two kids. She was unemployed. They spent a lot of time drinking together.

"It was a combination of things," Kris says. "It was a matter of time before it would blow up."

In 2011 Hunter got a phone call from Floyd "Shad" Meshad, a nationally known, highly regarded veterans' advocate. Meshad had been a medical service officer during the Vietnam War and founded the National Veterans Foundation. He was a leader in recognizing and treating soldiers with PTSD. He began stepping up for veterans during the early 1980s, when a wave of Vietnam vets were getting arrested for murders and violent assaults across the country. He helped pioneer the PTSD defense by educating lawyers and judges about the condition and became part of a veterans' criminal defense trial team.

In the late 1980s Meshad's foundation published *Defending the Vietnam Combat Veteran,* a guide for attorneys representing veterans in criminal court. Now in 2011 Meshad had a proposition for Hunter: Would he be willing to help put together an updated version of his book to assist lawyers defending the more recently returned veterans? "He heard about the stuff I was doing and invited me in," Hunter says. "It was like getting a call from Elvis. He is an absolute hero."

Hunter did help assemble, write, and edit *The Attorney's Guide to Defending Veterans in Criminal Court.* With chapters written by experts from the fields of law, medicine, social work, psychology, and psychiatry, the book offers practical advice on defending veterans with PTSD, TBI, substance abuse, and other service-related disorders.

One contributor to the book is retired Brig. Gen. Stephen N. Xenakis, MD, a former army medical corps officer with twenty-eight years of active service, including stints as special adviser to the chairman of the Joint Chiefs of Staff and senior adviser to the Department of Defense on neurobehavioral conditions and medical management. He also serves as an antitorture adviser to Physicians for Human Rights. Xenakis began to see the effects of head injuries on soldiers in 2004, when he went to visit his father, who was recovering from a stroke, at Walter Reed Army Medical Center in Bethesda, Maryland. The first wave of injured soldiers were then coming back from Iraq and Afghanistan. Xenakis walked around the neurology and surgery wards and talked to some of them. "I felt that many of them really showed problems in attention and concentration, and just being able to track our conversation," he says. He approached his former Pentagon colleagues and suggested they look into the mental health of returning soldiers, especially those who suffered from blast injuries. "I thought these IED blasts were going to have profound mental effects on these soldiers," he says. "If a blast was strong enough to blow off their legs, then it was going to affect their brains."

Xenakis started to speak more openly about his concerns that many soldiers were suffering from invisible, undiagnosed TBI. In 2007 Adm. Mike Mullen, then chairman of the Joint Chiefs of Staff, invited him to serve as a senior adviser on the issue. Xenakis wanted to try to help recent veterans avoid the problems of Vietnam veterans who suffered from undiagnosed PTSD, lacked treatment, and behaved in ways that caused them legal troubles. Society had to recognize that "IED blast concussions, PTSD, chronic pain and sleep problems . . . are going to add up and cause problems for the soldiers when they get out," Xenakis warned. "They're going to get into legal problems. . . . Let's see what we can do early on to head off the consequences."

He advocated treatment and compassion. "We always have to ask ourselves: How dangerous is the person to society and to himself? Does prison rehabilitate these people? Will they get treatment in prison? If so, what's the best treatment?"

Xenakis often consults with criminal defense lawyers who represent veterans and cautions them to be careful in using a brain defense: "Because it's an emerging science, the prosecution can clearly find scientists and experts who will argue there's no evidence." Besides, criminal behavior is too complex to be reduced to neurological dysfunction—it is the culmination of many factors, Xenakis says. The courts must take into account the readjustment, reintegration, employment, substance abuse, homelessness, and the stress of a vet's family life before pronouncing judgment. He believes the court system absolutely should render special treatment to veterans: the country asked them to protect our nation and way of life, so we are responsible to give back to them.

Kris Parson got special treatment because he served the country. After his arrest, Hunter was able to get his domestic violence case transferred to the special veterans court in Anoka County. Hunter worked out a deal with the prosecutor: Kris would undergo therapy, check in with the court periodically, and stay out of trouble for eighteen months. If he could do that, he would not have a felony conviction.

Was it fair that Parson received special treatment because he was a veteran? Most people are grateful to those who serve and, politics aside, believe they deserve the best in care and compensation for their sacrifices. Veterans returning from Vietnam had to struggle to gain access to proper treatment for their physical and mental wounds. Those coming back from Iraq and Afghanistan have found a much different atmosphere. There's a greater recognition of TBI and of the mental toll of combat and an acknowledgment of PTSD as a legitimate diagnosis. Today's veterans are in a better position than their predecessors to cite mental health issues and brain injuries as contributing factors to criminal behavior.

Thomas L. Hafemeister, a professor at the University of Virginia School of Law and its School of Medicine, has written extensively about PTSD, veterans, and the criminal justice system. "The veterans from Iraq and Afghanistan were generally viewed as a sympathetic population," he told me. "They've done a great service for the country and through no fault of their own have gone through some horrific events. So it feels really wrong to throw the book at them. They don't seem as deserving of the full strength of the law as other criminal defendants."

But this line of reasoning poses constitutional problems, he points out: "Under our criminal justice system, we have fair and equal treatment under the law. So how do we defend carving out special rules for this population? Do we have one set of rules for a population seen as sympathetic and another for a population seen as unsympathetic? That goes against the notion that justice is blind."

Brock Hunter has an answer: America's justice system already has a decades-long history of using special courts for drug offenders and those with mental health problems. "These courts are based not on the philosophy of sympathy but upon the recognition that treating offenders' underlying issues, rather than just punishing their associated behaviors, dramatically reduces the likelihood of recidivism and enhances public safety," he says. "Veterans courts operate on the same philosophy."

The legal ground may already be shifting when it comes to handling veterans with brain injuries and PTSD. "The legal system has been hesitant about embracing the insanity defense," Hafemeister says. "But the question that came with all these veterans coming back with PTSD and these other mental disorders was whether the criminal justice system would change its view about this type of defense."

Kris Parson has a newly acquired skill in building computers, which he learned by trial and error and through online courses. To him, it's simple. "Can you add one plus one? That's computers," he says. He also studies marketing and business and takes free online computer courses from Microsoft and Cisco Systems. "I have to have a challenge in my head," he says.

He's extremely sensitive to light—especially sunlight. When he goes outside, he wears glasses that are nearly black. Inside his home, the curtains and shades are always drawn.

He still has nightmares. "I've had them so long that it's normal," he says. In these dreams, he is in a firefight and runs out of ammo. He destroys a building. He grinds his teeth at night so badly that he had to have five of them surgically removed and replaced. "Even if I might look good, there's always stuff going on inside," he tells me.

I ask Kris if he is afraid he might lose control of himself and hurt someone because of his brain injury. The TBI, he says, "really messed with me. . . . I've learned how to manage it better." But "if people cross my boundaries . . ." He pauses and stops, lost in thought. "People don't understand what's going on."

Hunter says he's not looking to excuse anyone's behavior. "Injuries like TBI and having PTSD can drive behavior that gets [veterans] in the criminal justice system," Hunter explains. "We're not saying they need to escape responsibility. If they can get the help they need, let's give it to them. If not for their service or experience with the military, they might not be involved in the criminal justice system."

Kris feels fortunate to have found Hunter help him through his legal and personal troubles. "I believe Brock has a lot of passion," he says. "He really connects the dots and puts all this stuff out there. It can look like I'm a terrible person, but I'm not."

CHAPTER 18

The Head-Banger Defense

On an August afternoon in 2011, a 911 operator in St. Joseph County, Indiana, answered a call from a woman pleading for help. The operator heard children screaming in the background, then what sounded like a gunshot. Minutes later police officers were headed to a two-story redbrick house in the town of Granger, about ten miles northwest of Notre Dame University. As they arrived, the officers heard more gunshots and took cover. Three children were on the lawn, apparently unharmed. Their mother was still inside but emerged a few moments later with a bruise on her head.

Inside the house, clutching a gun, was her husband, Corwin Brown, a former NFL defensive back who had played with the Detroit Lions, the New York Jets, and the New England Patriots. Most recently he had been a defensive coach with Notre Dame.

Officers contacted Brown by cell phone to try to coax him out of the house. A SWAT team arrived, and police cordoned off the neighborhood subdivision. Brown remained inside, and was in and out of phone contact with police. One officer used a bullhorn: "We'd appreciate it if you let us know you're okay." Brown stepped outside a few times, then went back in. Officers remained patient and withheld fire. For the next seven hours, they held their positions and tried to contact Brown again.

Then the sound of two gunshots came from the garage. Brown staggered out—he had shot himself in the stomach. He was taken to a hospital. Prosecutors eventually charged him with holding his wife against her will and beating her.

His friends and family reacted with disbelief. That wasn't really Corwin Brown, they said. This was completely out of character for him. And then came the apparent explanation: his brain was damaged from repeated blows during his years as an NFL player, and he was not in his right mind. Five days after his arrest, his family released a statement to the press. "Many are asking, what would cause a young man who has been blessed beyond all measure, with a life so promising that he would put himself and his family in harm's way?" his wife, Melissa, read aloud from the statement. "We believe Corwin is suffering from symptoms similar to those experienced by the late Dave Duerson and were caused by the many notable collisions during Corwin's career in the NFL."

Duerson was the former Chicago Bears defensive back who five months earlier had committed suicide by shooting himself in the heart. He had been in mental decline for some time—he was arrested for domestic violence, got divorced, and suffered from memory loss, mood swings, and headaches. Before he killed himself, he wrote a note asking that his brain be studied alongside those of NFL players who had been diagnosed with chronic, progressive brain damage—a condition known as chronic traumatic encephalopathy (CTE). It turned out that Duerson had it, too. Years of head collisions while playing professional football apparently had taken a toll.

Since Duerson's suicide, the incidence of CTE among NFL players and the league's failure to address the issue have unleashed volumes of investigations, stories, books, and documentaries as well as a class action lawsuit claiming the league failed to inform and protect players. Another side of the story developed along the way. Some players began suggesting that CTE might be responsible for their criminal behavior, giving rise to a variation of the brain defense.

After his arrest, Corwin Brown's family said they suspected he had CTE. "The Corwin we know and love is gifted intellectually and athletically and loves his family," Melissa said. But after he retired from the NFL, he became suspicious, distant, gloomy, exhausted, and depressed. "He finally cried for help, surrendered, and prayed for forgiveness," she added. "We pray for those who may have answers to please come forth and help our family. . . . We pray that his former teams and the league that he adored hear our cries and provide assistance. Most of all we pray for studies to better understand and prevent this from happening to another player, as well as current families dealing with the same situation."

Brown played eight seasons in the NFL and four years at the University of Michigan. That he banged his head many times was not in dispute. But did it cause him to become violent and attack his wife and shoot himself?

CTE has been associated with many psychiatric symptoms, including depression, aggression, and suicidal behavior, but researchers differ on whether it causes aggressive or criminal behavior—or is another form of brain blame. Yet criminal defense attorneys are taking their chances on using it as a defense.

A month before Corwin Brown's arrest, Nathaniel Fujita, an eighteen-year-old high school football star from Wayland, Massachusetts, about twenty miles west of Boston, was charged with killing his ex-girlfriend, Lauren Astley. Police said he lured Astley, also eighteen, to his home and then beat, strangled, and slashed her to death in his garage. The motive for the killing was clear, according to the prosecutor: Fujita was angry because Astley had broken up with him.

Fujita's defense lawyer had a different take. Yes, Fujita's murder of his ex-girlfriend was a terrible thing. But he had done it during a brief psychotic episode, during which he had been unable to control his actions. Years of playing high school football had left him with concussive injuries that had caused him to lose his sense of reality. Fujita's murder trial would be the first criminal trial in which a defense lawyer linked football concussions to homicidal behavior.

Four months after Corwin Brown was arrested, his attorney, William Stanley, filed a notice in court that he intended to pursue a defense based on mental disease or defect, arguing that Brown was "not responsible for his conduct . . . because he lacked the substantial capacity to appreciate the wrongfulness of his conduct or to conform his conduct to the requirements of the law." On January 10, 2012, St. Joseph Superior Court judge Jane Woodward Miller appointed a psychiatrist and a psychologist who had not previously seen Brown to evaluate him.

By this time the NFL was facing scrutiny for its apparent indifference to players suffering from concussive head injuries. Lawyers had found what they claimed was a disturbing pattern of players who had developed CTE as a result of their years on the field. More than five thousand players had joined a multimillion-dollar class action suit against the league, seeking damages.

CTE is a progressive degenerative brain disease that can develop in people with a history of repetitive brain trauma. That trauma includes repetitive blows to the head that can cause concussions, as well as hits that might not register as concussions. Whether they are concussions or not, blows to the head create acceleration and deceleration stresses to the brain when the head suddenly jerks backward, forward, or sideways. The effects of CTE were long referred to by another term, *punch-drunk,* used to describe boxers who have suffered from repeated blows to the head. Hockey players can get it, military veterans who experience repeated exposure to blasts can get it, and those who play high school, college, and professional football can get it. The repeated brain trauma triggers progressive degeneration of brain tissue, building up the abnormal protein deposits known as tauimmunoreactive neurofibrillary tangles, similar to those found in Alzheimer's patients. Those afflicted with CTE have degenerated frontal lobes, medial temporal lobes, hippocampi, amygdalae, and brainstems.

"Punch Drunk" was actually the title of a 1928 article in the *Journal of the American Medical Association* about behavioral problems in patients who had received serious blows to the head. The author, Harrison S. Martland, called their behavior, for lack of any proper medical terms, "cuckoo, goofy or slug nutty." And he identified long-term physical and behavioral symptoms associated with the syndrome: speech problems, gait disorders, vertigo, Parkinson's, cognitive confusion, depression, neuroses, and psychoses. In some cases, the mental deterioration was so severe that it required the patient to be admitted to a psychiatric hospital. The syndrome also became known as dementia pugilistica, chronic progressive traumatic encephalopathy, and, most recently, chronic traumatic encephalopathy. The symptoms often begin years or even decades after the last brain trauma or end of active athletic involvement.

Chris Nowinski, a former professional wrestler with the WWE, has suffered from concussive brain injuries from his years battling on the mats. In 2007 he co-founded the Sports Legacy Institute (SLI), a Boston-based nonprofit organization, along with Dr. Robert Cantu, a world-renowned concussion expert. Nowinski met Cantu in 2003 while seeking treatment for severe postconcussion syndrome. Nowinski helped publicize the NFL concussion issue through his 2006 book, *Head Games: Football's Concussion Crisis,* and a 2014 documentary of the same name. The SLI's focus has been to expose the problem, create educational programs, and promote concussion safety.

As part of their work with the SLI, Nowinski and Cantu acquired the brains of deceased athletes for study. In 2008 the institute formed a partnership with Boston University School of Medicine, forming the Center for the Study of Traumatic Encephalopathy. Since then more than 350 current and former athletes, including 60 retired NFL players, have pledged to donate their brains for study, while others have agreed to be monitored over the years for mental and physical changes. By 2016 researchers had found CTE in 90 of 94 deceased former NFL players whose brains were analyzed.

Nowinski and Cantu, along with Ann McKee, a professor of neurology and pathology at Boston University, have published a number of papers on the effects of CTE. Their review of the CTE literature from 1928 through 2009 examined personality and behavioral changes in fifty-one individuals with CTE. It found that personality or behavioral changes occurred in 65 percent of them. The changes included aggression or violence in 70 percent, paranoia in 42 percent, agitation in 24 percent, and hypersexuality in 3 percent.

While Cantu and Nowinski have associated numerous psychological and behavioral problems with CTE, they have not gone so far as to advocate its use as a criminal defense. "People have to be accountable for their actions," Nowinski told me over coffee during a recent visit to Chicago. "But we can also learn a lot about how they got there." He strongly believes that CTE has triggered a host of unusual behaviors and often hears from concerned families of athletes who are showing shifts in their personalities. "We've seen a good amount of domestic violence and people making bad business decisions," he told me. "Drug issues are coming up. Those who had never taken drugs are now in their forties and starting to get addicted to drugs."

"How about O. J. Simpson?" Nowinski added, referring to the former running back and murder suspect who later was convicted for his involvement in the attempted robbery of his own sports memorabilia. "He is the most obvious example. He's been hit on the head more than anyone else. Guaranteed he has CTE." Dr. Bennet Omalu, the neuropathologist credited with first identifying CTE in NFL players and the subject of the 2015 movie *Concussion,* agrees. In an interview with ABC News, Omalu said Simpson was clearly suffering from the disease: "I would bet my medical license on it." Simpson himself tried to link his concussions to his criminal behavior and poor judgment when he sought, unsuccessfully, to overturn his 2008 conviction.

Blows to the head were cited as one reason the murder defendant Nathaniel Fujita was mentally unsound. To support his case at trial, Fujita's defense attorney, William Sullivan, called a forensic psychiatrist, Dr. Wade Myers, to testify that years of head injuries from football had left the teenaged Fujita with CTE. The doctor testified that in the weeks before Fujita killed his ex-girlfriend, he had slipped into a severe depression. To ease the pain, he had self-medicated with marijuana.

The prosecutor, Lisa McGovern, considered the CTE defense nonsense. Fujita's actions showed forethought and calculation, she argued—proof that he was thinking clearly and was not psychotic. After he killed Astley, he drove her car to a local beach and tossed her keys into a storm drain. He dumped her body into a marsh, then came home to shower and clean himself of evidence. "Say what you will about tooth fairies or fairy godmothers—there is no psychosis fairy who magically sprinkles a temporary dose of psychoses on this defendant," McGovern said. "It goes against everything we know scientifically about psychosis."

If Fujita really did experience a brief period of psychosis, proving that it was caused by brain damage was impossible—at least as long as he was alive. One problem with using CTE as a defense is that diagnosing the condition is possible only after the person has died. CTE cannot be confirmed until microscopic examination of the brain is performed. Some researchers have made strides in using PET scanning to diagnose CTE in the living, but the work is still preliminary.

Dr. Douglas Smith, director of the Center for Brain Injury and Repair and a professor of medicine at the University of Pennsylvania, told me in an interview that despite the growing body of literature about CTE, it is far from fully understood. "We're at the starting line. Right now CTE is neither a psychiatric diagnosis nor a neuropathological diagnosis," he says. "We don't have a clinical definition for CTE. No criteria have been developed to diagnose it. So this term is almost ahead of itself."

Pathologically, he says, CTE looks a lot like Alzheimer's disease. New PET imaging is making it possible to look for tau protein or amyloid. But the question remains whether the person who exhibits uncharacteristic behavior has CTE or a TBI or a combination of both. "You definitely need your frontal lobe for impulsive behavior management," Smith says. "In severe TBI, yes, it's not uncommon that someone is combative, but one person's aggression is different from another's. Can someone change personalities? Absolutely. Can they become more impulsive or disinhibited? Yes."

The criminal court would not decide whether Corwin Brown suffered from CTE or whether the condition led to his violent behavior. In June 2012 he pleaded guilty but mentally ill to felony confinement and domestic battery. During his appearance before Judge Miller, Brown's other attorney, Mike Tuszynski, said that his client remembered some but not all of the events that led to the police standoff outside his house that ended with Brown shooting himself in the stomach. Brown admitted to confining his wife inside their house and hitting her in the head with his arm, causing bruising. He also admitted to becoming upset after she took away his car keys. But Brown's lawyer did not push him to offer many more details. The results of the mental health evaluations were not publicly released or discussed.

During the hearing, Judge Miller asked Brown if he was in treatment and was taking medication. Brown said yes, he was.

"Do you know what medication you are on?" she asked.

Brown said he was unable to remember.

"Do you know what it's for?" she asked.

"Psychosis," he answered.

Melissa Brown told the judge that her husband's mental health had been deteriorating for a while. Chief deputy prosecutor Ken Cotter said he normally would seek prison time, but after talking with Brown's wife and doctors, he felt the plea agreement was the best choice.

Stepping back from his original position, defense attorney William Stanley did not, after all, suggest to Judge Miller that Brown's brain injuries were factors in his actions that day. The judge gave

Brown a suspended four-year sentence and placed him on probation. She said sending him to prison would do further harm to him and his family. She ordered him to continue counseling and taking the prescribed medications as part of his probation. She also told him that he could not own a gun.

Brown gave a tearful apology in court. His wife handed him a tissue and rubbed his arm. "I have a long way to go," he said. "It's disappointing I put you guys in this situation."

After the hearing, outside the courthouse, Stanley said Brown's head injuries were no longer an issue. "I think the real issue before the court today was what was best for the community, what was best for the family, and what was best for him," he said. "I didn't want to cloud it with any discussions about the perils of playing football and concussions or anything else we read about. If that's an issue, it will come up later on."

Four months later Corwin Brown, represented by two attorneys in Miami, joined the class action lawsuit against the NFL. More than five thousand players accused the league of hiding information about the dangers of concussions. As regards Brown, the suit claimed that while playing in the NFL, he sustained mild TBI caused by concussive and subconcussive impacts and that the league allowed him to return to the field too soon after his injuries, never telling him that he risked severe and permanent brain damage. His lawyers stated that he suffered from headaches, anxiety, severe depression, and suicidal thoughts and that he was also at heightened risk of developing further adverse neurological symptoms.

In 2015 the NFL settled the lawsuit. The settlement, estimated at about a billion dollars, would cover more than twenty thousand retired players for the next sixty-five years and would pay them up to $5 million each, depending on their neurological conditions.

If football players—from high school to the pros—are legally recognized as being at risk of developing CTE, could CTE become a brain defense for those in trouble with the law? Two years after the Corwin Brown incident, Titus Young, a former NFL wide receiver with the Detroit Lions, was charged with sixteen criminal counts, including burglary and fleeing police in Southern California. His father told *USA Today* that Titus was "sort of uncontrollable" and the family had been unable to help him. Richard Young said Titus has "had a problem since his concussion," though he did not indicate when the injury occurred. "The CAT scan shows that," Richard said.

Richard Young may have had good reason to think that brain damage led his son to allegedly commit a string of felonies. Other football players had also seemingly lost their way. Junior Seau, a Hall of Famer who played twenty seasons in the NFL from 1990 to 2009 as a linebacker, was charged with assaulting a girlfriend, gambled away much of his fortune, and survived driving his car off a cliff. He fatally shot himself in the chest in May 2012. After his death, tests showed Seau had CTE. Seven months later, in December, Jovan Belcher, a starting linebacker for the Kansas City Chiefs, shot and killed his girlfriend, Kasandra Perkins, then killed himself. An autopsy found that Belcher had also likely suffered from CTE.

Some researchers believe that such acts of domestic violence may be rooted in TBI. Dr. Ann McKee told the HBO program *Real Sports* that she and her colleagues found lesions in the anterior temporal lobes of many retired football players, which could cause them to lose control over anger and other emotions. The 2013 study, conducted with the Sports Legacy Institute, found that more than half of the thirty-three players had never been violent prior to sustaining head injuries. McKee cited CTE as a possible cause of violent behavior among players. "There are plenty of variables that can lead to it," she said. "But we know CTE leads to a short fuse. These guys used to be fine. . . . But now these guys are assaultive, they're overreacting."

For Titus Young, whose father believed concussions contributed to his behavior, a Los Angeles judge offered the former player compassion and an opportunity for drug and alcohol treatment as an alternative to prison. The judge sentenced him to five years of probation and one year of inpatient treatment at rehab center.

Daniel Antonius, an assistant professor of psychiatry at the University at Buffalo, is not convinced that the science has demonstrated a direct link between CTE and aggression, violence, depression, or suicide. CTE currently has no value in a courtroom setting, he says. He is the lead author of a 2014 article that challenges the assumptions that CTE causes a host of behavioral issues, because of the absence of research on the subject, especially longitudinal, prospective studies. Moreover, as Douglas Smith at Penn says, there are no definitive or widely accepted diagnostic criteria for identifying those at risk for CTE. Antonius argues that to show a causal relationship between CTE and behavioral changes, the phenomenon must be systematically studied in a large sample of athletes—in both contact and noncontact sports—over a long period of time, ideally starting early in their careers.

The peer-reviewed literature on CTE, he notes, consists primarily of case review studies about specific individuals and postmortem research. But case studies, while illuminating and important, can't be used to establish clinical criteria for diagnosing a condition. Continual media coverage of athletes being linked to CTE pathology has often led to premature conclusions about the relationship between CTE and behavioral problems. "Despite the widely held perception that CTE is linked with changes in personality, mood, and behavior, there is a dearth of research addressing these behavioral health features of CTE," Antonius said.

Antonius's paper is part of a long-term research project that involves working with former professional football and hockey players, among others, to see what happens to their brains and mental health as they age. The goal is to help them and their families identify treatment and counseling opportunities. Several factors, says Antonius, obscure the relationship between CTE and behavior. For example, those at risk of acquiring CTE also belong to groups that commonly are exposed to potentially stress-inducing experiences such as competitive sports, war and combat, and serious medical illnesses. Many of these athletes showed aggressive behavior before they experienced head trauma. NFL players are tough guys who play a violent game in which they are lauded for their fierceness.

"The evidence for a causal link, at this point, is still up in the air," Antonius tells me. He's concerned that criminal defense lawyers, in blaming CTE for their clients' behavior, are overreaching. "Is CTE really the cause behind some of these behaviors, when we're not even taking into account who these people are?" he says. "What are their personalities? It takes a certain personality to play football and to play football in the NFL."

Peter A. Carfagna, who teaches at Cleveland-Marshall College of Law and Case Western Reserve University School of Law, says the use of concussion injuries as a legal defense for professional football players doesn't work. The biggest barrier remains the inability to diagnose CTE in a living brain. "For now, the courts must rely upon psychological profiles and symptoms of those committing the crimes, often reducing these proceedings to a battle of expert witnesses," he says. "Until there are more reliable methods of diagnosing CTE in living persons, this defense will not be complete, but only mitigating."

But Carfagna does see a future for CTE with advances in technology: "I expect that over the next five to ten years, maybe sooner, CTE will become more reliable as a criminal defense." And the effects of CTE on behavior, he believes, do have a place in the courtroom: "Anything that diminishes capacity and renders a person unable to control themselves and their actions needs to be discussed within our criminal justice system." But we must also "ensure that no one takes advantage of using CTE as a defense to get away with a crime."

Nathaniel Fujita didn't get away with anything. A jury dismissed his lawyer's contention that he experienced a psychotic episode that may have been induced by CTE. He was found guilty in the murder of Lauren Astley and sentenced to life without parole. Fujita's uncle, attorney George Mattingly, said afterward that his nephew's verdict was morally wrong—that he needed treatment, not incarceration. On the television news program *48 Hours,* Mattingly said Nathaniel suffered from mental illness. His nephew had once led a life of promise, but his behavior had begun to change long before the murder occurred. His nephew, he said, had not been in his right mind.

I called Mattingly to ask him to elaborate, but he hesitated because the case was on appeal. Instead, he wanted to talk about the insanity defense, which he says never seems to work. "There are many psychiatrists and neuroscientists who will tell you that some people have more free will than others," he told me.

I asked Mattingly about the claim that his nephew had CTE and how it might have affected him. "It was part of the case," he said. "The symptoms vary and the symptoms that arise can mimic those of bipolar disorder or schizophrenia, and they can manifest in major depression. But when you say someone suffers from CTE, you have a problem. Unfortunately, it's not possible as of yet to diagnose CTE in a reliable way. You cannot prove CTE in a living person. You're left with the symptoms."

How was his nephew doing in prison? "His mental health is not good," he said. "Let me leave it at that."

Whether CTE can be conclusively linked to aggressive behavior or mental health problems or serve as a credible criminal defense remains a contentious issue, with no resolution in sight. Research into its causes and effects continues to be met with skepticism, depending on who's funding it. In the spring of 2016, less than a year after the NFL settled the class action lawsuit, the league got slammed by a congressional report alleging it had improperly tried to influence government research it had promised to fund. The charges were laid out in a ninety-one-page report issued by Democratic members of the House Energy and Commerce Committee. The report noted that in 2012, under intense criticism for its handling of the concussion controversy, the NFL had agreed to donate thirty million dollars in unrestricted funds to concussion-related research. But the NFL pressured the National Institutes of Health to steer away from a sixteen-million-dollar project by a group of Boston University researchers who were among the league's harshest critics and instead give the money to members of the NFL's own committee on brain injuries. While a league spokesman denied the allegations, the congressional report found that the NFL's actions "fit a long-standing pattern of attempts to influence the scientific understanding of the consequences of repeated head trauma."

CHAPTER 19

The Future of Neurolaw and the Brain Defense

In a basement on the campus of Vanderbilt University Medical Center in Nashville, graduate student Matt Ginther is briefing a young woman who's about to lie down in a darkened room to have her brain scanned. Ginther explains to the twenty-two-year-old that she's going to be reading various scenarios that describe one person causing harm to another. She'll then be prompted to decide whether to punish the person doing the harm. If so, then she must decide how severely. Was the harm intentional, accidental, or something in between? The study is intended to detect those regions in the brain that become active when the test subjects choose the punishment they deem appropriate for the scenario.

The woman is to press buttons to make her responses. "That allows us to pin down the time when they are making decisions, which is critical for imaging," Ginther tells me as we see structural images of the woman's brain appear on a glowing screen in an adjacent room.

He has to be efficient while using the new machine, a Philips Achieva scanner, which costs five hundred dollars an hour to rent. It's rated at three teslas of magnetic power, a force so strong that wearing a watch or jewelry or holding any loose metallic object while inside the room is not recommended as it could break free and rocket toward the magnet.

At the control panel, Ginther will be able to view images on three screens. The machine is set to take thirty-four cross-section images of the woman's brain every two seconds. The raw data will upload to a server that has a computer program designed to smooth out the images spatially, which eventually will be color-coded to illustrate brain activity. The final images will show areas of the woman's brain where neurons were activated when she was making decisions about punishing someone.

She lies on her back in the scanner for nearly an hour, viewing various narratives on a mirrored screen and pressing buttons that rate how severely she wants to punish the hypothetical person for harming the other. The scenarios include descriptions of people getting injured or killed with power tools, falling while putting up Christmas lights, getting run over by a camping trailer, and being poisoned by eating Thai peanut sauce. The person who causes the harm has varying levels of intent, which the woman must evaluate. Her responses will indicate whether she engages emotion in her decision making.

When the test is finished, Ginther pulls a twenty-dollar bill from his wallet, hands it to the woman, and thanks her for her time. He is among a new generation of researchers who represent the future of law and neuroscience. This program at Vanderbilt combines graduate degrees in both fields, and Ginther is the first student to enroll. It's one of two such programs in the country (the other is at the University of Wisconsin–Madison), but may be a sign of things to come, as more universities recognize the melding of these disciplines and their importance in helping to shape future research. Programs dedicated to law and neuroscience have been formed at about a dozen colleges and universities across the country.

The Vanderbilt program attracts students like Ginther who are eager to explore the legal, moral, and philosophical questions that arise with the use of neuroscience. Over lunch at a sushi restaurant near campus, he tells me he's always been interested in human behavior but only recently considered combining it with law. "We are a society of neurological constructs," he says. "And I'm interested in understanding the human condition by understanding the brain. At lot of what we do in public policy is about what we consider fair. Why do we have this intuition of what's fair compared to the person next to you?"

Owen Jones, the head of the MacArthur Foundation Research Network on Law and Neuroscience and a professor of law and biology at Vanderbilt, is co-director of the joint degree program. Jones is an easygoing, friendly academic who speaks in clear, accessible language, having authored many papers that introduce the complexities of neuroscience to nonscientists. He greets me in his office, an expansive room with floor-to-ceiling bookcases on one side, a small sofa on the other, and stacks of papers and books across the floor that require nimble navigation to get across the room. Posted on one wall are data from dozens of studies that are under way among research network members. Jones explains that the research network is interested in much more than analyzing whether neuroscience can or should be used to excuse criminal behavior. "We took the view that the legal system already was becoming enamored with neuroscience, and we thought: How can we separate the wheat from the chaff?"

A critical problem has been the misinterpretation of the science and what can be gleaned from it. For years, lawyers have been trying to apply scientific data, collected from groups of people, to individual cases, which Jones says is a fundamental flaw. Can the results of a study that shows people with frontal lobe damage tend to exhibit violent behavior be used to prove that one defendant who has frontal lobe damage committed a crime because of it? "It's very difficult to figure out how science relates to a particular case," Jones says. The lawyer for serial killer Randy Kraft showed the jury PET scans during the sentencing hearing to show that his client suffered frontal lobe dysfunction compared to a group of control subjects. But the jury found they proved nothing. And to underscore that such images really can't prove someone has violent tendencies, the neuroscientist Adrian Raine found that a PET scan of his own brain looked like Kraft's. Jones and his colleagues are working to develop guidelines for properly using such data.

The research network also continues to fund studies to investigate, by observing brain activity, how and why people behave the way they do. The research is designed not to arm lawyers with brain scans and excuses for their clients but to illuminate how we decide to punish people, how we can rehabilitate them, and how we might create a fair system of justice by understanding how people process information when weighing whether to commit a crime. These studies may or may not have practical courtroom applications, but the research is shifting away from questions that focus on blame.

Other neuroscientists are taking this approach as well. One of them is David Eagleman, who has a lot on his mind as he hustles down the hallway at Baylor College of Medicine. He's just returned to Houston from London, after completing voiceovers for his upcoming PBS series on the brain. He's facing deadlines for four books in various stages of completion, directing a dozen or so scientific studies, mentoring graduate students, running a neuroscience research lab, and on this sunny and humid spring day, arriving just in time to give a lunchtime talk.

About two dozen students are seated in a lecture hall and eating free slices of pizza as they listen to Eagleman discuss one of his programs, the Initiative on Neuroscience and Law. Eagleman, who is in his midforties, could easily pass for a student himself with his full head of black hair, young face, casual jeans, and tight black T-shirt. He paces as he tells the group of students that his program is seeking to use neuroscience to shape social policy and create a more effective criminal justice system. He's not interested in using neuroscience to assess whether criminals should be blamed for their deeds, he explains; nor does he believe anyone should use the science to excuse or to diminish responsibility. His work is about using science to build smarter sentencing policies, to prevent criminals from becoming repeat offenders, and to bring mental health treatment or therapy to those who need it. Neuroscience really doesn't have a place in the courtroom as it's now being used, he tells the students, but it can have value in shaping the criminal justice system.

As the U.S. prison population increases, he explains, there's a great need to reduce incarceration and create better opportunities for rehabilitation—and neuroscience can help. "We're trying to develop an evidence-based, forward-looking legal system," he says. Currently one-third of prisoners have some type of mental illness. Many don't belong behind bars, in his view, and he proposes finding the right place for them. "It's not that people get off the hook," he says. "We still need to keep society safe. But this is about routing people through the system in a way that leads to meaningful rehabilitation instead of mass incarceration."

Eagleman's lab was awarded a grant from the National Science Foundation for a study of criminal behavior using big data methods. As part of his Initiative on Law and Neuroscience, he and his students have been building the Neurolaw Criminal Record Database, which includes more than thirty million crime records they obtained through

Freedom of Information requests. The group will sort and analyze demographic information and characteristics of crime and criminals to look for trends. This large-scale data analysis, Eagleman says, has the potential to reveal patterns that will better inform presentencing decisions.

Later that Wednesday afternoon at Baylor, the Neurolaw Group, composed of three Harvard Law School graduates, a chemical engineer, a forensic psychologist, and students in electrical engineering and computer science, gathers for its weekly meeting in the Eagleman lab. On this day the students are discussing an app they've designed to measure whether a person convicted of a crime is at risk of becoming a repeat offender, and how serious that risk might be. It's an interactive program for a computer tablet that measures a person's propensity for risk taking through a series of neurological tests. The goal is to cast light on the relationship between decision-making traits and the decision to commit (or not commit) a crime. Research has found that lack of self-control is a strong and consistent predictor of criminal behavior.

The computer tablet app uses a series of standard neurological tests to measure empathy, aggression, planning, and risk taking. The "Reading the Mind Through the Eyes" test measures empathy by asking subjects to read the emotions of a person in a photo. "The Balloon Analogue Risk Task" measures a subject's risky behavior by asking him to inflate an animated balloon as far as he's willing before it pops: the bigger the inflation, the more points the person receives, but if the balloon pops, the subject receives no points. Eagleman says these tests promise to yield a deeper understanding of the interplay between deficits in impulse control and aggression and the opportunistic and reckless nature of crime. Improved knowledge of individual differences in these areas, he suggests, could inform policies aimed at crime prevention. Eventually, the group hopes to use such knowledge at sentencing hearings to demonstrate the likelihood that a convicted criminal would reoffend or to show how much promise he or she has for rehabilitation. The group has already been testing the program with detainees at the Harris County Community Supervision and Corrections Department in Houston.

Developing programs like the risk assessment app fits right into the mission of Eagleman's neurolaw program. "There are many contact points in the intersection of neuroscience and law," he says over coffee at the medical center. "There are so many places where defense lawyers are just trying stuff out in a field where there is something really important going on." For Eagleman, assigning blame is less important than predicting how likely a criminal is to break the law again. His vision is to create a system that accounts for people's individual characteristics rather than imposing prescribed sentences on them. The law already recognizes that some people are less likely than others to repeat the crimes they committed, like crimes of passion and crimes that aren't premeditated. In Eagleman's new system, there would still be guidelines. "You have a minimum—if you murder someone, there is a minimum of time [served], but a range of punishment," he says. "But if you have a psychopath or someone who has problems, it's not good to put him on the street. The thing about psychopathy is that there are no known rehabilitation strategies."

The choices we make are always connected to our neural circuitry, Eagleman tells me, so there's no meaningful way to separate our biology from our behavior—whether you're a psychopath or a so-called normal person. "I think neuroscience has a hard time determining whether we have free will or not," he says. "It's a tougher question to answer than some people pretend it is. If we have free will at all, it's a bit player in the system to the extent that asking the question of blameworthiness is essentially meaningless." The complex interaction of genetics and environment gives people different perspectives, personalities, and capacities for decision making. "You'll never be able to disentangle all the genetic and experiential differences that led a guy to be in court."

Rather than try to introduce this complexity into the current legal system, Eagleman envisions specialized courts that have on-call experts in mental health, drug addiction, and juvenile decision making. Such courts would allow judges and lawyers to better address their specific needs. Many of these proposals are spelled out in a Neurocompatibility Index, a term Eagleman coined in a 2012 paper that proposed a shakeup of the current system. The index is a measure of how compatible a criminal justice system is with the lessons of modern neuroscience. It includes criteria such as understanding mental illness, evaluating methods of rehabilitation, sentencing based on risk assessment, and other factors that Eagleman says can contribute to a brain-compatible system that prizes fairness and long-term crime prevention over harsh yet inconsequential punishment. "Where are the really important places where you can make social policy compatible with science and compatible with what we know?" he says.

Eagleman, a best-selling author of fiction and nonfiction and, more recently, television host, tells me that he got interested in the criminal justice system thanks to his father, a retired forensic psychiatrist who had examined and assessed serial killers. His father told him, he says, about a serial killer who had no remorse, explaining that you can't compare people like that with regular folks. "You just can't put yourself in other people's shoes 'neurally' speaking," Eagleman says his father told him. "We like to think we know what it's like to step into someone else's shoes, but it's illusory. If you sit with a guy like that for two or three hours, it's clear. He's running on different algorithms."

Poor impulse control, Eagleman believes, is the hallmark characteristic among most people in prison. Their actions supersede their ability to make reasonable choices about consequences "because the brain operates like a team of rivals." In other words, brain processes compete to control good and bad behavior, like the devil and an angel on each shoulder. The challenge is to find ways to regulate negative impulsive behavior consciously.

In his lab, Eagleman has been experimenting with different methods to help people resist the desire to succumb to their cravings and perhaps put the brakes on impulsive behavior. He's created a program to give the frontal lobes practice in squelching impulsive behavior, a method he calls the "prefrontal workout." It operates very much like biofeedback, in which people learn to use their thoughts to influence body functions such as heart rate. The prefrontal workout uses real-time brain imaging so people can watch their brains work and learn how to control that neural activity through their thoughts. For example, suppose a smoker wants to quit. During brain imaging, he looks at pictures of cigarettes and feels the craving. The images shows which brain regions are activated. As he looks at more cigarette pictures, he sees a vertical bar on a computer screen that represents his level of craving. The smoker tries to suppress the urges, using his thoughts, and when he succeeds, the bar goes down. If he is able to make the bar go all the way down, it means he recruited frontal circuitry to suppress the activity in the networks involved in impulsive craving. Practicing making the bar go down over and over would strengthen the frontal circuits. The ultimate goal, Eagleman says, is to use the method with prisoners who are approaching release, so they learn to control their criminal impulses.

This is the important work of neuroscience in the legal system, Eagleman argues—not brain scans introduced as evidence in the courtroom. Lawyers who try to make neuroscience part of their defense, he believes, are working against themselves. "Lawyers are just looking for excuses," he says. "I get a lot of calls from lawyers asking if I'll do a brain scan on their clients to see if there's something wrong. I don't do it." Most lawbreakers have no obvious, measurable biological problems—they freely choose their deeds and misdeeds. Neuroscience, Eagleman believes, has in many ways complicated, rather than illuminated, the question of culpability.

Others share Eagleman's view that neuroscience can and should be used not to assign blame but to redefine society's concepts of guilt and punishment. Joshua D. Greene, an assistant professor of psychology at Harvard University, and Jonathan D. Cohen, a psychology professor and director of the neuroscience program at Princeton University, designed an experiment they hoped would illuminate how people's brains react when making moral decisions—and whether these choices spring from emotional or reasoned responses. The study, which was published in 2001, used a well-known moral dilemma known as the trolley problem, which asks subjects to make a complicated, gut-twisting life-and-death decision. The scenario is this: a trolley is moving toward five people who will surely die if you don't intervene. You have the option of hitting a switch that will redirect the train to another track, where one person stands in the way and will get killed. Most people will choose to save the five people at the cost of one getting killed. In another scenario, the subject is standing with an obese person on a bridge over the tracks as the trolley heads toward five people who will get run over. The only way to save the five people is to push the obese man onto the tracks, where his body will stop the train from hitting the five. In this test, most people do not think it's okay to push the man over and kill him.

For their study, Greene (who was a graduate student at Princeton at the time) and Cohen scanned people's brains as they made their decision, to see which regions became engaged. They found that in the first scenario, the most active area was the dorsolateral prefrontal cortex, an area associated with problem solving and self-control. In the second scenario, the scans showed greater activation in the emotional centers of the brain—the subjects were debating whether to intentionally harm another. This finding suggests that even when people are rational, there are forces at work beyond their control, a struggle between emotional and cognitive responses that challenges the idea that they have free will. If we accept that our brains may drive us to make decisions we're not consciously guiding, Greene and Cohen argue, then our criminal justice system would benefit by shifting away from one that punishes to one that focuses on rehabilitation.

In 2004, following their study utilizing the trolley dilemma, Greene and Cohen published a paper in which they predicted that neuroscience will likely transform the law, not by undermining its current assumptions, but by transforming people's intuitions about free will and responsibility. Like Eagleman, they envision a shift away from a criminal justice system that metes out punishment for retribution toward one that is more progressive and "consequentialist," or concerned about promoting the welfare of society. Neuroscience, as it progresses, will dismantle people's commonsense view of free will, replacing it with the idea that many of our actions are not entirely under our own control, and that we should take that reality into account when judging and sentencing criminals and do so humanely.

I asked Greene to explain what he meant by *humanely*. "Humane treatment means that we regard punishment as a necessary evil, not as an aggrieved society's path to emotional satisfaction and 'true justice,'" he said. "We should punish only to the extent that the punishment causes people—both the person punished and others who may be deterred—to behave better. Punishment that makes it harder for people to return to society as law-abiding, productive citizens should be eliminated—even if it feels good and right. Punishment that destroys poor communities rather than helping them advance should be eliminated."

Did he think that if we understood the underlying mechanisms of criminal behavior, we might punish criminals differently? "We could recognize that all people are ultimately the products of forces beyond their control. This doesn't mean that people don't make choices, including very bad choices," he answered. "This doesn't mean that punishment isn't often necessary to induce people to make better choices. But the idea is that, if you take any bad choice and trace its causes all the way back, you get to critical factors that are beyond the person's control—both genetic and environmental. This doesn't mean the person is not responsible—it means that the person is not *ultimately* responsible. And I think this recognition of lack of ultimate responsibility makes it easier to take a more pragmatic, less moralistic, approach to the problems of criminal justice."

Whether neuroscience can be useful in determining how to punish criminals is also a question that researchers are asking at Vanderbilt. Owen Jones and his colleagues are interested in learning how jurors and judges assess criminal intent and culpability and how that affects the way they punish people—the question at the heart of Matt Ginther's research study. Ginther is trying to better understand the emotional reactions that go into punishing someone based on the perpetrator's perceived blameworthiness. "When it comes to evaluating the intentions of others, and the culpability of others, we're seeing the theory of mind network at work," he tells me. "It's the concept of taking on the thoughts of others, the idea of putting yourself in someone else's shoes. When people are actually evaluating the culpability of the actor, the theory of mind is actively engaged."

Such research may eventually be useful for judges who "are making decisions in arbitrary ways," Ginther says. "The point is, why do we punish in the way we do, and what are the biological underpinnings? How can we make the decision process better? This [research] is more likely to have an impact on educating judges about the nature of their mental processes."

Since 2013 Vanderbilt researchers have been scanning the brains of real judges to examine their punishment decision-making process so that they can compare it with a similarly educated population. "Why are we driven to do certain things? Is it our emotions that drive us to do it? Is our drive to punish the same as our drive for food and water? Is there a biological imperative?" Ginther asks. "To what extent are our punishment decisions the best ones we can make? When you start making people think about these things, it affects the decisions they make."

Educating judges about developments in law and neuroscience is one of the research network's most important missions, Jones tells me. Since its inception, the network has been offering programs and conferences for judges to give them crash courses on neuroscience, such as one for a group of federal judges. Among those who attended was Mark W. Bennett, a U.S. district court judge of the Northern District of Iowa, based in Sioux City. Bennett's interest in neuroscience intensified after he heard an appeal from a death row inmate whose lawyer failed to present neuropsychological information during the trial. It might have provided a better understanding of the defendant, which could have been used as mitigating evidence during sentencing. Bennett granted a new trial on the grounds of ineffective assistance of counsel. "They missed a lot of stuff, and that kind of heightened my interest in neuroscience," Bennett tells me. "As a judge, this issue would pop up [in my courtroom] every once in a while."

Bennett became particularly interested in the neuroscience of addiction because addicts frequently appear in his courtroom, and he struggles with how to sentence them in ways that are meaningful and productive. For example, one woman had had multiple drug-related arrests due to her addiction. "I understand her brain works differently because of her addiction—she's not acting like a rational human being," Bennett says. "We have a hard time understanding why addicts don't act like we do."

The annual meeting of the Society for Neuroscience is the world's largest gathering of neuroscientists. For the 2015 conference, on a fall weekend in Chicago, more than 27,000 people are registered at the McCormick Place convention center near Lake Michigan. Here they'll attend lectures and seminars, present their work, and mingle among like-minded people from around the world. The exhibition hall is a vast maze of booths and displays, banners, giant flat screens, and vendors selling neuro-related products and services. Companies are pitching brain scanners, microscopes, hardware for housing laboratory rats and mice, electrophysiology equipment, and all manner of instruments and tools for exploring and analyzing the brain. There's even a gallery of artists whose work celebrates the brain: photos and paintings depicting colorful images of neural networks and jewelry in designs inspired by brain anatomy.

This is the heart of the neuroscientific community, where most research addresses disease, injury, and aspects of cognition and behavior. The extent and variety of scientific papers being presented is staggering. Row after row of posters and displays explain recent studies on addiction, aging, decision making, degenerative disorders, depression, learning, memory, Parkinson's, Alzheimer's, spinal cord injuries, emotions, exercise—no human endeavor, process, or characteristic, it seems, is not being studied by neuroscientists.

Yet the opening keynote speaker on the first day of the conference is a federal judge. Judge Jed Rakoff, of the Southern District of New York, will speak on "Law and Neuroscience: Strange Bedfellows." He steps into a cavernous auditorium, his image projected on three giant screens. "I feel a little intimidated being here," he says, adding that he studied English, not science, as an undergraduate before going on to law. But he wants to make something clear right away. "The attitude of judges toward neuroscience is one of ambivalence and skepticism," he says. "You ask them about the hippocampus, they say it's something at the zoo."

Rakoff tells the assembled scientists that history has given judges reason for caution. During the last century, the law embraced science in ways that were inhumane and harmful and were eventually discredited. Eugenics, the theory that humans could employ selective breeding and sterilization to improve the genetic makeup of a new breed of people, was a supposedly scientifically supported theory once practiced in the United States. Lobotomies were accepted in the medical community for years, and courts ordered the procedure for people whether they wanted them or not. In the 1990s so-called recovered memories led to people being convicted of crimes, often child sexual abuse, on shoddy evidence with no solid scientific basis. "I use these stories to explain why judges have great hesitation accepting this kind of evidence," Rakoff says. "Neuroscience is not yet at the stage where it can be introduced with individual cases with much scientific validity."

While he's skeptical that neuroscience is a game-changing force in the judicial system, Rakoff says science can still play "a fantastic role" in sentencing of drug addicts. He also sees value in better understanding of the adolescent brain, in deciding how to handle juvenile defendants. But in the end, he says, judges are cautious about neuroscience "because we've been burned in the past."

"The worst thing that can happen with neuroscience is that it gets into the courtroom before it's ready," he says. "There is a communication barrier between lawyers and scientists. We need to learn to speak the same language."

Some lawyers and scientists are certainly trying to communicate. Judith Edersheim, a doctor *and* a lawyer, founded the Center for Law, Brain and Behavior at Massachusetts General Hospital in Boston with Bruce H. Price, MD. Edersheim's medical specialty is psychiatry, and for years she's performed mental health evaluations of criminal defendants and testified in competency hearings. She found herself increasingly frustrated with lawyers who sought her out to find ways to excuse their clients' behavior and asked her to testify using a brain defense. "I finally said enough is enough. I got a call from a defense lawyer asking me to say something completely outrageous about a defendant," she tells me. "And I knew that I would say no and he would find someone to say yes. And that needed addressing."

The clash between expert witnesses trying to translate—or extrapolate—science to answer questions of law and judges and juries unschooled in these areas is at the heart of the problem. "How can we make neuroscience speak the language of the law? And how can we make the law understand the neuroscience in a cogent and applicable way?" Edersheim says.

The group brings together leaders in law and neuroscience to tackle the contentious issues. Edersheim is in the unique position of understanding both how a lawyer thinks and how a doctor—a psychiatrist—thinks. "Now I'm going to put on my lawyer hat. The doctors all faint when I do this, but then I talk to them in their own language," she says. "Many of them are offended by this criminal defense tendency to pluck what's new in science and move it into the courtroom very quickly, but that's their job. Lawyers are supposed to zealously defend their clients," she says. "You will be subject to sanctions, reversible error, and just be a rotten defense lawyer if you don't zealously defend your client. And what that means is that the arguments that might be exculpatory for your defendant really ought to be something that you're paying attention to."

For some defense lawyers, that means anything goes, but "that runs completely counter to the ethos of a scientist. The ethos of a scientist is to be careful and measured," Edersheim says. "In what other field do you have a great discovery and spend the entire last paragraph saying what its limitations are? 'We did this and not that, we can't apply this too far because it's preliminary, our threshold was this, the confounders might be that.' It's what makes science so wonderful and so inapplicable."

The result has been a culture clash. "There are always lawyers who are perhaps less responsible than others and scientists who are less responsible than others, and when those two meet, the cases come out poorly. Some experts are unscrupulous. Some lawyers are unscrupulous. [Dr. Price and I] really wanted to make sure that bad science wasn't imported into the law to create bad law."

But preventing bad law is not the center's sole mission. Edersheim believes neuroscience has shown its value to the criminal justice system in many ways. "We understand that neuroscience is now corroborating psychological, behavioral, and commonsense notions of how juveniles are different from grownups. It is tremendously helpful to have that added value of neuroscience," she says. "And I think that's what neuroscience is going to do for the subject of self-control. We're beginning to see—not just in criminal law but in behavioral economics—that why people make the decisions they make is a very fruitful avenue of inquiry, and you can begin to parse out different components of good and bad decision making. And that is going to inform the law over the next fifty years."

While the future of law and neuroscience is a serious endeavor to people like Edersheim and her colleagues, popular neuroscience has taken some hard knocks. In their 2013 book *Brainwashed: The Seductive Appeal of Mindless Neuroscience,* psychiatrist Sally Satel and psychologist Scott O. Lilienfeld argued that the value of neuroscience—including its use in the criminal justice system—has been greatly exaggerated, and the science itself misapplied. Studies that claim to show what parts of the brain "light up" when people make decisions, fall in love, or feel pleasure are used (or misused) by "neuromarketers" and hyped in breathless media stories. Neuroscience, the authors point out, must be accurately translated into concepts that have meaning within the law. "I'm personally very skeptical that it will be able to resolve the major legal questions," Satel tells me. "Most of the time it's rhetorical. If someone has so much brain damage that it's influencing their capacity to think and reason well or control themselves, it's probably pretty obvious. You don't need a brain scan for it."

Satel observes that "neuromania," as she calls this love affair with neuroscience, seems to have died down during the past decade and may be leveling off. "That hysteria has really subsided," she says. "It's conceivable that the neuroscience will be promising. I don't have a principled objection to it. Does it work, and does it work better than we're doing now? Right now the answer is no. It's possible it may someday. But I don't think it can tell us anything we can't already get from established means."

Satel argues that scientists and medical professionals can't know, except possibly in extreme cases of brain injury or damage, whether a brain abnormality is relevant or is linked to specific criminal behavior. Even the best imaging techniques can't prove that a person's brain activity—or lack of it—in a particular region means they fail to meet the legal definition of responsibility, rationality, or intent.

Like many others writing in the field, Satel uses the Herbert Weinstein case as a cautionary tale against the misuse of neuroscience in criminal cases, calling his cyst "an impressive-looking, though ultimately irrelevant brain defect." She tells me she's not dismissive of neuroscience altogether—it's how it's interpreted that matters. "We've learned a ton, but the translation domain is really modest," she says. "They're always learning about little parts of the system, but how it all comes together and whether you can use it in practical ways—I don't think anyone is talking about any great breakthroughs."

Whatever the breakthroughs, the burgeoning field of neuroscience and its relationship to society has attracted enough attention that President Barack Obama created an advisory panel that includes some of the nation's leaders in medicine, science, ethics, religion, law, and engineering as part of his BRAIN Initiative (Brain Research through Advancing Innovative Neurotechnologies). In 2015 the Presidential Commission for the Study of Bioethical Issues issued a report called "Gray Matters, Topics at the Intersection of Neuroscience, Ethics and Society" that includes a section dedicated to neuroscience and the legal system. Like Satel, the report warns of exaggeration and hype about neuroscience's ability to resolve complex legal questions. Nita Farahany at Duke University, a member of the commission and one of the lead authors of the section, believes its value will be in shaping criminal justice policy rather than in its application to individuals' criminal behavior. She points to how studies on adolescent brain development played a role in eliminating the death penalty and life without parole for juveniles. "Group-level data is the more promising aspect," she says. "It will be a while before neuroscience can tell us about an individual."

Owen Jones, along with colleagues at the MacArthur Research Network, offered the commission their take. They predicted that lawyers will likely increase the use of neuroscience in the courtroom and called the current state of affairs "messy, un-systemized, under theorized, under investigated, and—if left unattended—likely to get worse." They recommended educating judges and others and creating a system of best practices.

Stephen Morse, a member of the research network and a professor at the University of Pennsylvania, has been not only educating judges but offering his view to lawyers, policy makers, and students of neuroscience. The Weinstein case, he argues, is a glaring example of the misuse of neuroscience in the courtroom. It was, at its core, an insanity defense, concerning a person's mental state and behavior. Mental disorders are defined entirely by behavior, he says, not by brain scans, "so the question is always going to be—always—does whatever clinical or scientific information you're trying to use help you answer the behavioral question or not?" A person's mental state is based on observation and some clinical testing. So, he asks, does a brain image offer anything to help diagnose a mental disorder? "The answer is it does not." To underscore his point, he says that the *Diagnostic and Statistical Manual of Mental Disorders,* fifth edition, the definitive reference work for mental health professionals, does not include biomarkers or references to brain scans to diagnose mental illness.

In many of his lectures on law and neuroscience, Morse lays out the facts of the Weinstein case and asks audience members how they, as jury members, would view his brain defense. In a recent talk before forty federal judges, he presented the evidence in the Weinstein case, then asked the judges to vote guilty or not guilty. "Every judge thought he was guilty," Morse says. He then asked the judges how many would take into account Weinstein's cyst as a mitigating factor when sentencing him, "About a third raised their hands," Morse said. "I was astonished."

"I said that's not an excusing condition," he told me. "What does it translate into that's a mitigating condition, a genuine mitigating condition? He's got a hole in his head? Not one judge could come up with a bridge theory between that clear pathological, anatomical finding and a behavioral problem that was mitigating."

Had it not been for Weinstein's PET scan, and the judge's decision to allow it as evidence for the defense, the case would have remained largely unknown—just another domestic homicide in a city where hundreds of murders occur every year. I asked Dr. Abass Alavi, the PET scan pioneer who testified on Weinstein's behalf, whether in retrospect he thought he had done the right thing by assisting in his brain defense. Alavi told me that when he got the call from Diarmuid White asking him to perform the PET scan, he listened with an open mind. The case sounded intriguing and seemed to invite a legitimate inquiry by respected scientists, including Antonio Damasio, into the workings of a brain that was impaired in an unusual way. Alavi said he felt strongly about using his scientific research in pursuit of justice. "It's been my view all along that if this works in the clinical setting, it should work for the legal setting," he said. "I know many of my colleagues are against it."

Since the Weinstein case, however, Alavi told me he's witnessed the abuse of the technology within the legal system, as many had predicted. "People who have PET machines for nothing but lawyers who pay for them are misusing the technology," he says. "It's a crisis. As a scientist who has been instrumental in developing this technology to help patients, I feel very bad to see its misuse."

Owen Jones acknowledges that there is misuse, yet he's quite enthusiastic about the future of law and neuroscience. "There's a great cause for optimism that we're learning more," he tells me. "I think all this is putting the spotlight on the vulnerability of the brain. It represents a shift in how we are looking at human beings." Jones is deeply invested in exploring that shift and in educating a new generation of students. He and two colleagues—Jeffrey D. Schall, a professor of neuroscience at Vanderbilt, and Francis X. Shen, a law professor at the University of Minnesota Law School—recently published a book called *Law and Neuroscience,* a nearly eight-hundred-page volume of articles, case studies, and information for teaching law and neuroscience, a subject already offered at more than twenty schools. Theirs may be the most comprehensive textbook in the field. It contains what they consider a historically important case study: Chapter 2, "Individuals: The Case of the Murdering Brain," is dedicated to Herbert Weinstein. "The case illustrates the challenges that lawyers for both the prosecution and defense are likely to face in brain-based criminal defenses," Jones writes. And it raises questions that are still being asked today: "What, exactly, was going on inside Mr. Weinstein's brain and what caused him to murder his wife?"

Neuroscience still can't answer those questions. But decades of research do tell us that damaged brains—"broken brains," if you will—can alter behavior and impair the ability to make sound judgments and rational decisions. In the legal realm, that's not enough for a successful criminal defense. Neuroscience alone cannot absolve someone of committing murder—or any crime—or pinpoint the cause of a single act or demonstrate that someone is legally insane. But accepting that our behavior can be influenced by brain injuries, disease, genetics, and other abnormalities does have a place in our legal system, and neuroscience is an important adjunct that can be used responsibly to support it. The ancient Greek ideal of a justice system that holds people accountable for their actions, yet also strives to understand the mind of the offender, is a worthy model from which to build. Modern science empowers us to evaluate criminal defendants more fully and compassionately, which is not incompatible with holding them responsible or protecting society from those who can do harm. Neuroscience offers opportunities in the criminal justice system that can serve everyone's interests, and its greatest possibilities lie before us.

Acknowledgments

This book would not have been possible without the help, encouragement, and wise counsel of many friends, colleagues, and sources who gave their time and expertise and shared their stories. Thanks to you all for answering my many questions and responding to my e-mails and phone calls as I tried to navigate the complexities of law and neuroscience while telling the human stories intertwined with them. I'm grateful to Joni Weinstein, who provided me with stories about her father, Herbert, along with letters, photographs, articles, tips, and ideas about brain research. Kim Glazer Goldberg revisited a painful subject and generously provided me with information and photos of her mother, Barbara. It's important never to forget the victims and their families when writing about those who caused them such terrible grief.

I'm also indebted to Owen Jones of Vanderbilt University, director of the MacArthur Foundation Research Network on Law and Neuroscience, for guiding me into this new world, for introducing me to his many colleagues, and for providing great insights and ideas along the way. Others at Vanderbilt have been generous with their time: Rene Marois, Jeffery Schall, Matt Ginther, Sara Elizabeth Grove, and Mollie Bodin.

Attorney Diarmuid White, now retired, drew on his recollections of the Weinstein case and filled in some of the gaps that didn't appear in legal documents. Zach Weiss, the former assistant district attorney who prosecuted Weinstein, also provided me with recollections as well as behind-the-scenes information, for which I am grateful.

Debra and Malori Alonso were extremely generous as they recounted the story about David, whose violent attack on these two strong women was among the strangest and most puzzling stories I had heard about the brain going awry. When he was finally released, David Alonso spoke with me about the remarkable experience from which he's still recovering. I'm grateful to prosecutor Deborah Factor and defense attorney Joseph Ferrante for sharing their stories. And thank you, Michael Connelly, fellow writer and friend, for telling me about the Alonso story and sharing your research on this case.

A special thanks to Martha Farah and everyone at Neuroscience Boot Camp at the University of Pennsylvania, where I got an eight-day intensive crash course in brain science and made many friends in the process. Boot camp served as a great resource and teacher. I benefited from lessons and lectures from Geoff Aguirre, Anjan Chatterjee, Seth Gillihan, Joseph Kable, Mike Kaplan, and David Wolk. Sarah Strickland worked tirelessly to make things at Boot Camp work smoothly. Stephen Morse of the University of Pennsylvania offered great insights and measured skepticism. Others at Penn were generous with their time, including Adrian Raine, Ruben Gur, Abass Alavi, and Douglas Smith. At Harvard's Center for Law, Brain and Behavior, I'm grateful to Judith Edersheim. I'm also indebted to Antonio Damasio for sharing his analysis of the Weinstein case, and for reviewing sections of the manuscript explaining his somatic marker hypothesis and early work with patients suffering from frontal lobe damage.

Andrew Martin, my good friend and investigative journalist extraordinaire, did me a tremendous favor by trudging down to the New York Supreme Court building in Lower Manhattan on his lunch break when I asked him to see if there was anything interesting in the Weinstein case file. There was, and from it sprang much of this book. Andy and his wife, Ellen, offered their generous hospitality during my research trips to New York. I also had terrific hosts on the West Coast in Warren and Diana Karlenzig, and I'm deeply grateful to my friend Bob Knotts in Florida for his hospitality, wisdom, and generosity. Michael McColly, teacher, mentor, and friend, helped guide and encourage me through this project. I owe thanks to Douglas Foster, whose magazine writing class at Northwestern University inspired me to delve into neuroscience. Thanks to my many friends, colleagues, and mentors at Northwestern's MFA program, including Sandi Wisenberg, Reg Gibbons, Peggy Shinner, and Alex Kotlowitz. Julienne Hill, a classmate and professional colleague, was always encouraging, wise, and understanding. I'm grateful to Hana Yoo, a DePaul University graduate student, who assisted me with research on the insanity defense, transcribed interview tapes, and helped assemble an ever-growing source list.

I learned a great deal about traumatic brain injury from Dr. Elliot Roth at the Rehabilitation Institute of Chicago, who's not only a world-class physician and expert on the brain but also my dear cousin. Among his many accomplishments, Elliot was instrumental in creating a program that helped identify TBI in returning combat veterans. My friends and colleagues at the *American Bar Association Journal* recognized that law and neuroscience was a subject worthy of investigation and published my first story on the subject. Thank you to Jill Chanen, Molly McDonough, Reg Davis, and Allen Pusey for bringing me on board.

I can always depend on my talented friends to embrace or challenge my ideas, offer advice, and direct me to a better place. Miles Harvey, once again, has been there from proposal to final draft. I'm thankful to have such a talented writer, editor, and more important, great friend in my corner. Author and friend Rob Kurson also helped me as I struggled through the early days of this project, and he always asked the tough questions. Other friends have supported my work: Paul Budin, Zack Nauth, Rich Cohen, and Kenny Golub, who told me about William Seward's defense of William Freeman. Dave Cullen, an incredible journalist and friend, was there when I needed advice as well. My parents, Marc and Judy Davis, read my original proposal and early sections of this book and offered invaluable feedback and support. My sister, Laura, was always inspiring and full of advice and babysat on many days when I needed time to write. Ken Kurson graciously went through the archives of the *New York Observer* to track down an indispensable article about the Weinstein case. Paula Kamen provided first-rate, timely, and accurate transcription services. Jonathan Smith and Penelope Messina, two New York court reporters, dug through their old files and floppy disks to find critical transcripts from the Weinstein case.

So many others were instrumental in the creation of this book. They are, in no particular order: Nina Marino, Antoinette R. McGarrahan, Stephen Cobb, Daniel Amen, Cecile Wagner, Daniel Tranel, Dan Martell, Russell Swerdlow, Joshua Greene, Nita Farahany, Beatriz Luna, B. J. Casey, Daniel Schwartz, Terry Lenamon, Abbe Rifkin, Brock Hunter, Kris Parson, Marijane Placek, Stephen Xanakis, Chris Nowinski, Daniel Antonius, George Mattingly, Peter A. Carfagna, James Fallon, Joseph Wu, Helen Mayberg, David Eagleman, Mark Bennett, Tiffany Lesko, Jessica Patrick, Laura Howell, Pablo Ormachea, Chris Green, Bill Sullivan, Joshua Buckholtz, Sally Satel, Thomas L. Hafemeister, Deborah Denno, Hank Greely, James Castle, and A. J. Roop. Thanks to Anne Ryan of zrimeages.com for taking my author photo on short notice.

My agent, Philip G. Spitzer, once again believed in my book proposal, showed great enthusiasm for the project, and matched me with a first-rate publisher. I'm grateful to have someone as dedicated, generous, and kind as my literary advocate and friend. Thanks also to Lukas Ortiz at the Spitzer Agency for his hard work and support, and to Luc Hunt. I'm thankful to Emily Cunningham at Penguin Press for her careful, thoughtful editing and for pushing me to think a little harder and go a little deeper, and to Jeff Alexander, who saw the potential for this project and acquired the book.

My wife, Martie Sanders, gave me the room to make this book happen by taking care of our son and our home as I traveled, worked early mornings, nights, weekends, and many hours here and there. I could not have done this without her. My son, Jackson "Sonny" Davis, inspired me to keep going and served as a great model as I tried to understand how little brains develop and witnessed the struggles of impulse control.

This book was also made possible by a grant from the Alfred P. Sloan Foundation, which allowed me to travel around the country to conduct research and interview neuroscientists, lawyers, and many other sources vital to this project. I am deeply grateful to the foundation for its support.

Notes

INTRODUCTION

1 **On December 17, 2014, Eric Williams:** Jennifer Emily, "Kaufman DA Killer Seeks New Trial, Citing Newly Discovered 'Brain Damage,'" *Dallas Morning News,* January 26, 2015; Gary E. Lindsley, "Judge Says No to New Trial for Convicted Murderer Eric Lyle Williams," *Terrell Tribune (Texas),* March 2, 2015.

2 **Nearly 1,600 judicial opinions:** Nita Farahany, "Neuroscience and Behavioral Genetics in US Criminal Law: An Empirical Analysis," *Journal of Law and the Biosciences* 2, no. 3 (2015): 485–509; Nita Farahany, interview by author.

4 **"when historians of the future":** Jeffrey Rosen, "The Brain on the Stand," *New York Times Magazine,* March 11, 2007.

CHAPTER 1: WE FOUND SOMETHING IN MR. WEINSTEIN'S BRAIN

5 **It was January 7, 1991:** The scenes in Chapter 1 were drawn primarily from records from the Supreme Court of New York, New York County, including Herbert Weinstein's criminal case, as well as the appeal he filed challenging denial of his parole. The records include motions, hearing transcripts, depositions, and police reports. Dialogue is taken directly from the records as well as from the recollections of those present, including Diarmuid White, Zachary Weiss, and Joni Weinstein.

12 **Herald Fahringer:** Sam Roberts, "Herald Price Fahringer, a Defender of Free Speech, Dies at 87," *New York Times,* February 19, 2015.

12 **He was struck by how unusually calm:** Diarmuid White, interview by author.

15 **"HIGH-RISE HORROR":** Mike Wald, "High-rise Horror on East Side," *New York Daily News,* January 8, 1991.

15 **It was completely out of character:** Neighbors' accounts came from Joseph A. Gambardello, "Wife Tossed Out Window," *Newsday,* January 8, 1991; David Kocieniewski, "Ad Exec Charged in Wife's Death," *Newsday,* January 9,

1991; Robin Pogrebin, "Death Crashes Down onto East 72nd Street," *New York Observer,* January 28, 1991.

15 **Morton and Cecile Wagner:** The account of Weinstein's friendship, conversations, and visits with the Wagners was drawn from my two interviews with Cecile Wagner.

16 **Arachnoid cysts usually:** Daniel Martel, "Causal Relation Between Brain Damage and Homicide: The Prosecution," *Seminars in Clinical Neuropsychiatry* 1, no.3 (1996): 184–94.

16 **Weinstein decided not to have the cyst drained:** My account of Weinstein's medical exams and his decision not to have his cyst drained comes from the testimony of Dr. Norman Relkin and from my interviews with Joni Weinstein. Additional details came from Norman Relkin et al., "Impulsive Homicide Associated with an Arachnoid Cyst and Unilateral Frontotemporal Cerebral Dysfunction," *Seminars in Clinical Neuropsychiatry* 1, no. 3 (1996): 172–83.

16 **But when he learned about Weinstein's cyst:** Legal motions filed in Weinstein court case; Diarmiud White, interviews by author.

17 **Phineas Gage:** J. M. Harlow, "Passage of an Iron Rod Through the Head," *Boston Medical and Surgical Journal* 39 (1848): 389–93; Zbigniew Kotowicz, "The Strange Case of Phineas Gage," *History of the Human Sciences* 20 (2007): 115–31; Antonio R. Damasio et al., "The Return of Phineas Gage: Clues About the Brain from the Skull of a Famous Patient (1823?–1860?)," *Science* 264, no. 5162 (1994): 1102–5.

19 **"fitful, irreverent":** J. M. Harlow, "Recovery from the Passage of an Iron Bar Through the Head," *Publications of the Massachusetts Medical Society* 2 (1868): 327–47.

19 **"was no longer Gage":** Ibid.

20 **"slight fact, considerable fancy":** Malcolm Macmillan's *An Odd Kind of Fame: Stories of Phineas Gage* (Cambridge, MA: Bradford, 2002), is the definitive account of Gage's life and medical case. See also Macmillan, "A Wonderful Journey Through Skull and Brains: The Travels of Mr. Gage's Tamping Iron," *Brain and Cognition* 5 (1986): 67–107; John D. Van Horn et al., "Mapping Connectivity Damage in the Case of Phineas Gage," *PLOS ONE,* May 16, 2012.

21 **Franz-Joseph Gall:** On phrenology, see "Phrenology," *Encyclopedia Britannica Online,* June 2014; Renato M. E. Sabbatini, "Phrenology: The History of Brain Localization," *Brain and Mind* (1997).

21 **In 1834 a criminal defense attorney in Maine:** Geoffrey S. Holtzman, "When Phrenology Was Used in Court," *Slate,* December 2015.

CHAPTER 2: LAWYERS, BRAINS, AND COLORFUL PICTURES

23 **Geoff Aguirre, a cognitive neuroscientist:** Aguirre's comments were made during the conference "The Future of Law and Neuroscience" in Chicago on April, 27, 2013. Comments from other attendees were culled from interviews during and after the conference.

25 **Brian Dugan:** Background information on the Brian Dugan case comes from Michael Haederle, "A Mind of Crime: How Brain-Scanning Technology Is Redefining Criminal Culpability," *Pacific Standard,* February 23, 2010; and

Virginia Hughes, "Science in Court: Head Case," *Nature* 464 (March 17, 2010): 340–42.

27 **"Neuroscience could have an impact":** MacArthur Foundation, "New $10 Million MacArthur Project Integrates Law and Neuroscience," press release, October 9, 2007. The comments from Jonathan Fanton, Michael S. Gazzaniga, and Walter Sinnott-Armstrong are also taken from this press release.

CHAPTER 3: A CHARMING MAN

31 **"What's the matter?":** Joni Weinstein, interviews by author.

33 **Rita Levy, Barbara's cousin:** Mike Wald, "High-rise Horror on East Side," *New York Daily News,* January 8, 1991.

34 **"fat and extremely":** Descriptions of Weinstein's younger years were obtained from medical reports and interviews in the court records.

38 **She came from a moneyed past:** Kim Glazer Goldberg and Bradley Goldberg, interviews by author; "Jerome S. Glazer, 66, New Orleans Importer," *New York Times,* April 22, 1991.

CHAPTER 4: THE BRAIN BLAME EVOLUTION

41 **The idea that the law might excuse:** On the history of the insanity defense, see Walter A. Borden, MD, "Classically Insane," *Journal of the American Academy of Psychiatry and the Law Online* 39, no. 2 (April 2011): 255–57; Allen D. Spiegel and Marc B. Spiegel, "The Insanity Plea in Early Nineteenth-Century America," *Journal of Community Health* 23, no. 3 (1998): 227–47; "A Brief Summary of the Insanity Defense," *Psychiatry and the Law,* n.d.; Aeschylus, *Oresteia,* trans. George C. W. Warr, *Project Gutenberg;* Walter A. Borden, "A History of Justice: Origins of Law and Psychiatry," *American Academy of Psychiatry and the Law* 24, no. 2 (1999): 12–14; Richard E. Redding, "The Brain-Disordered Defendant: Neuroscience and Legal Insanity in the Twenty-First Century," *American University Law Review* 56 (2007): 51–127.

43 **"wild beast test":** Stephen Allnutt, Anthony Samuels, and Colman O'Driscoll, "The Insanity Defence: From Wild Beasts to M'Naghten," *Australian Psychiatry* 15, no. 4 (2007): 292–98; Kevin Crotty, review of *Wild Beasts and Idle Humours: The Insanity Defense from Antiquity to the Present* by Daniel N. Robinson, in *Bryn Mawr Classical Review,* October 14, 1997; Russell D. Covey, "Temporary Insanity: The Strange Life and Times of the Perfect Defense," *Boston University Law Review* 91 (2011): 1597–668.

43 **one hundred recorded pleas of insanity:** Richard Moran, "The Modern Foundation for the Insanity Defense: The Cases of James Hadfield (1800) and Daniel McNaughtan (1843)," *Annals of the American Academy of Political and Social Science* 477 (1985): 31–42.

44 **James Hadfield:** *Attempt on the Life of the King. The Trial of James Hadfield for High Treason in the Court of King's Bench,* . . . (London, 1800); Michael A. Peszke, "Insanity Plea: Doctors vs. Law," *New York Times,* August 7, 1983; Sara West and Stephen Noffsinger, "Is This Patient Not Guilty by Reason of Insanity?"

Current Psychiatry 5, no. 8 (2006): 54–62; New York Unified State Court System, "Cayuga County Courthouse and the Case that Helped Establish the Insanity Defense in New York," *Benchmarks,* Spring 2007.

46 **William Freeman, an ex-convict:** On the William Freeman trial, see Benjamin F. Hall, *The Trial of William Freeman, for the Murder of John G. Van Nest, Including the Evidence and the Arguments of Counsel, . . .* (Auburn, 1848); Andrew Aprey, *William Freeman Murder Trial: Insanity, Politics, and Race* (Syracuse, NY: Syracuse University Press, 2003); Fosgate Blanchard, "Case of William Freeman, the Murderer of the Van Nest Family," *New Jersey Medical Reporter and Transactions of the New Jersey Medical Society (1847–1854),* January 1848, 55; "The Murder Near Auburn," *Evangelical Magazine and Gospel Advocate* (1846): 117; "Five Reasons Why Freeman Should Be Hung," *Prisoner's Friend: A Monthly Magazine Devoted to Criminal Reform, Philosophy, Science, Literature, and Art* (1846): 131; "Trial of William Freeman," *Monthly Law Reporter* (1848): 289–303; "William Freeman," *Prisoner's Friend: A Monthly Magazine Devoted to Criminal Reform, Philosophy, Science, Literature, and Art* (1846): 55; Silas Wright, "Case of Freeman, the Murderer," *National Police Gazette* (1847): 131; "The Legacy of John Adams: William Seward's Defense of William Freeman," *New York News Publishers Association's NIE Program,* n.d.

53 **Britain was the first to codify:** John P. Martin, "The Insanity Defense: A Closer Look," *Washington Post,* February 27, 1998; Henry T. Miller, "Recent Changes in Criminal Law: The Federal Insanity Defense," *Louisiana Law Review* 46, no. 2 (1985): 337–60; Nigel Walker, "The Insanity Defense Before 1800," *Annals of the American Academy of Political and Social Science* 477 (1985): 25–30.

53 **Daniel M'Naghten:** James George Davey, *Medico-legal reflections on the trial of Daniel M'Naughten, for the murder of Mr. Drummond: . . .* (London, 1843); "Criminal Injustice," *Spectator,* December 21, 1844; "Punishment of Lunatics," *Spectator,* March 11, 1843; "Proceedings in Parliament," *Spectator,* March 18, 1843; "A Settlement Unsettled," *Spectator,* July 22, 1843; "M'Naughten: Murder, Hanging," *Spectator,* February 11, 1843.

54 **the American Law Institute:** Miller, "Recent Changes in Criminal Law," 345.

55 **the trial of John Hinckley, Jr.:** On the trial of John Hinckley, Jr., see Laura A. Kiernan and Eric Pianin, "Hinckley Found Not Guilty, Insane," *Washington Post,* June 22, 1982; Lincoln Caplan, *The Insanity Defense and the Trial of John W. Hinckley, Jr.* (Boston: D. R. Godine, 1984); James W. Clarke, *On Being Mad or Merely Angry: John W. Hinckley, Jr., and Other Dangerous People* (Princeton, NJ: Princeton University Press, 1990); Alan M. Dershowitz, *America on Trial: Inside the Legal Battles That Transformed Our Nation* (New York: Warner Books, 2004); Charles P. Ewing and Joseph T. McCann, *Minds on Trial: Great Cases in Law and Psychology* (Oxford: Oxford University Press, 2006); John Files, "No Appeal on Hinckley Ruling," *New York Times,* January 17, 2004; Shamael Haque and Melvin Guyer, "Neuroimaging Studies in Diminished-Capacity Defense," *Journal of the American Academy of Psychiatry and the Law Online* 38, no. 4 (2010): 605–7; Brad Knickerbocker, "Should President Reagan Shooter John Hinckley Get More Freedom?" *Christian Science Monitor,* November 30, 2011; M. L. Perlin,

"His Brain Has Been Mismanaged with Great Skill: How Will Jurors Respond to Neuroimaging Testimony in Insanity Defense Cases?" *Akron Law Review* 42, no. 3 (2009): 885–916; Rita J. Simon and David E. Aaronson, *The Insanity Defense: A Critical Assessment of Law and Policy in the Post-Hinckley Era* (New York: Praeger, 1988); Michael Sokolove, "Should John Hinckley Go Free?" *New York Times,* November 16, 2003; Alan A. Stone, *Law, Psychiatry, and Morality: Essays and Analysis* (Washington, D.C.; American Psychiatric Press, 1984); Stuart Taylor, Jr., "CAT Scans Said to Show Shrunken Hinckley Brain," *New York Times,* June 2, 1982; William J. Winslade and Judith W. Ross, *The Insanity Plea* (New York: Scribner, 1983).

57 **a federal judge determined that Hinckley:** Spencer S. Hsu, "Would-be Reagan Assassin John Hinckley, Jr. to Be Freed After 35 Years," *Washington Post,* July 27, 2016.

CHAPTER 5: INSIDE WEINSTEIN'S BRAIN

59 **He spent his days laboring:** Details of Diarmuid White's work and his personal biography were drawn from my interviews with him.

61 **Dr. Norman Relkin:** The account of Weinstein's medical appointments is drawn from court transcripts, medical reports, and motions filed in his criminal case, along with recollections of his daughter, Joni. The details of Weinstein's medical examination by Dr. Norman Relkin and the subsequent meeting with colleagues at Cornell Medical Center is taken directly from Dr. Relkin's testimony and from his report in the court file.

63 **eight patients with intracranial cysts:** Robert Kohn et al., "Psychiatric Presentations of Intracranial Cysts," *Journal of Neuropsychiatry* 1, no. 1 (1989): 60–66.

63 **the case of a seventeen-year-old boy:** S. Colameco and R. A. DiTomasso, "Arachnoid Cyst Associated with Psychological Disturbance," *Journal of the Medical Society of New Jersey* 79, no. 3 (1982): 209–10.

CHAPTER 6: "THAT'S NOT MY DAD"

67 **David Alonso:** This account of David Alonso's actions, arrest, and court case came from interviews with Debra and Malori Alonso, court documents, newspaper accounts, and interviews with friends, family, defense attorney Joseph Ferrante, and Hunterdon County assistant prosecutor Deborah Factor.

69 **A neighbor who was walking her dog:** Jaccii Farris, "Police: Man Attacked Daughter, Before Harming Himself," WFMZ-TV News, June 13, 2012.

70 **more than 1.7 million people suffer brain injuries:** Centers for Disease Control and Prevention, "Basic Information about Traumatic Brain Injury and Concussion" and "Traumatic Brain Injury in the United States: Fact Sheet," n.d.; Page Walker Buck, "Mild Traumatic Brain Injury: A Silent Epidemic in Our Practices," *Health and Social Work* 36, no. 4 (2011): 299–302.

71 **One study found that TBI:** L. Turkstra, D. Jones, and Hon. L. Toler, "Brain Injury and Violent Crime," *Brain Injury* 17, no. 1 (2003): 39–47.

71 **people in prison have higher incidences of TBI:** Rebecca Bennett,

"Pilot Program Identifies Brain Injuries in Inmates," *Fox 59,* February 8, 2015; "Brain Scans of Inmates Turn Up Possible Link to Risks of Reoffending," *Los Angeles Times,* July 15, 2013; Katherine Harmon, "Brain Injury Rate Seven Times Greater Among U.S. Prisoners," *Scientific American,* February 4, 2012; William J. Winslade, "Traumatic Brain Injury and Criminal Responsibility," *Medical Ethics* 10, no. 3 (2003).

72 **a meta-analysis:** Thomas J. Farrer and Dawson W. Hedges, "Prevalence of Traumatic Brain Injury in Incarcerated Groups Compared to the General Population: A Meta-Analysis," *Progress in Neuro-Psychopharmacology and Biological Psychiatry* 35, no. 2 (2011): 390–94. For background and understanding of TBI and criminal justice, I consulted Bob Fleischner, "Traumatic Brain Injury and Competency to Stand Trial: Issues and Advocacy," Webcast, National Disability Rights Network, February 8, 2010; Lydia D. Johnson, "Guilty or Innocent? . . . Just Take a Look at My Brain—Analyzing the Nexus Between Traumatic Brain Injury and Criminal Responsibility," *Southern University Law Review* 37, no. 1 (2009): 25–40; Adam Lamparello, "Neuroscience, Brain Damage, and the Criminal Defendant: Who Does It Help and Where in the Criminal Proceeding Is It Most Relevant?" *Rutgers Law Record* 39, no. 2 (2013): 161–80.

75 **Anthony Kearns III, released a statement:** Office of the Hunterdon County Prosecutor, "Bloomsbury Man Not Guilty by Reason of Insanity for Attempted Murder of his Family," press release, December 6, 2012.

78 **Kenneth Parks:** Berit Brogaard, "Sleep Driving and Sleep Killing: The Kenneth Parks Case," *Psychology Today,* December 13, 2012; Lindsay Lyon, "7 Criminal Cases That Invoked the 'Sleepwalking Defense,'" *U.S. News & World Report,* May 8, 2009.

79 **Benjamin Libet:** Benjamin Libet, Walter Sinott-Armstrong, and Lynn Nadel, *Conscious Will and Responsibility: A Tribute to Benjamin Libet* (New York: Oxford University Press, 2011); Dean Mobbs et al., "Law, Responsibility, and the Brain," *PLOS Biology* 5, no. 4 (2007): e103.

82 **"there is no one thing":** Michael S. Gazzaniga, *Who's In Charge?* (New York: Ecco, 2012).

CHAPTER 7: A TRIP TO IOWA

85 **In the mid-1980s a forty-four-year-old:** For Elliot's story, I've drawn on Antonio R. Damasio, *Descartes' Error* (New York: Putnam, 1994), as well as e-mail correspondence with Dr. Damasio. Related articles include Antionio R. Damasio, Daniel Tranel, and Hanna Damasio, "Individuals with Sociopathic Behavior Caused by Frontal Damage Fail to Respond Autonomically to Social Stimuli," *Behavioural Brain Research* 41 (1990), 81–94; Antonio R. Damasio and Paul J. Eslinger, "Severe Disturbance of Higher Cognition After Bilateral Frontal Lobe Ablation, Patient EVR," *Neurology* 35 (December 1985): 1731–41; and Antonio R. Damasio and Jeffrey L. Saver, "Preserved Access and Processing of Social Knowledge in a Patient with Acquired Sociopathy Due to Ventromedial Frontal Damage," *Neuropsychologia* 29, no. 12 (1991): 1241–49.

88 **Damasio's somatic marker hypothesis:** Damasio, *Descartes' Error;* Anto-

nio R. Damasio, "The Somatic Marker Hypothesis and the Possible Functions of the Prefrontal Cortex," *Philosophical Transactions of the Royal Society B: Biological Sciences* 351, no. 1346 (1996): 1413–20; Antonio R. Damasio, "Emotions Create Our Preferences: The Somatic Marker Hypothesis," *NeuroRelay,* May 15, 2012; and Carl Marziali, "Emotional Rescue," University of Southern California, *USC Trojan Family Magazine,* Summer 2006.

91 **When Weinstein arrived at the lab:** My account of Weinstein's visit to Damasio's lab is drawn from an interview with Daniel Tranel, who was present during the visit; from testimony of Dr. Norman Relkin during Weinstein's court hearings; and from Damasio's report in the court record.

CHAPTER 8: THE YOUNG BRAIN DEFENSE

95 **Ronnie Cordell lived in fear:** Details of Cordell's early childhood come from court documents from Cordell's trial and sentencing hearing, especially Christine Penry, "Presentencing Report for Ronnie Cordell to the Honorable Jan R. Jurden, Superior Court of Delaware, New Castle County"; Penry interviewed Ronnie Cordell, his sister-in-law Terri Cordell, his brothers Randy Cordell and Larry Cordell, his half-brother David Cordell, and his sister Debra Cordell, March 26, 2014; and "Ronnie Cordell Psychiatric Report," University of Pennsylvania, August 22, 2013, written by John Northrup and Susan Rushing of the Department of Psychiatry.

96 **Early on the morning of June 4, 1982:** The account of the attack on Howard Marshall is drawn from Cordell's own description of events to authorities; trial testimony; and news accounts, including Obituary, "Howard W. Marshall," *Wilmington Morning News,* June 7, 1982; Tom Greer, "2 Testify to Seeing Fatal Attack," *Wilmington Morning News,* March 15, 1984; Tom Greer, "Suspect Linked with Talk of Beating," *Wilmington Morning News,* March 17, 1984; Tom Greer, "2 Youths Convicted of Killing," *Wilmington Morning News,* March 21, 1984; Tom Greer, "Teens Get Life Terms in Murders," *Wilmington Morning News,* March 22, 1984.

97 **a growing body of research has:** Lizzie Buchen, "Arrested Development," *Nature* 484 (2012): 304–6; "The Adolescent Brain: Beyond Raging Hormones," *Harvard Health Publications,* March 7, 2011.

97 **Abuse, neglect, and mistreatment:** U.S. Department of Health and Human Services, Children's Bureau, Child Welfare Information Gateway, *Supporting Brain Development in Traumatized Children and Youth,* 2011.

98 **"incubated in terror":** Bruce D. Perry, "Incubated in Terror: Neurodevelopmental Factors in the 'Cycle of Violence,'" in J. Osofsky, ed., *Children, Youth and Violence: The Search for Solutions* (New York: Guilford Press, 1997); Bruce D. Perry, "Effects of Traumatic Events on Children," Child Trauma Academy, 2003.

98 **"induces a cascade of effects":** Martin H. Teicher, "Wounds That Time Won't Heal: The Neurobiology of Child Abuse," *Cerebrum: The Dana Forum on Brain Science* 2, no. 4 (2000).

100 **"vicious will":** William Blackstone, "Of the Persons Capable of Committing Crimes," *Commentaries on the Laws of England* (Oxford: Clarendon Press, 1765–69).

100 **Thomas Graunger:** Lisa M. Lauria, "Capital Offences: Buggery," *Plymouth Colony Archive Project,* n.d.

101 **the nation's first juvenile court system:** "The History of Juvenile Justice," *in Dialogue on Youth and Justice* (Chicago: American Bar Association Division for Public Education, 2007); Shay Bilchik, "The Juvenile Justice System Was Founded on the Concept of Rehabilitation Through Individualized Justice," *1999 National Report Series, Juvenile Justice Bulletin: Juvenile Justice: A Century of Change,* December 1999; Sheila Merry, "Cook County Juvenile Court: The Juvenile Court in the 21st Century," *Cook County Justice for Children,* n.d.

101 **364 persons have been executed in the United States:** "Execution of Juveniles in the U.S. and Other Countries," Death Penalty Information Center, February 3, 2011.

102 **The youngest person ever executed:** Elliot C. McLaughlin, "New Trial Sought for George Stinney, Executed at 14," CNN, January 23, 2014; Karen McVeigh, "George Stinney Was Executed at 14. Can His Family Now Clear His Name?" *Observer,* March 22, 2014.

102 **Ronnie Cordell admitted to beating up Howard Marshall:** Tom Greer, "Teen Admits Hitting, Kicking, Man Who Died," *Wilmington Morning News,* March 16, 1984.

102–103 **Supreme Court eliminated the death penalty for juveniles:** *Roper v. Simmons,* 543 U.S. 551 (2005); Linda Greenhouse, "Supreme Court, 5–4, Forbids Execution in Juvenile Crime," *New York Times,* March 2, 2005; "Supreme Court Bars Death Penalty for Juvenile Killers," *New York Times,* March 1, 2005.

103 **filed briefs:** Amicus briefs filed by the American Medical Association, the American Psychiatric Association, the American Society for Adolescent Psychiatry, the American Academy of Child and Adolescent Psychiatry, the American Academy of Psychiatry and the Law, the National Association of Social Workers, the Missouri Chapter of the National Association of Social Workers, and the National Mental Health Association in *Roper v. Simmons,* 543 U.S. 551 (2005). See also Aliya Haider, "*Roper v. Simmons:* The Role of the Science Brief," *Ohio State Journal of Criminal Law* 3 (2006): 369–77.

103 **executing the mentally ill:** *Atkins v. Virginia,* 536 U.S. 304 (2002).

104 Terrance Jamar Graham: Graham v. Florida, 560 U.S. 48 (2010); amicus briefs filed by the American Medical Association and the American Academy of Child and Adolescent Psychiatry in Graham v. Florida, July 23, 2009; Adam Liptak, "Justices Limit Life Sentences for Juveniles," New York Times, May 17, 2010.

106 **Cautiously, she helped write a letter:** Beatriz Luna, interview by author. A draft copy of the letter was supplied by Luna. See also Beatriz Luna, "The Relevance of Immaturities in the Juvenile Brain to Culpability and Rehabilitation," *Hastings Law Journal* 63 (2012): 1469–86; Beatriz Luna, et al. to E. Joshua Rosenkrantz, July 16, 2009.

108 **Virginia Babicki:** Attorney A. J. Roop, interview by author.

108 **Evan Miller:** *Miller v. Alabama,* 567 U.S. (2012); James Swift, "Miller v. Alabama: One Year Later," *Juvenile Justice Information Exchange,* June 25, 2013; amicus brief filed by the American Psychological Association, the American

Psychiatric Association, and the National Association of Social Workers in *Miller v. Alabama* and *Jackson v. Hobbs.*

110 **Bryan Stevenson:** Adam Liptak and Ethan Bronner, "Justices Bar Mandatory Life Terms for Juveniles," *New York Times,* June 25, 2012.

111 **The psychiatrists found:** "Ronnie Cordell Psychiatric Report," University of Pennsylvania, August 22, 2013, John Northrup and Susan Rushing, Department of Psychiatry.

112 **Casey led a study:** Tim Requarth, "Neuroscience Is Changing the Debate Over What Role Age Should Play in the Courts," *Newsweek,* April 8, 2016; B. J. Casey et al., "When Is an Adolescent an Adult? Assessing Cognitive Control in Emotional and Nonemotional Contexts," *Psychological Science* (April 2016): 549–62; B. J. Casey, "The Teenage Brain: An Overview," *Current Directions in Psychological Science* 22. no. 2 (April 2013): 80–81; B. J. Casey and Kristina Caudle, "The Teenage Brain: Self Control," *Current Directions in Psychological Science* 22, no. 2 (April 2013): 82–87.

113 **Ronnie Cordell arrived:** Sean O'Sullivan, "Teen Who Killed Set Free 32 Years Later," *News Journal,* December 19, 2014. On adolescent brain development and neuroscience, see Jay D. Aronson, "Neuroscience and Juvenile Justice," *Akron Law Review* 42 (2009): 917–30; Jess Bravin, "U.S. Supreme Court to Review Juvenile Life Sentences," *Wall Street Journal,* March 23, 2015; Alexandra O. Cohen and B. J. Casey, "Rewiring Juvenile Justice: The Intersection of Developmental Neuroscience and Legal Policy," *Trends in Cognitive Sciences* 18, no. 2 (2014): 63–65; Judith Edersheim, "Could Tsarnaev Argue, 'My Immature, Pot-Impaired Brain Made Me Do It'?" *Massachusetts General Hospital, Center for Law, Brain and Behavior,* January 9, 2015; "The Juvenile Brain: Why Science, the Supreme Court Says Minors Should Be Treated Differently," *Youth Project,* n.d.; Terry A. Maroney, "The False Promise of Adolescent Brain Science in Juvenile Justice," *Notre Dame Law Review* 85, no. 1 (2009): 89–176; John Monterosso and Barry Schwartz, "Did Your Brain Make You Do It?" *New York Times,* July 27, 2012; Sally Satel and Scott O. Lilienfeld, "The 'Immature Teen Brain' Defense and the Dzhokhar Tsarnaev Trial," *Washington Post,* May 12, 2015; Beth Schwartzapfel, "Would You Let This Man Go Free?" *Boston Magazine,* July 2014; John Simerman, "George Toca, La. Inmate at Center of Debate on Juvenile Life Sentences, to Go Free," *New Orleans Advocate,* January, 30, 2015; Matt Stroud, "Prisoners Sentenced to Life as Kids Just Lost Their Best Chance for Freedom," *Bloomberg Business,* February 19, 2015.

CHAPTER 9: THE RICH MAN'S DEFENSE

115 **Zachary Weiss:** The material for this chapter was drawn from interviews with Daniel Martell and Zachary Weiss as well as Zachary Weiss, "The Legal Admissibility of Positron Emission Tomography Scans in Criminal Cases: People v. Spyder Cystkopf," *Seminars in Clinical Neuropsychiatry,* 1, no. 3 (1996): 202–10; Daniel Martell, "Causal Relation Between Brain Damage and Homicide: The Prosecution," *Seminars in Clinical Neuropsychiatry,* 1, no. 3 (1996): 184–94; Richard Dooling, "The Evil Mind," *George,* February 1998.

CHAPTER 10: WHEN NEUROSCIENTISTS COME TO COURT

123 **Adrian Raine:** The story of Raine's visit to the College of Charleston is drawn from my interviews with Raine, as well as Dave Munday, "Controversial Talk by Psychologist Adrian Raine Draws Big College of Charleston Crowd," *Post and Courier,* Charleston, SC, November 14, 2013; Diane Knich, "Murder Victim's Family, Friends Object to Defense Witness' College of Charleston Visit," *Post and Courier,* November 3, 2013.

127 **Raine and Buchsbaum designed:** Adrian Raine, Monte Buchsbaum, et al., "Selective Reductions in Prefrontal Glucose Metabolism in Murderers," *Biological Psychiatry* 36, no. 6 (1994): 365–73; Adrian Raine, "Murderous Minds: Can We See the Mark of Caine," Dana Foundation, n.d.

128 **James Castle:** Adrian Raine, interviews by author; James Castle, interviews by author; Adrian Raine, *The Anatomy of Violence* (New York: Pantheon, 2013); Steve Jackson, "Dead Reckoning," *Westword,* June 28, 2001; Mike McPhee, "Page 'Deliberate' in Killing," *Denver Post,* November 18, 2000.

132 **Fallon has, by his own conclusion:** James Fallon, interviews by author; James Fallon, "How I Discovered I Have the Brain of a Psychopath," *Guardian,* June 2, 2014; Judith Ohikuare, "Life as a Nonviolent Psychopath," *Atlantic,* January 21, 2014; Dean A. Haycock, "This Is Your Brain on Murder: What the Mind of a Psychopath Looks Like," *Salon,* March 9, 2014.

136 **The reporter Rex Dalton:** Rex Dalton, "Controversy Follows UC Irvine Scientist's Brain Scan Testimony," *Voice of OC,* April 3, 2014.

136 **Ruben Gur is probably the most sought-after:** This claim is based on Gur's own account and from my interviews with neuroscientists and lawyers familiar with his work.

137 **Bobby Joe Long:** Ruben Gur and Oren Gur, "Linking Brain and Behavioral Measures in the Medical-Legal Context," in Robert Sadoff, ed., *The Evolution of Forensic Psychiatry: History, Current Developments, Future Directions* (New York: Oxford University Press, 2015); Ruben Gur, "Brain Maturation and the Execution of Juveniles: Some Reflections on Science and the Law," *Pennsylvania Gazette,* January 5, 2005.

138 **John McCluskey:** Greg Miller, "Did Brain Scans Just Save a Convicted Murderer From the Death Penalty?" *Wired,* December 12, 2013.

140 **Gregory Scott Smith:** "Brain Damage Attributed at Penalty Trial to Slayer of Boy, 8," *Los Angeles Times,* January 16, 1992.

141 **The jury voted to sentence him:** Mack Reed, "Jury Urges Death Penalty for Boy's Killer," *Los Angeles Times,* January 29, 1992.

CHAPTER 11: THE BRAIN SCIENCE BATTLE

144 **Richard D. Carruthers:** Judge profile, *New York Law Journal,* n.d.

144 **James Alphonso Frye:** *Frye v. United States,* 593 F.1013 (D.C. Cir. 1923); K. J. Weiss, C. Watson, and Y. Xuan, "Frye's Backstory: A Tale of Murder, A Retracted Confession, and Scientific Hubris," *Journal of the American Academy of Psychiatry and the Law Online* 42, no. 2 (2014): 226–33.

145 **The Frye hearing began:** This account of Weinstein's court hearings is

taken from hearing transcripts and from my interviews with Daniel Martell, Zachary Weiss, and Diarmuid White.

156 **took issue with a study:** N. D. Volkow and L. Tancredi, "Neural Substrates of Violent Behaviour: A Preliminary Study with Positron Emission Tomography," *British Journal of Psychiatry* 151, no. 5 (1987): 668–73.

159 **Barry Wayne McNamara:** Associated Press, "McNamara Convicted of Murders, Death Penalty Possible," December 12, 1985; Steve Emmons, "Hunting for Brain Disorders: Attorneys Turn to UCI Scanner as Defense Tool," *Los Angeles Times,* July 14, 1989; "The Region" (news brief), *Los Angeles Times,* January 14, 1986.

161 **"If the jury's position is":** Jerry Hicks, "Brain Scan on Kraft Shows Abnormality, Professor Testifies," *Los Angeles Times,* July 27, 1989.

CHAPTER 12: DEADLY TUMOR

163 **"I don't quite understand":** For Charles Whitman's suicide letter and the Texas Tower massacre, see Gary M. Lavergne, *A Sniper in the Tower: The Charles Whitman Mass Murders* (Denton: University of North Texas Press, 1997); "Whitman letter," Austin History Center; "Report on the Charles J. Whitman Catastrophe," Texas Governor's Committee and Consultants, Archives and Information Services Division, Texas State Library and Archives Commission; "Whitman Autopsy," Austin History Center; Brenda Bell, "An Anniversary with No Answers," *Austin American-Statesman,* August 1, 2006; David Ray, "The Road to Violence—World Events and a Brain Tumor Seem to Have Pushed Charles Whitman up UT Tower," *San Antonio Express-News,* July 28, 1996; Cara Santa Maria, "The Mind of a Mass Murderer: Charles Whitman, Brain Damage, and Violence," *Huffington Post,* March 28, 2012.

166 **In 1986 authorities in Travis County:** Associated Press, "UT Sniper Was Sane, Ex-DA Says—Time Was Right to Release Files on Whitman, Former Prosecutor Says," *Dallas Morning News,* July 9, 1986.

167 **"nearly all the physicians":** Lavergne, 268.

167 **Nathan Malamud:** Nathan Malamud, "Psychiatric Disorder with Intracranial Tumors of Limbic System," *Archives of Neurology* 17 (August 1967): 113–23.

168 **"with little more than lip service":** Frank A. Elliott, "Neurological Findings in Adult Minimal Brain Dysfunction and the Dyscontrol Syndrome," *Journal of Nervous and Mental Disease* (November 1982): 680–87.

168 **A forty-year-old married schoolteacher:** Jeffrey M. Burns and Russell H. Swerdlow, "Right Orbitofrontal Tumor with Pedophilia Symptom and Constructional Apraxia Sign," *Archives of Neurology* (March 2003): 437–40.

CHAPTER 13: WHAT'S A PICTURE WORTH?

173 **Judge Richard Carruthers signed:** Judge Carruthers's decision and other court proceedings are in *People v. Weinstein,* 156 Misc. 2d 34 (1992), 591 N.Y.S. 2d 715. Transcripts of Weinstein's sentencing hearing were provided by former court reporters Jonathan Smith and Penelope Messina.

181 **"This decision opens":** Joe Rojas-Burke, "PET Scans Advance as Tool in Insanity Defense," *Journal of Nuclear Medicine* 34, no. 1 (1993): 13N–16N.

183 **"In our opinion":** Norman Relkin et al., "Impulsive Homicide Associated with an Arachnoid Cyst and Unilateral Frontotemporal Cerebral Dysfunction," *Seminars in Clinical Neuropsychiatry* 1, no. 3 (1996): 172–83.

184 **"These findings began to suggest":** Daniel Martell, "Causal Relationship Between Brain Damage and Homicide: The Prosecution," *Seminars in Clinical Neuropsychiatry* 1, no. 3 (1996): 184–94.

184 **"It could be argued":** Zachary Weiss, "The Legal Admissibility of Positron Emission Tomography Scans in Criminal Cases: The People v. Spyder Cystkopf," *Seminars in Clinical Neuropsychiatry* 1, no. 3 (1996): 202–10.

CHAPTER 14: NOT ONE HEALTHY BRAIN

190 **Dr. Daniel Amen:** Neely Tucker, "Daniel Amen Is the Most Popular Psychiatrist in America. To Most Researchers and Scientists, That's a Very Bad Thing," *Washington Post Magazine,* August 9, 2012; Robert T. Rubin, "Brain Scans, The New Snake Oil," *Los Angeles Times,* December 11, 2007; Harriet Hall, "Dr. Amen's Love Affair with SPECT Scan," *Science-Based Medicine,* March 19, 2013.

195 **Peter Chiesa:** Martin Lasden, "Mr. Chiesa's Brain: Can High-Tech Scans Prove that Criminal Acts Are the Result of a Damaged Brain?" *California Lawyer,* 2004.

198 **Jeffrey Glenn Hutchinson:** Associated Press, "Suspect Was Diagnosed with Gulf Syndrome," *Lakeland Ledger,* September 15, 1998.

CHAPTER 15: THE DEATH PENALTY ATTORNEY AND THE BROKEN BRAIN

201 **Terry Lenamon:** Details of Lenamon's biography were obtained during interviews with him and from his self-published book, *Heinous, Atrocious and Cruel,* written with Brooke Terpening (Telemachus Press, 2011).

202 **The bloody attack occurred:** Carol Marbin Miller, "Rape, Fear, Murder Destroy a Family," *Miami Herald,* April 24, 2005. Additional details of Nelson's crimes were drawn from the court records, Lenamon's book, and the attorney's own account.

207 **Dr. Gerald Gluck:** Grady Nelson's QEEG testing is drawn from the trial testimony of Dr. Gerald Gluck, a deposition of Dr. Robert Thatcher, and my interviews with Terry Lenamon.

209 **In the new trial, Lenamon and Markus:** David Ovalle, "Miami-Dade Jury: Man Guilty of Murdering His Wife," *Miami Herald,* July 10, 2010.

209 **Prosecutor Abbe Rifkin:** Abbe Rikfin, interview by author.

210 **The judge ordered a Frye hearing:** *State of Florida v. Grady Nelson,* case no. F05-00846," 11th Judicial Circuit Court, Miami-Dade County, Florida, Frye Hearing, volume 1, October 9, 2010.

210 **Dr. Robert Thatcher:** Robert W. Thatcher affidavit, *Florida v. Nelson.*

211 **After only an hour of deliberations:** David Ovalle, "Ex-Miami-Dade

Worker Gets Life for Murder, Rape," *Miami Herald,* December 3, 2010; David Ovalle, "Novel Defense Helps Spare Perpetrator of Grisly Murder," *Miami Herald,* December 12, 2010.

213 **Deborah W. Denno:** Deborah W. Denno, "The Myth of the Double-Edged Sword: An Empirical Study of Neuroscience Evidence in Criminal Cases," *Boston College Law Review* 56, no. 2 (2015): 493–551.

CHAPTER 16: "WHAT POSSIBLE HARM CAN I BE?"

217 **build a record of good behavior:** Weinstein's prison education programs, incarceration, parole hearings, and administrative appeal are in the record in his lawsuit challenging denial of parole in *People v. Weinstein,* 156 Misc. 2d 34 (1992). See also Mark Fass, "Elderly Inmate Wins New Parole Hearing; Article 78 Hearing," *New York Law Journal,* April 18, 2005. My account of Weinstein's parole hearings in 1999, 2001, and 2003 was taken directly from transcripts from the New York Parole Board.

CHAPTER 17: DEFENDING AMERICA'S DEFENDERS

236 **He soon began to see lots of veterans in the system:** Brockton Hunter, interviews by author; Brockton Hunter, "Echoes of War: The Combat Veteran in Criminal Court"; Brockton Hunter and Ryan Else, "Echoes of War Part Two: Legal Strategies for Defending the Combat Veteran in Criminal Court," *Champion* (2013): 18–26.

238 **Blast injuries like those Kris suffered:** This discussion of TBI and its effects on cognition and behavior was drawn from interviews with Dr. Elliot Roth, medical director of patient recovery at the Rehabilitation Institute of Chicago; U.S. Department of Defense, *Traumatic Brain Injury: Department of Defense Special Report,* 2014; Cyrus A. Raji et al., "Functional Neuroimaging with Default Mode Network Regions Distinguishes PTSD from TBI in a Military Veteran Population," *Brain Imaging and Behavior* (2015); Ronald Glasser, Chrisanne Gordon, and Peter Demitry, "Traumatic Brain Injury: The Invisible Injury," in Brockton D. Hunter and Ryan C. Else, eds., *The Attorney's Guide to Defending Veterans in Criminal Court* (Veterans Defense Project, 2014); Maj. Jason M. Elbert, "A Mindful Military: Linking Brain and Behavior Through Neuroscience at Court-Martial," *Army Law* 4, September 2012.

240 **a special veterans treatment court:** Matthew Daneman, "N.Y. Court Gives Veterans Chance to Straighten Out," *USA Today,* June 1, 2008.

240 **Arthur Torgeson:** Paul Levy, "'Everything Is Over for Me,' Distraught Vet Said," *Minneapolis Star Tribune* (Minneapolis), July 22, 2008.

241 **In Fort Carson, Colorado:** Lizette Alvarez and Dan Frosch, "A Focus on Violence by Returning G.I.s," *New York Times,* January 1, 2009; U.S. Army Center for Health Promotion and Preventative Medicine, "Epidemiologic Consultation No. 14-HK-OBIU-09, Investigation of Homicides at Fort Carson, Colo., November 2008–May 2009," July 2009.

242 **Army Staff Sgt. Robert Bales:** Jack Healy, "Apology, but No Explanation, for Massacre of Afghans," *New York Times,* August 23, 2013; Eric Johnson,

"U.S. Soldier Who Killed Afghan Villagers Gets Life Without Parole," *Reuters,* August 23, 2013; Gene Johnson, "U.S. Soldier Robert Bales Sentenced to Life in Prison Without Parole for Afghanistan Massacre," *World Post,* August 23, 2013.

242 **Anthony Klecker:** Matt McKinney, "Convicted Drunk Driver Gets Four-Year Sentence," *Star Tribune* (Minneapolis), June 17, 2011.

245 **Brig. Gen. Stephen N. Xenakis, MD:** Stephen Xenakis, interview by author; Stephen Xenakis, "Combat Trauma in the 21st Century: An Overview of Psychological Injuries in Modern War," in Hunter and Else, *Attorney's Guide to Defending Veterans;* Stephen Xenakis, "Posttraumatic Stress Disorder: Beyond Best Practices," *Psychoanalytic Psychology* 31, no. 2 (2014): 236–44; "The Role and Responsibilities of Psychiatry in 21st Century Warfare," *Journal of the American Academy of Psychiatry and the Law* 42, no. 4 (2014): 504–8.

247 **Those coming back from Iraq and Afghanistan:** Thomas L. Hafemeister and Nicole A. Stockey, "Last Stand? The Criminal Responsibility of War Veterans Returning from Iraq and Afghanistan with Posttraumatic Stress Disorder," *Indiana Law Journal* 85, no. 1 (2010). On PTSD and head injuries, see Lisa M. Shin, Scott L. Rauch, and Roger K. Pittman, "Structural and Functional Anatomy of PTSD: Findings from Neuroimaging Research," in Jennifer J. Vasterling and Chris R. Brewin, eds., *Neuropsychology of PTSD: Biological, Cognitive and Clinical Perspectives* (New York: Guilford, 2005); Daniel E. Dossa and Ernest G. Boswell, "Post Traumatic Stress Disorder: A Brief Overview," in Hunter and Else, *Attorney's Guide to Defending Veterans;* Betsy J. Grey, "Neuroscience, PTSD and Sentencing Mitigation," *Cardozo Law Review* 34, no. 53 (2012): 53–103; Jordan Grafman et al., "Frontal Lobe Injuries, Violence, and Aggression: A Report of the Vietnam Head Injury Study," *Neurology* 46 (1996): 1231–38.

CHAPTER 18: THE HEAD-BANGER DEFENSE

251 **On an August afternoon:** For Corwin Brown's case, see Associated Press, "Ex-ND Coach Hospitalized After Standoff," *Post-Tribune* (Indiana), August 13, 2011; Cliff Brunt, "Former NFL Player Corwin Brown Faces Three Felonies," Associated Press, August 16, 2011; Cliff Brunt, "Family Says Brown May Suffer from Brain Trauma," Associated Press, August 16, 2011; Mark Cannizzaro, "Concern for Corwin—Tragic Shift in Character Stuns Family of Ex-Jet," *New York Post,* August 18, 2011.

252 **Duerson was the former Chicago Bears:** Alan Schwartz, "Before Suicide, Duerson Said He Wanted Brain Study," *New York Times,* February 19, 2011; Sean Gregory, "Dave Duerson: Football's First Martyr Can't Die in Vain," *Time,* February 25, 2011.

252–253 **the incidence of CTE among NFL players:** Daniel J. Kain, "'It's Just a Concussion': The National Football League's Denial of a Causal Link Between Multiple Concussions and Later-Life Cognitive Decline," *Rutgers Law Journal* 40, no. 3 (2010): 697–736; Caleb Korngold, Helen M. Farrell, and

Manish Fozdar, "The National Football League and Chronic Traumatic Encephalopathy: Legal Implications," *Journal of the American Academy of Psychiatry and the Law* 41 (2013): 430–36.

253 **Some players began suggesting:** Paul D. Anderson, "Criminal Defendants Add New Tool to War Chest," *NFL Concussion Litigation,* August 3, 2014; Dan Diamond, "Does Playing Football Make You Violent? Examining the Evidence," *Forbes,* September 16, 2014; Linda Carroll, "Could Brain Injuries Be Behind the NFL Rap Sheet?" *NBC News,* October 22, 2014; Daniel Engber, "Did Concussions Make Him Do It?," *Slate,* April 24, 2013.

253 **CTE has been associated with many psychiatric:** Jennifer Carr, "Hard Knocks: The Science of Concussions," Society for Neuroscience, BrainFacts .org, October 3, 2012; Naomi Shavin, "Does Head Trauma Cause People to Be More Violent?" *New Republic,* September 17, 2014; Ellen Goldbaum, "How Are CTE and Behavior Linked? The Answer Requires More In-Depth Research, Scientists Say," *News Center,* University at Buffalo, December 2014.

253 **Nathaniel Fujita:** Norman Miller, "Fujita Pleads Not Guilty; Prosecutor Provides More Details of Murder," *MetroWest Daily News,* August 23, 2011.

254 **"not responsible for his conduct":** "Corwin Brown Claims Mental Defect," Associated Press, November 30, 2011; Mary Kate Malone, "Ex-Coach Offers Insanity Defense," *South Bend Tribune,* December 1, 2011.

254 **Jane Woodward Miller:** Tom Coyne, "Psychiatrist, Psychologist to Evaluate Mental Status of Former Notre Dame Assistant Brown," Associated Press, January 11, 2012.

255 **used to describe boxers:** Harry L. Parker, "Traumatic Encephalopathy ('Punch Drunk') of Professional Pugilists," *Journal of Neurology and Psychopathology* 15, no. 57 (1934): 20–28; Jef Akst, "Punch Drunk," *Scientist,* December 1, 2011.

256 **Their review of the CTE literature:** A. C. McKee et al., "Chronic Traumatic Encephalopathy in Athletes: Progressive Tauopathy After Repetitive Head Injury," *Journal of Neuropathology and Experimental Neurology* 68, no. 7 (2009): 709–35.

257 **Dr. Bennet Omalu:** Adam Chandler, "Is O.J. Simpson the NFL's Latest Concussion Casualty?" Atlantic.com, January 29, 2016.

257 **Dr. Wade Myers:** Norman Miller, "Expert: Fujita Not Criminally Responsible for Murder," *MetroWest Daily News,* March 2, 2013.

259 **he pleaded guilty but mentally ill:** Dave Stephens, "Ex-ND Coach Pleads Guilty, but Mentally Ill," *South Bend Tribune,* June 29, 2012.

260 **a suspended four-year sentence:** Tom Coyne, "Ex-Notre Dame Coach Gets Four-Year Suspended Sentence," Associated Press, August 21, 2012.

260 **Corwin Brown, represented by two attorneys:** *Corwin Brown et al. v. National Football League,* U.S. District Court, Southern District of Florida, Miami Division, December 3, 2012.

260 **In 2015 the NFL settled the lawsuit:** "Judge Approves Deal in NFL Concussion Suit," *New York Times,* April 22, 2015; "Appeals Court Upholds $1 Billion Concussion Settlement," ESPN.com, April 18, 2016.

261 **Titus Young:** David Leon Moore, "Dad Says Ex-NFLer Son Titus Young Is 'Uncontrollable,'" *USA Today,* July 15, 2014.

261 **Junior Seau:** Mary Pilon and Ken Belson, "Seau Suffered From Brain Disease," *New York Times,* January 11, 2013; Gary Milhoces, "Junior Seau's Family Sues NFL Over Brain Injuries," *USA Today,* January 23, 2013.

261 **Jovan Belcher:** Sam Mellinger, "Jovan Belcher's Brain Showed Signs of CTE, According to Post-Mortem Exam," *Kansas City Star,* September 29, 2014.

261 **Dr. Ann McKee:** Michael O'Keeffe, "Boston University Study Finds Possible Link Between Traumatic Brain Injuries and Domestic Violence," *New York Daily News,* October 18, 2014; Soraya Nadia McDonald, "Study Finds a Strong Correlation Between Repeated Head Trauma and Domestic Abuse," *Washington Post,* October 22, 2014.

262 **a Los Angeles judge:** David Leon Moore, "L.A. judge Spares ex-Lion Titus Young Prison Term, Gives Him Long Probation," *USA Today,* May 5, 2015.

262 **a 2014 article that challenges the assumptions:** Daniel Antonius et al., "Behavioral Health Symptoms Associated with Chronic Traumatic Encephalopathy: A Critical Review of the Literature and Recommendations for Treatment and Research," *Journal of Neuropsychiatry and Clinical Neurosciences* 26 (2014): 313–22. The study was funded in part by NFL Charities.

263 **"For now, the courts must rely":** Peter A. Carfagna, "The Possible Use of Sports-Related Concussion 'Brain Trauma' as a Legal Defense for Violent Crimes Committed by Professional Football Players," presentation at *Journal of Law and Health* Lecture Series, Cleveland, OH, March 2015.

264 **He was found guilty:** Evan Allen and Lisa Kocian, "Nathaniel Fujita Found Guilty in Wayland Murder," *Boston Globe,* March 8, 2013.

264 **Mattingly said Nathaniel suffered:** "Loved to Death," *48 Hours,* CBS News, October 26, 2013.

265 **the league got slammed by a congressional report:** John Branch, "N.F.L. Tried to Influence Concussion Research, Congressional Study Finds," *New York Times,* May 23, 2016; Steve Fainaru and Mark Fainaru-Wada, "Congressional Report Says NFL Waged Improper Campaign to Influence Government Study," ESPN.com, May 24, 2016. For further information about concussions and CTE, see "League of Denial: The NFL's Concussion Crisis," *Frontline,* PBS, October 8, 2013; John J. Mann, "Suicide in Professional Athletes: Is It Related to the Sport?" *Dana Alliance,* Dana Foundation, July 26, 2012; Douglas H. Smith, Victoria E. Johnson, and William Stewart, "Chronic Neuropathologies of Single and Repetitive TBI: Substrates of Dementia?" *Nature Reviews Neurology* 9 (2013): 211–21; Nick Tate, "Are Brain Injuries Behind NFL Domestic Violence?" *NewsmaxHealth,* September 18, 2014; Matt Wilhalme, "Brain Disease CTE Found in 87 of 91 NFL Players Tested, Researchers Say," *Los Angeles Times,* September 18, 2015.

CHAPTER 19: THE FUTURE OF NEUROLAW AND THE BRAIN DEFENSE

274 **Neurocompatibility Index:** David M. Eagleman and Sarah Isgur Flores, "Defining a Neurocompatibility Index for Criminal Justice Systems: A Frame-

work to Align Social Policy with Modern Brain Science," *Law of the Future* 1 (2012): 161–72.

276 **the trolley problem:** Joshua D. Greene et al., "An fMRI Investigation of Emotional Engagement in Moral Judgment," *Science* 293 (2001): 2105–8; Sandra Blakeslee, "Watching How the Brain Works As It Weighs a Moral Dilemma," *New York Times,* September 25, 2001.

277 **transforming people's intuitions:** Jonathan Cohen and Joshua Greene, "For the Law, Neuroscience Changes Nothing and Everything," *Philosophical Transactions Royal Society, London B, Biological Science* (November 26, 2004): 1775–85.

286 **Stephen Morse:** Morse's extremely helpful writings on law and neuroscience include "Brain and Blame," *Georgetown Law Journal* 84 (1996): 527–49; "Lost in Translation?: An Essay on Law and Neuroscience," in Michael Freeman, ed., *Law and Neuroscience,* vol. 13 in *Current Legal Issues* (Oxford: Oxford University Press, 2010); "The Status of NeuroLaw: A Plea for Current Modesty and Future Cautious Optimism," *Journal of Psychiatry and Law* 39 (2011): 595–626.

288 **"Individuals: The Case of the Murdering Brain":** Owen D. Jones, Jeffrey D. Schall, and Francis X. Shen, *Law and Neuroscience,* Aspen Casebook Series (New York: Wolters Kluwer Law & Business, 2014), 41.

Index